Stafford County, Virginia Tithables

Quit Rents, Personal Property Taxes
and Related Lists and Petitions,

1723-1790

in two volumes

compiled by

John Vogt
&
T. William Kethley, Jr.

with an introduction by Michael Burgess

volume two
Iberian Publishing Company
Athens, Georgia

ISBN 0-935931-50-3

Printed in the United States of America
The Iberian Publishing Company
548 Cedar Creek Drive
Athens, Georgia 30605-3408

Stafford County
Virginia

Personal Property
Tax List

1787

Source: Virginia State Library, Archives Division. County Records. Stafford County Tax lists.

Form of return of taxable property to be made by the commissioners

List No. 1.

A List of Taxable property within the district of William Mountjoy, Commissioner in the County of Stafford for the year 1787

[Categories]:

Date of receiving lists from individuals;
Persons names chargeable with the tax;
Names of white male tithables above 21;
[col. 1] - No. of white males above 16 and under 21;
[col. 2] - Blacks above 16;
[col. 3] - Blacks under 16;
[col. 4] - Horses mares colts & mules;
[col. 5] - Cattle;
[other] - Coaches wheels;
Faetons & wagons;
chairs wheels;
Ordinary licence;
Billiard tables;
Studs;
Rate pr season.

List No. 2.

A List of Taxable property within the district of William Alexander, Commissioner in the County of Stafford for the year 1787

[Categories]:

Date of receiving lists from individuals;
Persons names chargeable with the tax;
Names of white male tithables above 21;
[col. 1] - No. of white males above 16 and under 21;
[col. 2] - Blacks above 16;
[col. 3] - Blacks under 16;
[col. 4] - Horses mares colts & mules;
[col. 5] - Cattle;
[other] - Coaches wheels;
Faetons & wagons;
chairs wheels;
Ordinary licence;
Billiard tables;
Studs;
Rate pr season;
Physicians.

[folio 1]

A List of Taxable property within the district of William Mountjoy, Commissioner in the County of Stafford for the year 1787

Date chargeable w/tax	white males over 21	" 16-21	/blks/H/ 16+	-16	C/	other
Mar 12 George Abbet	George Abbet				4	11
Mar 12 Elijah Abbet	Elijah Abbet				3	10
Mar 12 James Abbet	James Abbet				1	1
Mar 13 James Arrosmith	James Arrosmith				3	4
Mar 15 Sarah Ashby	Robert Ashby				2	4
Mar 21 John Agin	John Agin					1
Mar 24 William Anderson	William Anderson				1	2
Mar 29 William Aleson	William Aleson				1	
Apr 9 John Achison	John Achison	1			1	
Apr 9 Nathan Atchison	Nathan Achison	2	2	2	2	8
Apr 9 Daniel Antrum	Daniel Antrum	*[see next line]*				
Apr 9	Levy Antrum	1			4	
Apr 9 Benjamin Adie	Benjamin Adie		5	2	4	0
Apr 9 William Adie	William Adie	*[see next line]*				
Apr 9	William Adie		9	14	6	14 2whl. carr.
Apr 14 Amus Atchison	Amus Atchison	1			3	13
Mar 12 John Bannister	John Bannister				2	
Mar 12 William Browne	William Browne				2	5
Mar 12 Thomas Barby	Thomas Barby				1	4
Mar 12 William Barby	William Barby				3	5
Mar 13 James Billingslee Sr.	Ja.S Billingslee	*[see next line]*				
Mar 13	Ja.S Billingslee	2			4	3
Mar 14 William Byrum Sr.	William Byrum				1	2
Mar 15 William Bridwell Jr.	William Bridwell				2	
Mar 17 Joseph Beagle	Joseph Beagle				1	5
[folio 2]						
Mar 17 William Bridwell	William Bridwell	3	3	3	3	13
Mar 20 James Barnot	James Barnot	1	3	2	2	
Mar 20 John Bruin	John Bruin	1			2	6

Date	chargeable w/tax	white males over 21	" 16-21/	/blacks/ 16+	H/ -16	C/	other
Mar 21	William Barnot	William Barnot				1	
Mar 21	John Beagle	John Beagle	1			2	6
Mar 21	Mary Bell			3	1	3	4
Mar 22	William Baul	William Baul		3	3	6	14
Mar 22	Benjamin Bowlin	Benjamin Bowlin					3
Mar 22	Robert Buchan	Robert Buchan		5	2	8	11
Mar 23	George Barns	George Barns					
Mar 23	John Browne	John Browne				1	
Mar 27	Nathan Bannister	Nathan Bannister	1			3	6
Mar 27	Elijah Bell	Elijah Bell				1	3
Mar 27	George Bell	George Bell	1	1	1	5	7
Mar 28	John Bell	John Bell			1	2	5
Mar 28	John Bridges	John Bridges				1	2
Mar 28	Clem. Billingslee	Clement Billingslee	1			2	2
Mar 28	George Bell	George Bell				2	3
Mar 29	Bassell Burroughs	Bassell Burroughs				1	3
Mar 29	Samuel Burroughs	Samuel Burroughs				1	2
Mar 29	John Butler	John Butler	1	2	3	3	7
Mar 31	Jacob Bridwell	tax free		2		3	8
Apr 3	William Bradly	William Bradly		[see next line]			
Apr 3		Cha.ˢ Bradly				2	6
Apr 3	Jonathan Bell	Jonathan Bell				1	
Apr 4	Francis Brooks	Francis Brooks				2	7
[folio 3]							
Apr 4	Magdalin Betty					2	4
Apr 9	George Byrum	George Byrum	1			1	
Apr 9	George Bridwell Jr.	George Bridwell				2	4
Apr 9	George Bridwell	George Bridwell				2	5
Apr 9	William Botts	William Botts		3	5	4	9
Apr 9	Aron Botts	Aron Botts		5	6	7	15
Apr 9	Moses Bridwell	Moses Bridwell	1	4	3	3	7
Apr 9	John Browne	Jn.ᴼ Browne		[see next line]			
Apr 9		Nathaniel Williams		12	13	6	19
Apr 9	Enough Benson	Enough Benson		3	5	5	11
Apr 9	Walter Browne	Walter Browne				4	10
Apr 9	John Botts	John Botts	1	5	2	6	11
Apr 17	Thomas Beach	Thomas Beach				3	

Date	chargeable w/tax	white males over 21	" /blacks/ H/ C/ 16-21/ 16+ -16	other
Apr 19	Edward Bethel	Edward Bethel	1 2 1	
Apr 19	Joseph Browne	Joseph Browne	[see next line]	
Apr 19		Tho.s Browne	1 5 4 6 13	
Apr 20	Samuel Bridwell	Samuel Bridwell	2 1	
Apr 20	Joseph Botts	Joseph Botts	[see next line]	
Apr 20		John Prince	3 3 7 11	
Apr 20	William Battoe	William Battoe	3 4	
Apr 28	James Bridges	James Bridges	1 2	
May 4	William Branson	William Branson	2	
May 14	George Burroughs	George Burroughs	2 2 2 6	
May 14	Richard Brent	Richard Brent	3	
May 14	Derk Benear	Derk Benear	2 4	
May 14	Benjamin Brock	Benjamin Brock	1 5	
May 14	Ann Brent	Ann Brent	23 29 6	
May 14	George Brent	George Brent	[see next line]	
May 14		Izaah Corbin	115 910 46	
May 14	John Brent's estate		4	
May 14	George Bussel	George Bussel	2 9	
May 14	John Bradly	John Bradly	1 1	
May 14	John Bridwell	John Bridwell	1 2 3	
[folio 4]				
May 14	Zachariah Benson	Zachariah Benson	1 1 4 5	
May 14	Joseph Buchanon	tax free	1 2	
May 14	Mary Ann Bronaugh		110 10 9 6	
May 14	Joseph Barby	Joseph Barby	1 1 3 4	
May 14	Daniel C. Brent	D. C. Brent	[see next line]	
May 14		Jones Garner	[see next line]	
May 14		Wm Fritter	30 2413 6	
May 14	Eleoner Brent	John Blake	20 2011 48	
			4-wheeled carriage	
May 18	Robert Brent	in Maryland	1 2 3 5 stud @ 1.10.0	
May 18	Joseph Burroughs	Joseph Burroughs	1 1	
May 19	Benjamin Bridwell	Benjamin Bridwell	1 1	
May 19	Simon Bridwell	Simon Bridwell	1 3	
May 19	John Brooker	John Brooker		
May 24	Rawleigh T. Browne	R. T. Browne	[see next line]	
May 24		Pearson Williams	16 2012 15	

Date	chargeable w/tax	white males over 21	16-21	/blacks/ H/ 16+	-16	C/	other
May 25 Thomas Bridwell	Thomas Bridwell	2				1	2
May 25 Peter Byrum	Peter Byrum					1	4
May 25 Cuthbert Byrum	Cuthbert Byrum					1	
May 25 James Battoe	James Battoe Levy free			2	10		
Mar 13 James Carter	James Carter			2	3	4	
Mar 14 William Cummins	William Cummins					3	2
Mar 14 Joseph Combs	Joseph Combs		3	3	3		15
Mar 16 Peter Cook	Peter Cook					2	3
Mar 20 John Carter	John Carter					2	
Mar 20 Asey Cummins	Asey Cummins	3				6	3
Mar 20 William Cole	William Cole						
Mar 23 Henry Clifton	H. Clifton	*[see next line]*					
Mar 23	Lawrence Butler		3	5	5	5	13
Mar 23 Brian Chadwell	Brian Chadwell		1	2	4	4	15
Mar 24 Cuthbert Combs	Cuthbert Combs			6	9	4	11
[folio 5]							
Mar 24 John Cloe	John Cloe					1	3
Mar 29 John Carter	John Carter						
Mar 29 Jedediah Carter	Jedediah Carter					2	4
Mar 30 James Cloe Sr.	tax free					4	10
Mar 31 James Cloe Jr.	James Cloe					1	
Mar 31 Eliab Cooper	under 21			1	1	1	
Mar 31 Joseph Cooper	tax free					1	4
Apr 3 Daniel Cane	Daniel Cane					2	1
Apr 3 George Coats	George Coats			2	6	1	
Apr 3 Harris Carter	Harris Carter					1	5
Apr 9 Josua Carney	Josua Carney	*[see next line]*					
Apr 9	Benj.a Carnet		2	1	1	7	14
Apr 28 Perry Chinn	Perry Chinn					1	2
May 4 Elizabeth Chissom			1			1	2
May 4 Wilkinson Chandler	Wilkinson Chandler					4	3
May 14 Charles Carter	C. Carter	*[see next line]*					
May 14	Able Holloway			20	17	16	32
May 14 Mary Chesshire			1			2	5
May 14 John Cook	John Cook			20	34	12	36
May 19 Seth Combs			1	9	8	8	34
May 19 John Chiverall	John Chiverall					1	4

Date	chargeable w/tax	white males over 21	16-21	blacks 16+	-16	H	C	other
May 19 Jessey Cooper	Jessey Cooper					2	4	
May 25 William Chadwell	William Chadwell					1		
Mar 12 Bradly Dent	Bradly Dent	1				2	6	
Mar 12 Charles Davis	Charles Davis					1		
Mar 22 Jerremiah Day	Jerremiah Day							
Mar 22 William Davis	William Davis					2	6	
Mar 24 James Dent	James Dent							
Mar 27 Elizabeth Dunaway		2				3	4	

[folio 6]

Date	chargeable w/tax	white males over 21	16-21	blacks 16+	-16	H	C	other
Mar 27 William Dunaway	William Dunaway					1	5	
Mar 27 William Devene	William Devene					1		
Mar 30 John Dillon	John Dillon					1	2	
Mar 30 William Dorson	William Dorson					1	3	
Mar 31 Christopher Dorson	Christopher Dorson					1	1	
Apr 4 Hannah Dickenson	Anthony Latham		6	8		9	23	stud1.4.0
Apr 9 Dennis Doyall Sr.	Dennis Doyall	1				4	6	
Apr 9 Rawleigh Wm Downman	Nathaniel Elkins		9	16		4	16	
Apr 9 Travers Daniel Sr.	Travers Daniel	1	16	6		14	41	2whl carr.
Apr 9 Travers Daniel Jr.	Travers Daniel	5	1	5		3		
Apr 9 Sarah Daniel			14	16		12	43	4whl carr.
Apr 19 Patterson Doyall	Patterson Doyall					3	1	
Apr 19 Dennis Doyall	Dennis Doyall	1				4	5	
May 25 Archebald Douglis		1				6	10	
Mar 12 Jessey Edwards	Jessey Edwards	*[see next line]*						
Mar 12	Thomson Edwards	1				2	8	
Mar 12 William Edwards Sr.	William Edwards	1				2	10	
Mar 15 William Ensey	William Ensey	2	2			3	3	
Mar 20 William Edwards Jr.	William Edwards	3	1			1	3	
Mar 24 William Edrington	William Edrington	1	2	6		6	11	
Mar 29 Willis Edwards Sr.	Willis Edwards			1		1	3	
Mar 30 Backer Edwards	Backer Edwards	1				2	8	
Apr 4 Margaret Eaton						1		
Apr 9 Haden Edwards	Haden Edwards		5	4		5	20	2whl carr.
Apr 9 Thomas Edrington	Thomas Edrington	2	2			2	2	
Apr 20 William Eaton	William Eaton	1					1	

[folio 7]

Date	chargeable w/tax	white males over 21	16-21	blacks 16+	-16	H	C	other
May 5 Isaac Eustace	Isaac Eustace	1	10	5		7	14	2whl. carr.

Date	chargeable w/tax	white males over 21	" /blacks/ H/ C/ 16-21/ 16+ -16				other
May 5 George Enzor	George Enzor					1	
Mar 12 William Franklin	William Franklin			1	3	4	
Mar 12 John Franklin Jr.	John Franklin						
Mar 12 John Ford	John Ford				1	2	
Mar 13 John Fritter	John Fritter				2	4	
Mar 13 John Fristoe	John Fristoe		3	3	5	7	
Mar 15 James Ford	James Ford		3	3	5	8	
Mar 17 William French	William French	[see next line]					
Mar 17	Stephen French		5	5	8	21	
Mar 22 Francis Foushee	F. Foushee	[see next line]					
Mar 22	John H. Foushee		2	2	2	14	
Mar 29 William Fling	tax free				1	4	
Mar 30 John Franklin Sr.	John Franklin				2	8	
Mar 30 Joseph Franklin	Joseph Franklin						
Mar 31 Reuben Franklin	Reuben Franklin				3	6	
Apr 9 John Finch	John Finch						
Apr 9 Samuel Faunt	Samuel Faunt				4	11	
Apr 9 Anthony Ficklin	Anthony Ficklin		1	7 8	6	15	
Apr 9 Joseph Franklin	tax free				5	5	
Apr 9 Richard Fristoe	do.			1	1	12	
Apr 9 Moses Fritter Sr.	Moses Fritter Sr.		1		2	7	
Apr 9 William Fritter	William Fritter				2	3	
Apr 16 Benjamin Ficklin	Benjamin Ficklin		1	2	2 4	9	
Apr 16 James Faunt	Ja.ˢ Faunt	[see next line]					
Apr 16	William Faunt				4	12	
Apr 20 Phillip Foxworthy	Phillip Foxworthy				1	2	
Apr 20 Vintsin Foxworthy	Vintsin Foxworthy				1	3	
May 14 Moses Fritter	M. Fritter	[see next line]					
May 14	John Latham				1	5	
[folio 8]							
May 19 William Fristoe	William Fristoe		1		5	10	
May 26 Jerremiah Fugate	Jerremiah Fugate				1	1	
Mar 12 Samuel Groves	Samuel Groves				2	6	
Mar 12 Elisha Grigsby	Elisha Grigsby			2	2	6	
Mar 12 William Gollohorn	William Gollohorn		1	1	4	4	
Mar 12 John Garrison	John Garrison				1	4	
Mar 14 Richard Griffis	Richard Griffis		1		1	2	

Stafford Co., Va. personal property tax list - 1787

Date	chargeable w/tax		white males over 21	" 16-21	/blacks/ 16+ H/	-16 C/	other
Mar 14 Benjamin Grigory	Benjamin Grigory				2	3	
Mar 15 John Goldsmith	John Goldsmith		1	3	4	3	5
Mar 20 William Gant	William Gant			1	2	2	7
Mar 27 William Gui	William Gui		[see next line]				
Mar 27	Joseph Gui				4	5	
Mar 27 John Gui	John Gui				2	1	
Mar 27 Benjamin Gui	Benjamin Gui				1	4	
Mar 27 Kissiah Gui	Kissiah Gui				2	6	
Mar 28 William Groves	William Groves			1	2	2	
Mar 28 Henry Griffin	Henry Griffin		1	1	2	2	
Mar 29 Mary Garrard				8	14	3	12
Mar 29 William Garrard	William Garrard		1	2			
Mar 29 Ann Gaddis			1	3	2	5	15
Mar 30 Isaac Gaskins	Isaac Gaskins				3	6	
Mar 30 Aron Garrison	Aron Garrison				1	2	
Mar 31 Elizabeth Garrison					1	6	
Apr 9 George Garrison	George Garrison		1		2	3	
Apr 9 John Grigsby	John Grigsby				1	5	
Apr 17 John Green	John Green				2	4	
[folio 9]							
Apr 19 John Gunn	John Gunn				2		
Apr 20 Jemime Grigory					1	2	
Apr 28 Robert Green	Robert Green		[see next line]				
Apr 28	John Green				4	2	
May 4 Phillip Gardner	Phillip Gardner			3	3	3	12
May 19 William George	William George						3
May 25 Hannah Gough			1	1	2	3	2
May 25 Moses Grigsby	Moses Grigsby				1	5	
Mar 12 Henry Hiden	Henry Hiden				2	10	
Mar 12 George Harding	George Harding			1	3	5	
Mar 12 Peter Hansbrough	Peter Hansbrough			1	2	4	4
Mar 12 Henry Horton	Henry Horton		1		1	3	
Mar 12 John Scott Harding	John Scott Harding				3	9	
Mar 12 Samuel Hudson	Samuel Hudson			2	2	4	15
Mar 12 John Holloday	John Holloday		1		1	4	7
Mar 17 Richard Hiden	Richard Hiden						
Mar 21 John Hedgman	John Hedgman			20	18	13	20

Date	chargeable w/tax	white males over 21	" 16-21	/blacks/ 16+	-16	H/	C/	other
Mar 22	John Harrison	John Harrison		1	1	3	4	
Mar 22	Thomas Hay		1			2	7	
Mar 24	William Harding	William Harding	1	1	5	5	15	
Mar 24	John Harding	John Harding				2	2	
Mar 24	Cuthbert Harding	Cuthbert Harding		1	2	1	3	
Mar 27	Mary Hore	William Hore		7	7	3	20	
Mar 27	John Hore	John Hore			1			
Mar 27	Elias Hore	Elias Hore		1	2	1	4	
[folio 10]								
Mar 27	Thomas Heth			1			5	
Mar 27	Rachel Hewitt	Richard Hewitt		4	9	3		
Mar 30	James Hore	James Hore		1	2	2	11	
Mar 21	John Hardy	John Hardy		7	14	6		7 2whl. carr.
Apr 9	Causom Horton	Causom Horton	1			3	4	
Apr 9	William Honey	William Honey				2	7	
Apr 9	John Horton	John Horton		5	7	7	18	
Apr 9	Elijah Horton	Elijah Horton				1	6	
Apr 9	Thomas Harding	Thomas Harding			1	2	8	
Apr 9	John Holloway Sr.	John Holloway				2	3	
Apr 9	James Horton	James Horton				3	4	
Apr 16	James Henderson	James Henderson				1		
Apr 17	Isaac Holloway	Isaac Holloway	1			3	9	
Apr 28	James Holloway	James Holloway	1			2	4	stud 18.0
Apr 28	George Holloway	George Holloway					2	
May 3	William Holloday	William Holloday			1	3	2	
May 5	Asey Holloway Sr.	Asey Holloway	*[see next line]*					
May 5		Rich.d Ketchen				2	9	
May 5	Asey Holloway Jr.		1			1	1	
May 14	John Holloway	John Holloway	1			2	10	
May 19	Virgen Huse					1	5	
May 25	Ledia Hansbrough				1	2	3	
Mar 12	William Jones	William Jones				3	7	stud 7.0
Mar 12	Alexander Jameson	Alexander Jameson				2	3	
Mar 12	John Jones Sr.	John Jones				5	19	
Mar 12	John Jones Jr.	John Jones				1		
[folio 11]								
Mar 12	James Jones	James Jones				1		

Date	chargeable w/tax	white males over 21	16-21	blacks 16+	-16	H	C	other
Mar 12	John Innis					1	2	
Mar 13	David Jones Sr.	David Jones	1			2	4	
Mar 15	William Innis	William Innis						
Mar 28	Steaphen Johnston	Steaphen Johnston		1				
Mar 29	John Jinkins	John Jinkins						
Mar 31	John Johnston	John Johnston		1				
Apr 9	Gabril Jones	Gabril Jones	*[see next line]*					
Apr 9		Fieldin Ficklin		4	6	4	4	
Apr 20	Elizabeth Jones						1	
--- --	Peter Knight	Peter Knight		1		3	4	

[the above entry is written in a different hand - T.E.S. Tyler?]

Date	chargeable w/tax	white males over 21	16-21	blacks 16+	-16	H	C	other
Mar 12	Christopher Knight	Christopher Knight				2	4	
Mar 13	Jeremiah Knight	Jeremiah Knight	1			5	12	
Mar 23	Jessey Kendall	Jessey Kendall				2	4	
Mar 23	Aron Kendall	Aron Kendall				2		
Mar 24	Peter Kendall	Peter Kendall				3		
Mar 31	Uriah Knight	Uriah Knight				3		
Apr 9	James Kirk	James Kirk				2		
Apr 9	Peter Knight Sr.	Peter Knight	2			4	12	
Apr 9	Henry Kendall	Henry Kendall		1	1	3	7	
Apr 9	Sarah Kirk					3	7	
Apr 16	Ann Knight		1	2	2	3	5	
Apr 16	Sarah Knight		1				2	
Apr 16	Daniel Kendall	Daniel Kendall				3	3	
Apr 18	James Kendall	James Kendall				1	7	
Apr 28	Charles Kendall	Charles Kendall		1	1	2	4	

[folio 12]

Date	chargeable w/tax	white males over 21	16-21	blacks 16+	-16	H	C	other
May 5	Josua Kendall	Josua Kendall					3	
May 5	John Kendall	Jn.º Kendall	*[see next line]*					
May 5		Moses Kendall	*[see next line]*					
May 5		James Kee Kendall		3	3	5	22	
May 10	Merryman Ketchen	Merryman Ketchen		2	5	2	3	
May 14	Josua Kendall Sr.	Josua Kendall	*[see next line]*					
May 14		Anthony Kendall		4	3	7	20	
May 14	John Knight	John Knight				2	6	
Mar 12	Edmund Lumdit	Edmund Lumdit	1			3	10	
Mar 12	John Lawlis	John Lawlis	1			2	16	

Date	chargeable w/tax	white males over 21	" 16-21	/blacks/ 16+	-16	H/	C/	other
Mar 13	John Lunsford	John Lunsford				4	15	
Mar 13	George Latham	George Latham		1	1	4	5	
Mar 22	James Lowry	James Lowry	2			2	7	
Mar 27	Charles Latham	Charles Latham		1				
Mar 30	Jane Lunsford					1	4	
Apr 9	Chondrid Lewis	Chondrid Lewis				1	1	
Apr 9	Gavin Lawson	Gavin Lawson	*[see next line]*					
Apr 9		David Bridges	*[see next line]*					
Apr 9		Charles Duncanson		18	18	13	46	4whl. carr.
Apr 9	Snodon Latham	Snodon Latham				2	7	
Apr 9	Moses Lunsford	Moses Lunsford				3	9	
May 15	Francis Linum	Francis Linum						
May 15	John Latham	John Latham				2	7	
May 15	Rob.ᵗ B. Morton	Rob.ᵗ B. Morton		7	6	4	12	2whl. carr.

[the above two entries are written in a different hand - T.E.S. Tyler?]

Date	chargeable w/tax	white males over 21	" 16-21	/blacks/ 16+	-16	H/	C/	other
Mar 12	Richard Mason	Richard Mason	1	1		7	8	
Mar 12	Charles Mifflin	levy free				2	5	
Mar 12	Henry Mcentire	Henry Mcentire		1	2	2	4	
Mar 12	John Murray	in Prince William		3	1			
Mar 12	Edward McKenzy	Edward McKenzy				1	3	
Mar 12	Alexander Mcentire	Alexander Mcentire		2	5	2	10	
Mar 13	William Mullin	William Mullin		6	8	4	11	2whl. carr.
Mar 13	Peter Mauzy Sr.	Thomas Loury		3	1	2	8	
Mar 13	Hugh McDaniel	Hugh McDaniel						
Mar 17	Margaret Matthews			3	4	5	2	2whl. carr.
Mar 20	Allen Mountjoy	Allen Mountjoy	1	1		3	9	
Mar 21	William Mawzy	William Mawzy		1		3	5	
Mar 21	Urslee Morton			1	5	2	16	
Mar 21	Richard Morton	Richard Morton		2				
Mar 21	James Morton	James Morton		1	1	1		
Mar 21	Peter Mawzy Jr.	Peter Mawzy		1	1	2	6	
Mar 22	Thomas Mallery	Thomas Mallery						
Mar 27	Thomas Mountjoy	Thomas Mountjoy	1			1	4	
Mar 28	Ann Moncure			9	6	5	21	2whl. carr.
Mar 28	Elizabeth Mason			6	5	5	4	4whl. carr.
Mar 29	Mary McDaniel					1	6	
Mar 30	Benjamin Million	Benjamin Million	1			2	10	

Date	chargeable w/tax	white males over 21	" 16-21	/blacks/ 16+	H/ -16	C/	other
Apr 4	James More	James More				1 7	
Apr 9	Lewis Mason	Lewis Mason				3 5	
Apr 9	Daniel Mason	Daniel Mason	2	1	1	6 16	
Apr 9	Lettace Massey		1			1 4	
[folio 13]							
Apr 9	Robert Million	Robert Million	2			6 9	
Apr 9	John Mason	John Mason	*[see next line]*				
Apr 9		Joel Mason	1	2	2	6 13	
Apr 15	John Fr.ª Mercer	Wᵐ Amrose Browne	*[see next line]*				
Apr 15		Wᵐ More	*[see next line]*				
Apr 15		David Habern		44	30	19120	
Apr 17	Francis Mcentosh	Francis Mcentosh				1	
Apr 19	John Minton	John Minton			1	1 2	
Apr 22	Thomas Mountjoy	Thomas Mountjoy		7	9	6 27	
Apr 27	John Mountjoy Sr.	John Mountjoy			1	3 4	
Apr 27	Edward Mountjoy	Edward Mountjoy	1			4 12	
May 12	George Mawzy	George Mawzy				1	
May 14	John McCullough	John McCullough				3	
May 14	William Mountjoy	William Mountjoy		4	6	9 24	
May 18	John Markham	John Markham	1	5	9	3	42whl. carr.
May 18	Michal Maze	Michal Maze	1				ord. lic.
May 18	Jonathan Mountjoy	Jonathan Mountjoy	1			1 5	
May 26	John Mountjoy	John Mountjoy	1	5	510	18	
Mar 15	John Nelson	John Nelson	2		2	2	
Mar 23	George Normon	George Normon	3		2	5 8	
Mar 27	Edward Normon	Edward Normon	4		4	6 17	
Mar 29	Phillip Nash	Phillip Nash				1 2	
Apr 9	James Nailer	James Nailer	1			7 9	
Apr 16	John Nicholson	John Nicholson				1 5	
[folio 14]							
Mar 12	James Ocane	James Ocane	1	1	2	5 6	
Mar 20	James Oglesby	James Oglesby				2 3	
Mar 22	Elizabeth Overall		1	6	4	7 22	
Mar 12	John Packston	John Packston	1			6 13	
Mar 12	Charles Porter Jr.	Charles Porter	1	2	4	3 1	
Mar 15	Benjamin Pritchet	Benjamin Pritchet		6	3	5 20	stud 15.0
Mar 17	James Parmer	James Parmer				2 2	

Date	chargeable w/tax	white males over 21	" 16-21/	/blacks/ 16+	H/ -16	C/	other
Mar 22	Jessey Payń	Jessey Payn			1	5	
Mar 22	Francis Payn	Francis Payn					
Mar 22	James Payn	James Payn			1	4	
Mar 23	John R. Peyton	John R. Peyton		*[see next line]*			
Mar 23		Zachariah Griffith		12	11	10	27	2whl.carr.
Mar 27	William Parmer	William Parmer					
Mar 27	Calvert Porter	Calvert Porter		*[see next line]*			
Mar 27		Thomas Porter		3	2	5	10	
Mar 28	Wharton Philbert	Wharton Philbert				2	
Mar 31	William Poats	William Poats			1 3	8	
Mar 31	John Poats	John Poats			1	4	
Mar 31	Richard Poats	Richard Poats			5	8	
Mar 31	Moses Poats	Moses Poats			2	4	
Apr 3	Elizabeth Peyton	Thomas Peyton		*[see next line]*			
Apr 3		Sam. H. Peyton		11	11	7	14	ord. lic.
Apr 3	John Patterson	John Patterson	1		3	17	
Apr 3	Hesekiah Patterson	Hesekiah Patterson			2	1	
Apr 9	Robert Painter	Robert Painter	1		4	12	
Apr 9	James Primm	James Primm		2	2	2	7	
Apr 9	Charles Porter Sr.	Charles Porter		4	9	5	11	
Apr 9	Vallentine Peyton	Vallentine Peyton		9	15	4	17	4whl.carr. physician's license
Apr 17	John Primm	John Primm		2	3	2	9	
[folio 15]								
Apr 17	Margaret Primm			1		3	10	
Apr 19	William Pattin	William Pattin			1		
Apr 19	William Phillips	William Phillips		7	3	2	10	
Apr 25	Thomas Powell	Thomas Powell					
Mar 12	Habern Rauls	under 21	1		2	2	1	
Mar 12	William Ross Jr.	William Ross		1	1	4	16	
Mar 12	Aron Read	Aron Read			3	10	
Mar 12	Kenez Rauls	Kenez Rauls			1	3	
Mar 12	Baily Riley	Baily Riley		1		2	5	
Mar 12	Jessey Riley	Jessey Riley			1	4	
Mar 12	Joel Readish	Joel Readish	1 5		5	6	15	
Mar 12	William Robeson	William Robeson	1 1		3	6	
Mar 15	James Ratliff	James Ratliff					

Date	chargeable w/tax	white males over 21	" 16-21	/blacks/ 16+	-16	H/	C/	other
Mar 15	Mary Ann Rauls			3	1	2	8	
Mar 15	Richard Read	Richard Read		2		3	15	
Mar 20	William Roles	William Roles				2	3	
Mar 20	Joseph Readish	Joseph Readish		4	4	5	12	
Mar 22	Reuben Rogers	Reuben Rogers					1	
Mar 22	Daniel Reads	Daniel Reads				3	9	
Mar 23	Presly Raimy	Presly Raimy		1		3	2	
Mar 24	Aihsah Rauls			1	2	1		
Mar 27	William Richards	William Richards		1	1	2	4	
Mar 29	Thomas Right	Thomas Right	1	3		5	15	
Mar 29	Winneford Ratliff			3	5	6	18	
Mar 29	Gowry Right	Gowry Right						
[folio 16]								
Apr 4	Burdit Readish	Burdit Readish	*[see next line]*					
Apr 4		John Smith	1			2	6	
Apr 9	James Robeson	James Robeson				2	6	
Apr 9	Rawleigh Rawls	Rawleigh Rauls		3	3	3	12	
								stud@0.15.0
Apr 9	William Rout	William Rout		1	3	3	11	
Apr 9	George Randol	Thomas Gill				2	9	
Apr 9	Charles Rauls	Charles Rauls	*[see next line]*					
Apr 9		George Williams	3	2	4	1	7	
Apr 9	William Randol	Wᵐ Randol	*[see next line]*					
Apr 9		John Randol	1			4	7	
Apr 19	John Rogers	John Rogers		1	1	3	1	
Apr 27	John Richards	John Richards						
May 4	William Right	William Right				3	11	
May 14	Richard Ratliff	Richard Ratliff		1	2	2	6	
May 14	Ann Rogers		1			3	4	
May 19	Nicholis Riley						1	
May 19	Jonathan Reid	Jonathan Reid					2	
[the above entry is written in a different hand - T.G. Tyler?]								
Mar 12	William Shelton Sr.	William Shelton		1		2	6	
Mar 12	John Stark	John Stark					1	
Mar 12	Jerremiah Stark	Jerremiah Stark	2	2	0	5	8	
Mar 12	William Stark	William Stark		1		2	2	
Mar 12	William Shelton Jr.	William Shelton			1	6	10	

Date	chargeable w/tax	white males over 21	" 16-21	/blacks/ 16+	H/ -16	C/	other
Mar 12	Edward Snoxall	Edward Snoxall	1		3	5	
Mar 12	Charles Stern	Charles Stern		2 6	1	2	
Mar 12	Richard Sims Jr.	Richard Sims			2	2	
Mar 12	John Stark Jr.	John Stark	1		4	6	
Mar 12	Presly Sims	Presly Sims			1		
Mar 20	Charles Stuart	Charles Stuart		5 2	5	13	
Mar 20	Craven Spiller	under age	1		1		
[folio 17]							
Mar 21	Henry Sudduth	Henry Sudduth			2	4	
Mar 22	Elizabeth Spilman				1	7	
Mar 22	John Shelket	John Shelket	1	1	4	7	
Mar 23	Francis Stern	Francis Stern	*[see next line]*				
Mar 23		Ralph Hughs		4	8 5	7	
Mar 23	Hawkin Stone	Hawkin Stone		4	12 7	20	
Mar 23	John Stern	John Stern	1	1	3	2	
Mar 27	Benjamin Shacklet	B. Shacklet	*[see next line]*				
Mar 27		Wm Shacklet	1		4	6	
Mar 28	John Smith	John Smith			2	4	
Mar 29	William Stone	William Stone		5	9 7	20	
Mar 29	William Stark	William Stark	1	1	3	5	
Mar 30	John Stork	John Stork		4	7	6	
							stud@0.15.0
Mar 30	Josius Stone	Josius Stone		5	5 3	13	
Mar 30	Robert Smith	Robert Smith					
Apr 3	Richard Stone	Richard Stone		2	4 3	5	
Apr 4	Thomas Sedden	T. Sedden	*[see next line]*				
Apr 4		Richard Taylor		14	14 9	34	
Apr 4	Thomas Sudduth	Thomas Sudduth			2	3	
Apr 9	Nathaniel Smith	Nathaniel Smith		2	3	12	
Apr 9	Richard Sims Sr.	Levy free			2	9	
[the above entry "Levy free" is written in a different hand - T.E.S. Tyler?]							
Apr 9	James Sims	James Sims			3	4	
Apr 9	Wilson Shelton	Wilson Shelton			1	6	
Apr 17	Jessey Stone	Jessey Stone	2			5	
May 14	Sarsfield Snoxall	Sarsfield Snoxall			1		
May 14	George Shelton	George Shelton			3	8	
May 14	John Snoxall	John Snoxall		1	1	2	

Date	chargeable w/tax	white males over 21	16-21	blacks 16+	-16	H	C	other
May 14 Ann Snoxall						1	3	
May 14 Hannah Stark		3				2	9	
[folio 18]								
Mar 12 William Tolsen	William Tolsen			1	1	2	7	
Mar 12 Mary Grigsby Travers				1	6			
Mar 13 William Tungate	William Tungate					3	4	
Mar 17 William Taylor	William Taylor	1		7	10	7	18	2whl.carr.
Mar 31 Elizabeth Tolson				4	6	8	36	
Mar 31 Benjamin Tolson	Benjamin Tolson			1	1			
Mar 31 John Tolson	John Tolson							
Apr 9 Samuel Thompson	Samuel Thompson			2	1	3	5	
Apr 27 George Thralekeld	George Thralekeld			1		2	1	
May 3 Elijah Thralekeld	Elijah Thralekeld			13	13	9	32	
May 5 Charles Thornton	Charles Thornton					2	7	
May 11 Alexander Taylor	Alexander Taylor	1				1	4	
May 18 Joannah Tolson						1	4	
May 18 T.S. Tyler	T.S. Tyler	1		1	3	4	9	
[the above entry is written in a different hand - T.E.S. Tyler?]								
Mar 31 Ann Vaun						3	4	
Mar 12 Charles Waters	Charles Waters					2	2	
Mar 12 James Waters	James Waters			1	2	2	4	
Mar 13 Richard Walker	Richard Walker			1	2	3	5	
Mar 13 William Williams	William Williams							
Mar 20 Mary Waller	Moses Grigsby	1		4	6	6	17	
Mar 20 Benjamin Willits	Benjamin Willits					2	2	
Mar 20 William Waller	Wm Waller			*[see next line]*				
Mar 20	Edw.d Waller			*[see next line]*				
Mar 20	Wm Waller			4	11	6	15	
Mar 21 John Withers	John Withers			4	1			
Mar 22 John Withers Sr.	John Withers			*[see next line]*				
Mar 22	Benj.a Withers			13	15	9	38	
Mar 22 George Withers	George Withers			1	1	3	16	
Mar 23 Barsheba Waller					1	2	5	
[folio 19]								
Mar 23 Peter Waters	Peter Waters					2	7	
Mar 24 Baily Washington Sr.	Baily Washington			11	4	9	30	4whl.carr.
Mar 24 Baily Washington Jr.	Baily Washington			10	13	4		2whl.carr.

Date	chargeable w/tax	white males over 21	16-21	blacks 16+	-16	H	C	other
Mar 27	William Williams	William Williams				4	4	
Mar 28	John Waters	John Waters	[see next line]					
Mar 28		Baily Waters		1		2	3	
Mar 29	Savanah Womsly			1		3	6	
Mar 30	John Warren	John Warren	1			3	8	
Mar 30	William West	William West	1			3	10	
Mar 30	John Waters Sr.	levy free		2	2	4	12	
Apr 3	William Wilson	William Wilson	1			3	1	
Apr 4	William West Jr.	William West		1				
Apr 4	William West Sr.	William West	1	1		2	4	
Apr 4	Benjamin Wine	Benjamin Wine						
Apr 9	George Wort	George Wort	1			6	6	
Apr 9	John Waters	John Waters				1	3	
Apr 9	Nathaniel Williams	Nathaniel Williams		6	10	5	7	
Apr 9	Peter Wood	Peter Wood		1		2	3	
Apr 9	George Williams	George Williams		7	10	2	11	
Apr 16	Sarah Williams					2	6	
Apr 16	William Waters	Wm Waters	[see next line]					
Apr 16		James Waters	1			1	5	
Apr 18	George Waters	George Waters				5	18	
Apr 20	George Wells	George Wells		1	2	4	8	
Apr 20	Elizabeth Wells			3	7	3	11	
Apr 27	Thomas Wells	Thomas Wells				1		
Apr 28	Allen Way	Allen Way				1	1	
May 4	Stacy Wilson	Stacy Wilson						
May 19	Margaret Williams			2	4	3	5	
May 19	Richard Woodgerd	Richard Woodgerd				2	2	
May 19	Henry Woodgerd	Henry Woodgerd	1			3	4	
May 19	William Watson	Wm Watson	[see next line]					
May 19		Ja.s Watson	1			1	5	

[folio 20]
Stafford Sct.   31 May 1787

Certified that I have examined & compared this aforegoing List with three others of some kind made by Mr. Wm. Mountjoy a Commissioner of said County & find them on addition to sum

- 480 White Males of & above 21 years @..
- 125 ditto of & above 16 years...
- 862 Blacks ditto...
- 959 ditto under 16 years...
- 1441 Horses @... each
- 3358 Cattle @.
- 34 Carriage Wheels
- 16 Viz. Chariots
- 12 ... Phaetons
- 26 ... Chairs
- 2 Ordinary License
- x Billiard Tables
- 8 Stud Horses am.^{t} in toto. £ 8.12.0
- 1 Practising Physician... £5.0.0.

[folio 21]

Stafford Sct.   March Court 1787

On motion of the Collectors of the Taxes in this County for year 1784 setting faith that there are Errors & overcharges arising on the Lists returned therefor, so that a just settlement can not be made therein - The Court do order & appoint that Arthur Morson, Baily Washington Junr & Daniel Triplet Gents. or either two of them do examine into the said Lists, rectify any errors that may appear, & make a state of the amount in order to a final settlement of the Taxes due by s.^{d} Lists.

Attest

T. E.S. Tyler CSC

*   *   *   *   *

*   *   *

*

[End of 1787 Personal Property Tax List]
[for William Mountjoy, Commissioner]

[folio 22]

A List of Taxable property within the district of William Alexander, Commissioner in the County of Stafford for the year 1787

Date	chargeable w/tax	white males	over 21	16-21	blks 16+	-16	H/	C/	other
Mar 7	Alexander William	William Alexander			7	7	6	25	2whl.rid.chr
Apr 27	Allison William	David Allison	1	2			1	2	
Apr 28	McAuslands Humpries	Humpries McAuslandsl			1				
Mar 17	Alexander Phillip Est.	Thomas Bowen			6	10	6	18	
Mar 23	Anderson John	John Anderson	1				3	5	
Apr 7	Arrosmith Thomas	Thomas Arrosmith	1	1			2	3	
Apr 9	Alexander William	William Alexander	*[see next line]*						
Apr 9		John Alexander	1				3	9	
Apr 11	Allentharp Jacob	Jacob Allentharp	1	1			5	9	
Apr 12	Archiball David	David Archiball					1	4	
Apr 30	Barrett Bartho^W	Bartholomew Barrett	1				1	2	
Mar 19	Bates Joseph tax free	Joseph Bates				1	1	2	
Apr 4	Buchannan Andrew	Andrew Buchannan			7	8	5	15	2whl.rid.chr
Apr 5	Briggs David	David Briggs	*[see next line]*						
Apr 5		George Patterson			10	7	7	47	2whl.rid.chr
Mar 17	Ball William	William Ball			3	4	6	8	
Mar 17	Bowen Thomas	*[name struck through]*			1	2	5	2	
Mar 17	Bolling William	William Bolling							
Mar 19	Bruce William	William Bruce	2	3	5		4	8	
Apr	Bowen Burkett	Burkett Bowen	*[see next line]*						
Apr		John Read			3	6	5	10	stud@.10.0
Apr 2	Banks Gerard	Gerard Banks			8	7	5	21	see next ln
		4 wheeled stage wagon & 2 wheeled *[riding]* chair							
Mar 19	Berry Sarah		1	2			2	4	
Mar 19	Butler William	William Butler	1	3			2	4	
Mar 19	Burnett William	William Burnett	2			4	4	7	
Mar	Bengey John	John Bengey	1				2	2	
Mar 22	Bolling Thomas	Thomas Bolling	1				1	2	
Mar 22	Bolling James	James Bolling	2				2	6	
Mar 22	Bolling Charles	Charles Bolling					1		

Stafford Co., Va. personal property tax list - 1787

Date	chargeable w/tax	white males over 21	16-21	blks 16+	-16	H	C	other
Mar 22	Beasley Phillips	Phillips Beasley				1		
Mar 23	Benson James	James Benson		2	5	2	2	
Mar 27	Black Margrett		1			4	6	
Mar 27	Berry Richard	Richard Berry					2	
Apr 2	Berry Thomas	Thomas Berry		1	3	2	1	
Apr 2	Briant John	John Briant				1	2	
[folio 23]								
Apr 2	Brown James	James Brown				3	2	
Apr 4	Ballard Thomas	Thomas Ballard		3	3	4	11	
Apr 4	Ballard William	William Ballard		1				
Apr 4	Bolling Simon	Simon Bolling						
Apr 4	Bolling William Senr	William Bolling				1	2	
Apr 5	Bussell Vincent	Vincent Bussell						
Apr 5	Burton John	John Burton	1			1		
Apr 7	Berry Anthony	Anthony Berry	1			3	9	
Apr 9	Burgess Rubin	Rubin Burgess	1			2	7	
Apr 9	Burton Girard	Girard Burton				2		
Apr 9	Brown William	William Brown				4	15	
Apr 11	Burton Rachel	Isaac Brimmer	1			3	10	
Apr 11	Bates John	John Bates						
Apr 11	Branson Isaac	Isaac Branson				2		
Apr 11	Burgess William	William Burgess				1	2	
Apr 12	Burton James	James Burton				3	7	
Apr 12	Brimmer John	John Brimmer	1			1	2	
Apr 14	Beach Thomas	Thomas Beach				3		
Apr 20	Bell John	John Bell		3	2	5	2	
Apr 20	Bower Michal	Michal Bower		1	6	3	2	
Mar 20	Bussell William	William Bussell	1	1		3	9	
May	Carter Charles Col.o	Simon Linn		11	22	4	4	
n.d.	McCullock John	John McCullock				1	2	
Mar 7	Casson Thomas	Thomas Casson		5	4	7	23	
Apr 28	Chapman Phillip	Phillip Chapman		1	1	4	4	
Apr 28	Curtice John	John Curtice						
Apr 28		John Curtice Jr.				3	9	
Mar 7	Curtice George	George Curtice Sr.		1		4	11	
Mar 7	Clark Ann					4	7	
Mar 7	Curtice George	George Curtice Jr.		0	1			

Date	chargeable w/tax	white males over 21	" 16-21/	/blks/ 16+	H/ -16	C/	other
Mar 24	Crop James Sr.	James Crop Sr.		6	4	4 13	
Apr 19	Colquhoun Walter	Walter Colquhoun		3	2	1	
Mar 19	Chilton William	William Chilton	1			2 2	
	[folio 24]						
Mar 19	Curtice Aaron	Aaron Curtice	1			1 3	
Mar 20	Cox George	George Cox				3 3	
Mar 20	Cox Vincent Jr.	Vincent Cox				4 7	
Mar 20	Chinn Susannah	Joseph Chinn			1	3 7	
Mar 20	Clemmons John	John Clemmons				2	
Mar 22	Conyers John	John Conyers	4	5	6	3 12	
Mar 23	Crop John	John Crop		[see next line]			
Mar 23		James Green		8	6	8 39	
Mar 23	Cook David	David Cook		[see next line]			
Mar 23		James Cook				1 2	
Mar 24	Crop James	James Crop		5	5	6 21	
Mar 24	Cotney John	John Cotney		3	2	4 12	
Mar 27	Cox Charnock	Charnock Cox			2	2 3	
Mar 27	Cox Presly	Presly Cox				1 4	
Apr 4	Carter Joseph	Joseph Carter		1	2	3 7	
Apr 5	Conner John	John Conner Con.				3 7	
Apr 7	Cox Enoch	Enoch Cox					
Apr 9	Cotney Elisha	Elisha Cotney				1	
Apr 9	Curtice William	William Curtice				2 4	
Apr 9	Callender Phillip	Phillip Callender				2 7	
Apr 9	Cox Vincent Sr.	Vincent & John Cox				3 5	
Apr 11	Carter Robert (Westm. Cy.)			[see next line]			
Apr 11		Leonard Hill Overseer	15	10		637	
Apr 12	Caves Thomas	Thomas Caves		0	3	4 2	
Apr 20	Collins Thomas	Thomas Collins		2	2	4 2	
Apr 20	McCloud James	James McCloud		[see next line]			
Apr 20		John McCloud	1	1			
Apr 25	Cook Christian	George Cook				1 4	
Mar 19	Carter Henry	Henry Carter					
Apr 20	Conyers Benjaman	Benj.a Conyers				1	
May 2	Curtice Richard	Rich.d Curtice				1 2	
Apr 17	Dalrymple John	John Dalrymple		[see next line]			
Apr 17		Joseph Darling	2	1		1	

Date	chargeable w/tax	white males over 21	16-21	16+	-16	H	C	other
Apr 14	Dunbar Robert	Robert Dunbar	*[see next line]*					
Apr 14		Alexander Rankins	1	4	2	3	1	
Mar 7	Donathan Gerard *[folio 25]*	Gerard Donathan		4	7	5	25	
Apr 9	Debaptist John	John Debaptist	*[see next line]*					
Apr 9		John Lucas	*[see next line]*					
Apr 9		John Faggott	1			1	4	
Mar 23	McDonnell Daniel	Daniel McDonnell	2	2	1			
Mar 26	Downman Joseph Ball	Q[uar]t[er] Little faul	*[see next line]*					
				7	14	5	35	
Apr 5	Doudle James	James Doudle	*[see next line]*					
Apr 5		Brawner Doudle	3	3	3	4		
Apr 14	Day John	John Day	1	1		1	2	
Apr 25	Day Elizabeth					1	4	
Apr 16	Drake John	John Drake						
Mar 20	Edwards Andrew	Andrew Edwards	1	7	7	10	24	
Apr 7	England John	John England	*[see next line]*					
Apr 7		John Froughner	1	1		2	3	
Mar 23	Ellison Thomas	Thomas Ellison		2	4	3	13	
Mar 20	Ellwell George	George Ellwell			1			
n.d.	Fox Nathaniel	Nath.a Fox		6	4	6	13	
n.d.	Follis Thomas	Thomas Follis	1			3	14	4rid.chr.whls
Apr 16	Fitzhugh William	William Fitzhugh	54	54	27	15		*[next line]* 8 chariot wheels & 4 chair wheels
Apr 13	Fitzhugh John	John Fitzhugh	*[see next line]*					
Apr 13		Elijah Curtice	1	18	20	9	23	*[next line]* 4 phaeton or stage wheels
Apr 13	Fitzhugh Henry	Henry Fitzhugh	*[see next line]*					
Apr 13		Lowry Henry	7	16		6	10	
Apr 16	Fitzhugh Thomas	Thomas Fitzhugh	*[see next line]*					
Apr 16		John Curtice	25	19	13	27		4char.whls.
Apr 4	Faunt John	John Faunt				2	10	
Mar 20	Fugett Benja	Benjaman Fugett	1	2	1			
Mar 19	Fletcher Rachal	Darby Souillivant	1			2	7	
Mar 20	Fugett Francis	Francis Fugett				2	4	
Mar 20	Fugett Daniel	Daniel Fugett	1					

Date	chargeable w/tax	white males over 21	" 16-21	/blks/ 16+	-16	H	C	other
Mar 20	Fugett Frances Jr.	Frances Fugett						1	
Mar 20	Finnell Jonathan	Jonathan Finnell			5	13	6	22	
Mar 23	Faunt George	George Faunt			3	1	2	15	
Mar 27	Fines Patrick	Patrick & James Fines	1				4	8	
[folio 26]									
Apr 6	McFarling Obediah	Obediah McFarling *[see next line]*							
Apr 6		John Pare					5	12	
Apr 7	Faunt Joseph	Joseph Faunt			3	1	4	15	
Apr 9	Fickling John	John Fickling			3	7	6	11	
Apr 11	Fields Samuel	Samuel Fields					1		
Apr 11	Foster Seth	Seth Foster					3	5	
Mar 27	Gollohorn Sollomon	Sollomon Gollohorn					2	4	
Apr 13	Groves Thomas	Thomas Groves	1				1	2	
Apr 17	Gordon Samuel	Samuel Gordon				1	1		
Mar 19	Green Sarah						1	1	
Mar 19	Garner John	John Garner	1				1	1	
Mar 21	Gilpin Israel	Israel Gilpin *[see next line]*							
Mar 21		Joseph Gilpin					1		
Mar 20	Green Jesse	Jesse Green					2	2	
Mar 21	Guttery Thomas	Thomas Guttery					1	3	
Mar 27	Gollohorn John taxfree	Tho.s Gollohorn					3	9	
Mar 27	McGuire Rachal		1				2	5	
Mar 27	Green James	James Green							
Apr 4	Groves William Sr.	Wm & Wm Groves	2	1			7	13	
Apr 4	Graves Benjaman	Benj.a Graves					1	5	
Apr 12	Gollohorn John Jr.	John Gollohorn					1	2	
Apr 14	Graves George	George Graves	1	1				3	
Mar 19	Garner Jacob	Jacob Garner							
Apr 19	Haner William	William Haner *[see next line]*							
Apr 19		Will Sutherly			5	1	3	7	
May 6	Graves Martha			1			3	6	
May 6	Hunter Adam	Adam Hunter *[see next line]*							
May 6		Chitton Hansdell *[see next line]*							
May 6		George Bane		3	40	35	20	76	2chr.whls.
Mar 24	Hord Peter Sr.	Peter Hord		1	6	3	4	18	
Mar 24	Hord Killis	Killis Hord		1	4	3	3	10	
[folio 27]									

Date	chargeable w/tax	white males over 21	" 16-21/	/blks/ 16+	H/ -16	C/	other
Mar 20 Hooe Harris Dust. Est.				9	13	9 35	
Mar 20 Hewitt Susanna				6	4	8 16	
Mar 23 Hord Thomas	Thomas Hord			1	1	7	
Mar 23 Hord Rody	Rody Hord			3	3	4 11	
Mar 23 Hord James	James Hord	[see next line]					
Mar 23	William Hord			8	2	8 22	
Mar 24 Hord Jesse	Jesse Hord			4	3	6 18	
Mar 24 Hord Peter Jr.	Peter Hord Jr.			1	1	3 14	
Mar 24 Humpfries William	William Humpfries	1				5 20	
n.d. Hughs McCagby	McCagby Hughs	1	1			1 2	
Mar 26 Hill Jesse		1	3	1		4 3	
Apr 4 Hord Edward	Edward Hord	1	2			8 28	
Apr 4 Heffertin Martin	Martin Heffertin					2	
Apr 5 Hall Hannah						2 6	
Apr 5 Hudson David	David Hudson			1	1	3 13	
Apr 7 Hume Francis	[name struck through]	1	2				
Apr 7 Harwood John	John Harwood	1	1			3 8	
Apr 7 Horner John	John Horner	1	5			2	
Apr 9 Horton William	William Horton					3 6	
Apr 11 Hill Leonard	William Barber			3	3	5 12	
Apr 13 Hewitt William	William Hewitt			14	14	8 20	2whl.rid.chr
Apr 14 Howard John	John Howard						
Apr 25 Hinson Sarah						2 6	
Apr 25 Hinson Elijah	Elijah Hinson					3 2	
Apr 6 Hall Benjaman	Benj.ᵃ Hall					3 6	
Apr 21 Hunter Adam @ forge	Abner Vernon	[see next line]					
Apr 21	Benj.ᵃ Bussell	[see next line]					
Apr 21	Joseph Lavender	[see next line]					
Apr 21	Robert Lavender	[see next line]					
Apr 21	John Rogers			3 43	10	25 23	2whl.rid.chr
Apr 6 Hall John	John Hall						
Mar 19 Jones Thomas	Thomas Jones					3 5	
Mar 20 Johnson Scarlott	Scarlott Johnson						
Mar 24 Jones George	George Jones					2 3	
[folio 28]							
Mar 24 Jett William	William Jett	2	1			3 11	
Mar 24 Jones Charles	Charles Jones	1	1			4 7	

Date	chargeable w/tax	white males over 21	" 16-21	/blks/ 16+	-16	H/	C/	other
Mar 27	Jones William tax free			1		1	1	
Apr 4	Jackson Rosanna	George Jackson				3	11	
Apr 4	Jackson Robert	Robert Jackson		*[see next line]*				
Apr 4		William Jackson				4	5	
Apr 6	Jones James	James Jones		*[see next line]*				
Apr 6		John Jones				3	6	
Apr 6	Jones Evins	Evins Jones		*[see next line]*				
Apr 6		James Phillips		1	1	3	8	
Apr 6	James George	George James		3	4	3	6	
Apr 7	Jones Henry	Henry Jones				5	10	
Apr 7	McIntosh James	James McIntosh				2	6	
Apr 9	Jett Presly	Presly Jett					3	
Apr 25	Jett Francis	Francis Jett		2	2	3	15	
Apr 25	Jett John	John Jett				2	3	
Apr 25	Jacobs William	William Jacobs		3	6	3	6	
Mar 19	Jones John	John Jones		1				
Apr 9	Jett George	George Jett						
Mar 6	James John	John James		*[see next line]*				
Mar 6		George James	2	13	7	10	35	*[next line]*
		4 wheeled stage wagon & 2 wheeled riding chair						
Apr 9	Kenyon James	James Kenyon		5	10	8	25	
Mar 19	Kenny Thomas	Thomas Kenny		3		4	21	
Mar 27	Kitchen James	James Kitchen		*[see next line]*				
Mar 27		Charles Kitchen				4	8	
Mar 27	Kenny John	John Kenny		1	1	2	9	
Apr 9	Kirk Jeremiah	Jeremiah Kirk		3	2	2	2	
Apr 19	McKittrick Anthony	Anthony McKittrick		1	9	2	13	22whl.rid.chr
Apr 7	Kirby James	James Kirby	1					
Apr 20	Lyon James	James Lyon		*[see next line]*				
Apr 20		Tunis Joue?		*[see next line]*				
Apr 20		Henry Hill	1	1	2	1	2	
Mar 7	Lang Robert tax free	James Lang	1			3	2	
Mar 19	Limbrick Lettice		1			2	7	
[folio 29]								
Mar 20	Limbrick William	William Limbrick				1	11	
Mar 21	Leach Andrew	Andrew Leach		1				
Apr 25	Lowry Jerry	Charg.d to Henry Fitzhugh						

Date	chargeable w/tax	white males over 21	16-21	blks 16+	-16	H	C	other
Mar 21	Lateman Daniel	Daniel Lateman				4	3	
Mar 22	Laverty Peggy			1	2	3	3	
Mar 23	Leach James	James Leach		3	5	4	7	
Mar 23	Logee Alexander	Alex.ʳ Logee	1			3	4	
Mar 24	Lanman Griffin	Griffin Lanman				1	2	
Mar 27	Leach Benjamin	Benj.ᵃ Leach		2				
Mar 27	Limbrick Francis	Francis Limbrick				3	10	
Mar 27	Limbrick George	George Limbrick						
Apr 4	Lathrum George	George Lathrum				1	2	
Apr 4	Lathrum John	John Lathrum	2			4	12	
Apr 11	Linn Simon given by C.L.		2			1	7	
Apr 11	Lunsford Joanah			1	3	4	6	
Apr 12	Limbrick John	John Limbrick				1	5	
Apr 13	Lowry James	James Lowry		1	1	3	2	
Apr 20	Lotspick William	William Lotspick		1		2	3	
Apr 25	Lathum John Sr.	John Lathum		1	3	3	11	
May 14	Lee Thomas & Mary	Thomas S. Lee	*[see next line]*					
May 14		Enoch Masson		27	42	20	61	*[next line]*
		4 wheeled stage wagon & stud horse @ 1.10.0						
Apr 20	Mortimore Charles	Charles Mortimore Jr.		1	1			
Apr 18	Middleton Thomas	Thomas Middleton	1	1				
Apr 20	McMillon William	William McMillon			1			
Apr 13	More Edward	Edward Moor *[sic]*		7	7	6	35	
Apr 20	Morison Alexander	Alex.ʳ Morison	1	2	2	1	2	
Apr 6	Morson Arthur	Arthur Morson	*[see next line]*					
Apr 6		John Andrews	*[see next line]*					
Apr 6		George Paten		7	15	15	57	
Mar 19	Miner Elizabeth			1	1	1	4	
Mar 21	Musselman Chrisʰer	Christopher Musselman				*[see next line]*		
Mar 21		Chris Musselman				4	10	
[folio 30]								
Mar 22	Massey Thomas	Thomas Massey		3	2	5	18	
Mar 22	Massey Benjaman tax free					1	1	
Mar 22	Mellett John	John Mellett				2	4	
Mar 23	Murrow Daniel	Daniel Murrow		1	2	3	4	
Mar 26	Masson Henry	Henry Masson		1				
Apr 4	Mulbury John	John Mulbury				2	11	

Date	chargeable w/tax	white males over 21	" 16-21	/blks/ 16+	-16	H/	C/	other
Apr 4	Marquess Anthony	Anthony Marquess		1		1	3	
Apr 4	Martin Daniel	Daniel Martin				2	1	
Apr 4	Massey Elizabeth					1	4	
Apr 4	Massey Tolliferro	Tolliferro Massey						
Apr 4	Martin Thomas	Thomas Martin				1	2	
Apr 6	Meal John	John Meal	*[see next line]*					
Apr 6		Samuel Meal				3	3	
Apr 6	Mattocks Lazarus	Lazarus Mattocks		1		5	6	
Apr 7	Miller John	John Miller				2		
Apr 9	Martin Charles	Charles Martin						
Apr 9	Miller Samuel	Samuel Miller	*[see next line]*					
Apr 9		Lewis Martin				4	14	
Apr 10	Manning John	John Manning				3	3	
Apr 11	Munrow Williamtaxfree	John Munrow				1	4	
Apr 12	Martin Ann	Charles Martin	1	1		3	13	
Apr 14	Mortimore Charles Sr.			3	1	3	4	
Apr 20	Moss John	John Moss						
Mar 20	Newton John	John Newton	1	5	7	5	14	
Mar 24	Norwood John	John Norwood	*[see next line]*					
Mar 24		George Robertson		3	1	5	2	
Mar 26	Newton Margrett			2	1	5	5	
Mar 26	Newton William	William Newton	*[see next line]*					
Mar 26		Isaac & Thomas Newton						*[see next line]*
Mar 26		James Dodd	*[see next line]*					
Mar 26		Theodotia Curtice		10	10	9	11	
Apr 19	Nooe Zepheniah	Zepheniah Nooe		3	5	2		22whl.rid.chr
Apr 19	Newell Ann					1	2	
Mar 22	Oliver John	John Oliver Sr.	*[see next line]*					
Mar 22		John Oliver				3	8	
[folio 31]								
Apr 7	Payne Daniel	Daniel Payne	1	1	3	1	1	
n.d.	Pollard Linsey	Linsey Pollard		1				
Mar 24	Pitcher Masson	Masson Pitcher		6	4	6	27	
Mar 17	Pitcher Richard	Richard Pitcher	1			3	8	
Mar 26	Pollard John	John Pollard		9	12	5	20	
Mar 19	Payn John	John Payn	*[see next line]*					
Mar 19		Thomas Payn	1			2	6	

Date	chargeable w/tax		white males over 21	" 16-21	/blks/ 16+	-16	H/	C/	other
Mar 19	Pitcher Mildred				1	4	1	10	
Mar 20	Pitcher Charles	Cha.s Pitcher						1	
Mar 23	Parmer Rawleigh	Rawley Parmer	1	1	4		3	7	
Mar 24	Pettet Benjaman	Benj.a Pettet	2	1			3	9	
Mar 27	Porch Thomas	Thomas Porch			8	12	7	25	
Mar 27	Pitcher Moses	Moses Pitcher			2	1	2	10	
Mar 26	Posey Thomas	Rodith White			12	10	25	41	
Apr 2	Peyton Ann	Charles Peyton	2	1	1		3	10	
Apr 4	Porch Esum	Esum Porch			1	4	3	10	
Apr 5	Patten Rachal						3	7	
Apr 5	Patterson Thomas	Thomas Patterson					3	3	
Apr 5	Patterson Perry	Perry Patterson			1				
Apr 6	Payn George over 16			1					
Apr 7	Puzey Stephen	Stephen Puzey	2				1	4	
Apr 12	Persifull Allen	Allen Persifull						3	
Mar 20	Pates Aaron	Aaron Pates			1		2	2	
Apr 12	Pitcher Peter	Peter Pitcher			1		1	4	
Apr 9	Roch Robert	Robert Roach tax free	2				2	6	
Apr 7	Richard William	William Richard	[see next line]						
Apr 7		& William Richard			6	8	3	5	
Mar 22	Rose William	William Rose					4	6	
Mar 26	Rods Mary							1	
Apr 2	Rose Jesse	Jesse Rose							
Apr 9	Reavley William	William Reavley	[see next line]						
Apr 9		William Burton			5	11	4		132whl.rid.chr
[folio 32]									
Apr 10	Roberts Griffin	Griffin Roberts							
Apr 11	Rankins John	John Rankings			1				
Apr 14	Robertson John	John Robertson			1				
Apr 25	Robertson Thomas	Thomas Robertson					3	7	
n.d.	Rawlings John	John Rawlings			2				
May 6	Read Margrett	William Read					4	9	
Mar 17	Strother Anthony	Anth.o Strother	[see next line]						
Mar 17		Geo & Anth.o Strother	1		4		6	6	12
Mar 17	Stone William	William Stone					2	3	
Apr 20	Stringfellow George	Geo. Stringfellow	[see next line]						
Apr 20		Henry Stringfellow	[see next line]						

Date	chargeable w/tax	white males over 21	16-21	/blks/ 16+	-16	H/	C/	other
Apr 20		Theodosia Wine			1	2	1	
Apr 6	Stringfellow James	James Stringfellow			2	3	10	
Mar 7	Stone Joseph	Joseph Stone				1	7	
Apr 9	Selden Samuel	Samuel Selden	*[see next line]*					
Apr 9		Pearce Perry			32	35	17	91	4whl.chariot
Apr 17	Sedden John	John Sedden			12	9	10	40	
Mar 19	Swillivant Lettice					3	8	
Mar 19	Swillivant Gabriel	Gabriel Swillivant		1			4	10	
Mar 20	Swillivant Darby	Darby Swillivant Sr. tax free				1	6	
Mar 20	Swillivant Benjaman	Benj.a Swillivant				3	7	
Mar 20	Simpson Elizabeth			1		2	4	
Mar 20	Snellings Enoch	Enoch Snellings		1		3	3	
Mar 20	Smith Samuel	Samuel Smith			4	3	3	16	
Mar 22	Siblee Benson	Benson Siblee		1		2	2	
Mar 22	Sharp Thomas	Thomas Sharp Sr.	*[see next line]*					
Mar 22		John Sharp			4	3	2	2	
Mar 22	Sharp Thomas Jr.	Thomas Sharp				1	1	2	
Mar 22	Sutor John	John Sutor	*[see next line]*					
Mar 22		Jesse Sutor						2	
Mar 22	Stringfellow Townshand	Tows.d Stringfellow					1	

[folio 33]

Date	chargeable w/tax	white males over 21	16-21	/blks/ 16+	-16	H/	C/	other
Mar 22	Smith John	John Smith			2	5	4	8	
Mar 26	Slaven Jesse	Jesse Slaven	*[see next line]*					
Mar 26		Alexander Lensey		1		3	4	
Mar 27	Swillivant Ann	Aaron Nonday				1	3	
Apr 2	Sharp Linsfield	Linsfield Sharp	*[see next line]*					
Apr 2		William Sharp			8	3	8	16	
Apr 2	Snipe Nathaniel	Nathaniel Snipe				2	5	
Apr 4	Stripling Joell	Joell Stripling			1			
Apr 4	Sutor Andrew	Andrew Sutor	*[see next line]*					
Apr 4		William Sutor		1	1	3	4	9	
Apr 9	Schooler Thomas	Thomas Schooler				1	7	
Apr 6	Simpson Alex.r	Alex.r Simpson tax free				2	6	
Apr 6	Simpson John	John Simpson					2	
Apr 7	Simmons William	Will Simmons						
Apr 7	Sudtherd William	William Sudtherd				1	7	

Date	chargeable w/tax	white males over 21	16-21	/blks/ 16+	H/ -16	C/	other
Apr 9 Skinker Thomas				5	9	6	33
Apr 9 Seydmore Joshua	Joshua Seydmore				1	1	
Apr 11 Scott Sarah		1				1	4
Apr 12 Smith Henry Sr.	Henry Smith		[see next line]				
Apr 12	Joseph Smith			6	3	6	23
Apr 12 Stripling Samuel	Sam.l Stripling						
Apr 24 Smith Joseph	Joseph Smith						
Apr 25 Sudtherd Moses	Moses Sudtherd					1	3
Apr 25 Stripling William	Will Stripling					1	2
May 3 Swillivant Francis	Fra.s Swillivant	1		4	3	4	
May 6 Snelling John	John Snelling					3	2
May 6 Snelling William	Will Snelling					3	6
May 6 Sanders James	James Sanders						2
May 6 Swann Phillip	Phillip Swann	1					
Apr 9 Swann Asa	Asa Swann						
Mar 27 Swillivant Daniel	Daniel Swillivant	1				3	7
Apr 4 Stripling Elizabeth		1				5	2
[folio 34]							
Apr 9 Thompson Zacha.a	Zachariah Thompson				1	2	4
Apr 20 Taylor William	William Taylor		[see next line]				
Apr 20	William Elkins		[see next line]				
Apr 20	Richard Gatewood	1		6	7	3	3
Apr 7 Triplett Daniel	Daniel Triplett	1		5	4	4	1
							4whl stage wag
Apr 7 Thompson James	James Thompson	1				6	14
Mar 19 Thornton Thomas	John Bern			7	7	6	8
Mar 19 Templeman Jane						1	4
Mar 23 Turner Benjaman	Benj.a Turner	1				3	11
Mar 26 Threlkell Jesse	Jesse Threlkell					1	
Mar 26 Turner James	James Turner		[see next line]				
Mar 26	William Turner					4	13
Apr 9 Turner Grif.n William	William G. Turner	1				3	7
Apr 9 Taylor Jesse	Jesse Taylor						1
Apr 9 Troop Thomas	Thomas Troop					1	2
Apr 9 Turner Absolum	Absolum Turner	1				3	6
Apr 11 Tate William	William Tate					1	5
Apr 17 Taylor Robert	Robert Taylor						

Date	chargeable w/tax	white males over 21	" 16-21	/blks/ 16+	H/ -16	H/	C/	other
Apr 25	Tinsley John	John Tinsley					1	
Apr 25	Tyler Alice	John Tyler	1	6	7	5	15	
Apr 5	Timmons William	William Timmons				3	6	
Apr 14	Travis Margrett			1	3		2	
Apr 14	Templeman Edward	Edward Templeman				3	11	
Apr 11	Underwood John	John Underwood						
Apr 20	Vowles Henry	Henry Vowles						*[see next line]*
Apr 20		Cha.s Vowles						*[see next line]*
Apr 20		Zacha.h Vowles		6	8	4		52whl.rid.chr
[folio 35]								
Apr 20	Vowles Thomas	Thomas Vowles						*[see next line]*
Apr 20		Andrew Chinn						*[see next line]*
Apr 20		Joseph Shepherd						*[see next line]*
Apr 20		James Doratha						*[see next line]*
Apr 20		Andrew McDonnell	3	2	2			
Apr 16	Waugh Lee George	George Lee Waugh		21	12	7	23	
Apr 9	Wallice James Doct.r			3	2	2	8	
								no physic.lic.
Apr 9	Wallice John	John Wallice		5	7	4	5	
Apr 13	Weathers James	James Weathers	1	8	8	7	36	
Apr 13	Weathers Charles	Cha.s Weathers					2	
Apr 17	Walker William	William Walker	1	3	3	3	8	
Apr 16	Waugh T. Robert	Robert T. Waugh		3	3	2	13	
Mar 19	Waugh McCagby	McCagby Waugh				3	7	
Mar 22	Wooderd Mary		1	2		2	11	
Mar 22	Webb Aaron	Aaron Webb	1			5	15	
Mar 22	White George	George White		1	4	4	8	
Mar 23	White Thomas	Thomas White		1		4	8	
Mar 23	West Edward Jr.	Edward West Jr.		2	1	3	4	
Mar 23	West Edward Sr.	Edward West & John	1	3		6	7	
Mar 26	White George	George White tax free				1	2	
Mar 26	Genl Washington George	Jesse Hill		7	4	4	23	
n.d.	Wallice B. William	Wm B. Wallice		2	6	4		
Apr 4	West John	John West				5	2	
Apr 4	Wood William	William Wood	1	1	3	6	14	
Apr 5	Walker Solomon	Solomon Walker				1	4	
Apr 9	Walker James	James Walker					2	

Date	chargeable w/tax	white males over 21	16-21	/blks/ 16+	H/ -16	C/	other
Apr 9	Weaks Thomas	Thomas Weaks			2	4	
Apr 9	White Nancy				1		
Apr 12	White George	George White Jr.			1	2	
Apr 19	Wilson William	Wm Wilson	2	2	1	1	
[folio 36]							
Apr 19	West Thomas	Thomas West		1			
Apr 19	Winlock William	Wm Winlock	3.		3	3	
Apr 19	Williams Kiziah	John Zyley	*[see next line]*				
Apr 19		Joseph Cornuck	1		1		
Apr 25	Walton James				3	5	
Apr 28	Wellford Robert		10	13	19	26	
Mar 19	Wisharts Esta	John Rawling	4	5	3	7	
n.d.	Young Joseph	Jos. Young	*[see next line]*				
n.d.		Wm Gimbo	*[see next line]*				
n.d.		John Andrew	8	6	10	12	
Mar 22	Young William	William Young	*[see next line]*				
Mar 22		Leonard Young		1	5	4	

On Oct. 16, 1787 Wm Alexander sent an addendum:

Date	chargeable w/tax	white males over 21	16-21	/blks/ 16+	H/ -16	C/	other
Jun 21	Ann Lewis			1	1		
Jun 22	James Donavan		1	1	5	3	6

* * * * *
* * *
*

[End of 1787 Personal Property Tax List]

[This page blank]

Stafford County
Virginia

Personal Property
Tax List

1787

[Arranged by date of tax enumeration]

Source: Virginia State Library, Archives Division. County Records. Stafford County Tax lists.

Form of return of taxable property to be made by the commissioners

List No. 1.

A List of Taxable property within the district of William Mountjoy, Commissioner in the County of Stafford for the year 1787

[Categories]:

Date of receiving lists from individuals;

Persons names chargeable with the tax;

Names of white male tithables above 21;

[col. 1] - No. of white males above 16 and under 21;

[col. 2] - Blacks above 16;

[col. 3] - Blacks under 16;

[col. 4] - Horses mares colts & mules;

[col. 5] - Cattle;

[other] - Coaches wheels; Faetons & wagons; chairs wheels; Ordinary licence; Billiard tables; Studs; Rate pr season.

List No. 2.

A List of Taxable property within the district of William Alexander, Commissioner in the County of Stafford for the year 1787

[Categories]:

Date of receiving lists from individuals;

Persons names chargeable with the tax;

Names of white male tithables above 21;

[col. 1] - No. of white males above 16 and under 21;

[col. 2] - Blacks above 16;

[col. 3] - Blacks under 16;

[col. 4] - Horses mares colts & mules;

[col. 5] - Cattle;

[other] - Coaches wheels; Faetons & wagons; chairs wheels; Ordinary licence; Billiard tables; Studs; Rate pr season; Physicians.

A List of Taxable property within the district of
William Mountjoy, Commissioner in the County of Stafford
for the year 1787

[arranged by date of tax enumeration]

Date chargeable w/tax	white males over 21	" 16-21	/blks/H/ 16+	-16	C/	other
Mar 12 James Abbet	James Abbet				1	1
Mar 12 George Abbet	George Abbet				4	11
Mar 12 Elijah Abbet	Elijah Abbet				3	10
Mar 12 John Bannister	John Bannister				2	
Mar 12 William Barby	William Barby				3	5
Mar 12 Thomas Barby	Thomas Barby				1	4
Mar 12 William Browne	William Browne				2	5
Mar 12 Charles Davis	Charles Davis				1	
Mar 12 Bradly Dent	Bradly Dent	1			2	6
Mar 12 Jessey Edwards	Jessey Edwards	*[see next line]*				
Mar 12 *Jessey Edwards*	Thomson Edwards	1			2	8
Mar 12 John Ford	John Ford				1	2
Mar 12 William Franklin	William Franklin		1		3	4
Mar 12 John Garrison	John Garrison				1	4
Mar 12 William Gollohorn	William Gollohorn		1	1	4	4
Mar 12 Elisha Grigsby	Elisha Grigsby		2		2	6
Mar 12 Samuel Groves	Samuel Groves				2	6
Mar 12 Peter Hansbrough	Peter Hansbrough		1	2	4	4
Mar 12 John Scott Harding	John Scott Harding				3	9
Mar 12 George Harding	George Harding		1		3	5
Mar 12 Henry Hiden	Henry Hiden				2	10
Mar 12 John Holloday	John Holloday	1	1		4	7
Mar 12 Henry Horton	Henry Horton	1			1	3
Mar 12 Samuel Hudson	Samuel Hudson		2	2	4	15
Mar 12 John Innis					1	2
Mar 12 Alexander Jameson	Alexander Jameson				2	3
Mar 12 James Jones	James Jones				1	
Mar 12 William Jones	William Jones				3	7 stud@0.7.0
Mar 12 John Jones Jr.	John Jones				1	

Date	chargeable w/tax	white males over 21	16-21	blks 16+	-16	H	C	other
Mar 12	Charles Porter Jr.	Charles Porter	1	2	4	3	1	
Mar 12	William Ross Jr.	William Ross		1	1	4	16	
Mar 12	John Franklin Jr.	John Franklin						
Mar 12	Richard Sims Jr.	Richard Sims				2	2	
Mar 12	John Stark Jr.	John Stark		1		4	6	
Mar 12	William Shelton Jr.	William Shelton			1	6	10	
Mar 12	Christopher Knight	Christopher Knight				2	4	
Mar 12	John Lawlis	John Lawlis		1		2	16	
Mar 12	Edmund Lumdit	Edmund Lumdit	1			3	10	
Mar 12	Richard Mason	Richard Mason	1		1	7	8	
Mar 12	Henry Mcentire	Henry Mcentire		1	2	2	4	
Mar 12	Alexander Mcentire	Alexander Mcentire		2	5	2	10	
Mar 12	Edward McKenzy	Edward McKenzy				1	3	
Mar 12	Charles Mifflin	levy free				2	5	
Mar 12	John Murray	in Prince William	3	1				
Mar 12	James Ocane	James Ocane	1	1	2	5	6	
Mar 12	John Packston	John Packston	1			6	13	
Mar 12	Habern Rauls	under 21	1		2	2	1	
Mar 12	Kenez Rauls	Kenez Rauls				1	3	
Mar 12	Aron Read	Aron Read				3	10	
Mar 12	Joel Readish	Joel Readish	1	5	5	6	15	
Mar 12	Baily Riley	Baily Riley		1		2	5	
Mar 12	Jessey Riley	Jessey Riley				1	4	
Mar 12	William Robeson	William Robeson	1	1		3	6	
Mar 12	Presly Sims	Presly Sims				1		
Mar 12	Edward Snoxall	Edward Snoxall	1			3	5	
Mar 12	John Jones Sr.	John Jones				5	19	
Mar 12	William Edwards Sr.	William Edwards		1		2	10	
Mar 12	William Shelton Sr.	William Shelton		1		2	6	
Mar 12	Jerremiah Stark	Jerremiah Stark	2	2	0	5	8	
Mar 12	John Stark	John Stark				1		
Mar 12	William Stark	William Stark		1		2	2	
Mar 12	Charles Stern	Charles Stern		2	6	1	2	
Mar 12	William Tolsen	William Tolsen		1	1	2	7	
Mar 12	Mary Grigsby Travers			1	6			
Mar 12	James Waters	James Waters		1	2	2	4	
Mar 12	Charles Waters	Charles Waters				2	2	

Date	chargeable w/tax	white males over 21	" 16-21/	/blks/ 16+	H/ -16	C/	other
Mar 13	James Arrosmith	James Arrosmith			3	4	
Mar 13	James Carter	James Carter		2	3	4	
Mar 13	John Fristoe	John Fristoe	3	3	5	7	
Mar 13	John Fritter	John Fritter			2	4	
Mar 13	Jeremiah Knight	Jeremiah Knight	1		5	12	
Mar 13	George Latham	George Latham	1	1	4	5	
Mar 13	John Lunsford	John Lunsford			4	15	
Mar 13	Hugh McDaniel	Hugh McDaniel					
Mar 13	William Mullin	William Mullin	6	8	4 11		2whl. carr.
Mar 13	Peter Mauzy Sr.	Thomas Loury	3	1	2	8	
Mar 13	David Jones Sr.	David Jones	1		2	4	
Mar 13	James Billingslee Sr.	Ja.s Billingslee		[see next line]			
Mar 13	*James Billingslee Sr.*	Ja.s Billingslee	2		4	3	
Mar 13	William Tungate	William Tungate			3	4	
Mar 13	Richard Walker	Richard Walker	1	2	3	5	
Mar 13	William Williams	William Williams					
Mar 14	Joseph Combs	Joseph Combs	3	3	3	15	
Mar 14	William Cummins	William Cummins			3	2	
Mar 14	Richard Griffis	Richard Griffis	1		1	2	
Mar 14	Benjamin Grigory	Benjamin Grigory			2	3	
Mar 14	William Byrum Sr.	William Byrum			1	2	
Mar 15	Sarah Ashby	Robert Ashby			2	4	
Mar 15	William Ensey	William Ensey	2	2	3	3	
Mar 15	James Ford	James Ford	3	3	5	8	
Mar 15	John Goldsmith	John Goldsmith	1 3	4	3	5	
Mar 15	William Innis	William Innis					
Mar 15	William Bridwell Jr.	William Bridwell			2		
Mar 15	John Nelson	John Nelson	2		2	2	
Mar 15	Benjamin Pritchet	Benjamin Pritchet	6	3	5	20	stud 15.0
Mar 15	James Ratliff	James Ratliff					
Mar 15	Mary Ann Rauls		3	1	2	8	
Mar 15	Richard Read	Richard Read	2		3	15	
Mar 16	Peter Cook	Peter Cook			2	3	
Mar 17	Joseph Beagle	Joseph Beagle			1	5	
Mar 17	William Bridwell	William Bridwell	3 3	3	3	13	

Stafford Co., Va. personal property tax list - 1787

Date	chargeable w/tax	white males over 21	" 16-21	/blks/ 16+	-16	H/	C/	other
Mar 17	William French	William French	[see next line]					
Mar 17	*William French*	Stephen French		5	5	8	21	
Mar 17	Richard Hiden	Richard Hiden						
Mar 17	Margaret Matthews			3	4	5	2	2whl. carr.
Mar 17	James Parmer	James Parmer				2	2	
Mar 17	William Taylor	William Taylor	1	7	10	7	18	2whl. carr.
Mar 20	James Barnot	James Barnot		1	3	2	2	
Mar 20	John Bruin	John Bruin	1			2	6	
Mar 20	John Carter	John Carter				2		
Mar 20	William Cole	William Cole						
Mar 20	Asey Cummins	Asey Cummins	3			6	3	
Mar 20	William Gant	William Gant		1	2	2	7	
Mar 20	William Edwards Jr.	William Edwards	3	1		1	3	
Mar 20	Allen Mountjoy	Allen Mountjoy	1	1		3	9	
Mar 20	James Oglesby	James Oglesby				2	3	
Mar 20	Joseph Readish	Joseph Readish		4	4	5	12	
Mar 20	William Roles	William Roles				2	3	
Mar 20	Craven Spiller	under age		1		1		
Mar 20	Charles Stuart	Charles Stuart		5	2	5	13	
Mar 20	Mary Waller	Moses Grigsby	1	4	6	6	17	
Mar 20	William Waller	Wm Waller	[see next line]					
Mar 20	*William Waller*	Edw.d Waller	[see next line]					
Mar 20	*William Waller*	Wm Waller		4	11	6	15	
Mar 20	Benjamin Willits	Benjamin Willits				2	2	
Mar 21	John Agin	John Agin					1	
Mar 21	William Barnot	William Barnot		1				
Mar 21	John Beagle	John Beagle	1			2	6	
Mar 21	Mary Bell			3	1	3	4	
Mar 21	John Hardy	John Hardy		7	14	6	7	2whl. carr.
Mar 21	John Hedgman	John Hedgman		20	18	13	20	
Mar 21	Peter Mawzy Jr.	Peter Mawzy		1	1	2	6	
Mar 21	William Mawzy	William Mawzy		1		3	5	
Mar 21	James Morton	James Morton		1	1	1		
Mar 21	Urslee Morton			1	5	2	16	
Mar 21	Richard Morton	Richard Morton		2				
Mar 21	Henry Sudduth	Henry Sudduth				2	4	
Mar 21	John Withers	John Withers			4	1		

Date	chargeable w/tax	white males over 21	* 16-21	/blks/ 16+	-16	H/	C/	other
Mar 22	William Baul	William Baul		3	3	6	14	
Mar 22	Benjamin Bowlin	Benjamin Bowlin					3	
Mar 22	Robert Buchan	Robert Buchan		5	2	8	11	
Mar 22	William Davis	William Davis				2	6	
Mar 22	Jerremiah Day	Jerremiah Day						
Mar 22	Francis Foushee	F. Foushee	*[see next line]*					
Mar 22	*Francis Foushee*	John H. Foushee		2	2	2	14	
Mar 22	John Harrison	John Harrison		1	1	3	4	
Mar 22	Thomas Hay		1			2	7	
Mar 22	James Lowry	James Lowry	2			2	7	
Mar 22	Thomas Mallery	Thomas Mallery						
Mar 22	Elizabeth Overall		1	6	4	7	22	
Mar 22	Jessey Payn	Jessey Payn				1	5	
Mar 22	Francis Payn	Francis Payn						
Mar 22	James Payn	James Payn				1	4	
Mar 22	Daniel Reads	Daniel Reads				3	9	
Mar 22	Reuben Rogers	Reuben Rogers				1		
Mar 22	John Shelket	John Shelket		1	1	4	7	
Mar 22	Elizabeth Spilman					1	7	
Mar 22	John Withers Sr.	John Withers	*[see next line]*					
Mar 22	*John Withers Sr.*	Benj.a Withers		13	15	9	38	
Mar 22	George Withers	George Withers		1	1	3	16	
Mar 23	George Barns	George Barns						
Mar 23	John Browne	John Browne		1				
Mar 23	Brian Chadwell	Brian Chadwell	1	2	4	4	15	
Mar 23	Henry Clifton	H. Clifton	*[see next line]*					
Mar 23	*Henry Clifton*	Lawrence Butler	3	5	5	5	13	
Mar 23	Jessey Kendall	Jessey Kendall				2	4	
Mar 23	Aron Kendall	Aron Kendall		2				
Mar 23	George Normon	George Normon		3	2	5	8	
Mar 23	John R. Peyton	John R. Peyton	*[see next line]*					
Mar 23	*John R. Peyton*	Zachariah Griffith		12	11	10	27	2whl.carr.
Mar 23	Presly Raimy	Presly Raimy	1			3	2	
Mar 23	Francis Stern	Francis Stern	*[see next line]*					
Mar 23	John Stern	John Stern		1	1	3	2	
Mar 23	*Francis Stern*	Ralph Hughs		4	8	5	7	
Mar 23	Hawkin Stone	Hawkin Stone		4	12	7	20	

Date	chargeable w/tax	white males over 21	16-21	/blks/ 16+	-16	H/	C/	other
Mar 23	Barsheba Waller				1	2	5	
Mar 23	Peter Waters	Peter Waters				2	7	
Mar 24	William Anderson	William Anderson				1	2	
Mar 24	John Cloe	John Cloe				1	3	
Mar 24	Cuthbert Combs	Cuthbert Combs		6	9	4	11	
Mar 24	James Dent	James Dent						
Mar 24	William Edrington	William Edrington	1	2	6	6	11	
Mar 24	William Harding	William Harding	1	1	5	5	15	
Mar 24	John Harding	John Harding				2	2	
Mar 24	Cuthbert Harding	Cuthbert Harding		1	2	1	3	
Mar 24	Baily Washington Jr.	Baily Washington		10	13	4		2whl.carr.
Mar 24	Peter Kendall	Peter Kendall				3		
Mar 24	Aihsah Rauls			1	2	1		
Mar 24	Baily Washington Sr.	Baily Washington		11	4	9	30	4whl.carr.
Mar 27	Nathan Bannister	Nathan Bannister	1			3	6	
Mar 27	Elijah Bell	Elijah Bell				1	3	
Mar 27	George Bell	George Bell	1	1	1	5	7	
Mar 27	William Devene	William Devene				1		
Mar 27	Elizabeth Dunaway		2			3	4	
Mar 27	William Dunaway	William Dunaway				1	5	
Mar 27	Kissiah Gui	Kissiah Gui				2	6	
Mar 27	Benjamin Gui	Benjamin Gui				1	4	
Mar 27	John Gui	John Gui				2	1	
Mar 27	William Gui	William Gui				[see next line]		
Mar 27	*William Gui*	Joseph Gui				4	5	
Mar 27	Thomas Heth					1	5	
Mar 27	Rachel Hewitt	Richard Hewitt		4	9	3		
Mar 27	Mary Hore	William Hore		7	7	3	20	
Mar 27	John Hore	John Hore				1		
Mar 27	Elias Hore	Elias Hore		1	2	1	4	
Mar 27	Charles Latham	Charles Latham				1		
Mar 27	Thomas Mountjoy	Thomas Mountjoy	1			1	4	
Mar 27	Edward Normon	Edward Normon		4	4	6	17	
Mar 27	William Parmer	William Parmer						
Mar 27	Calvert Porter	Calvert Porter				[see next line]		
Mar 27	*Calvert Porter*	Thomas Porter		3	2	5	10	
Mar 27	William Richards	William Richards		1	1	2	4	

Stafford Co., Va. personal property tax list - 1787

Date	chargeable w/tax	white males over 21	white males 16-21	blks 16+	-16	H	C	other
Mar 27	Benjamin Shacklet	B. Shacklet						*[see next line]*
Mar 27	*Benjamin Shacklet*	Wm Shacklet	1			4	6	
Mar 27	William Williams	William Williams				4	4	
Mar 28	George Bell	George Bell				2	3	
Mar 28	John Bell	John Bell		1		2	5	
Mar 28	Clem. Billingslee	Clement Billingslee		1		2	2	
Mar 28	John Bridges	John Bridges				1	2	
Mar 28	Henry Griffin	Henry Griffin	1	1		2	2	
Mar 28	William Groves	William Groves		1		2	2	
Mar 28	Steaphen Johnston	Steaphen Johnston		1				
Mar 28	Elizabeth Mason			6	5	5	4	4whl. carr.
Mar 28	Ann Moncure			9	6	5	21	2whl. carr.
Mar 28	Wharton Philbert	Wharton Philbert				2		
Mar 28	John Smith	John Smith				2	4	
Mar 28	John Waters	John Waters						*[see next line]*
Mar 28	*John Waters*	Baily Waters		1		2	3	
Mar 29	William Aleson	William Aleson				1		
Mar 29	Samuel Burroughs	Samuel Burroughs				1	2	
Mar 29	Bassell Burroughs	Bassell Burroughs				1	3	
Mar 29	John Butler	John Butler	1	2	3	3	7	
Mar 29	Jedediah Carter	Jedediah Carter				2	4	
Mar 29	John Carter	John Carter						
Mar 29	William Fling	tax free				1	4	
Mar 29	Ann Gaddis		1	3	2	5	15	
Mar 29	Mary Garrard			8	14	3	12	
Mar 29	William Garrard	William Garrard		1		2		
Mar 29	John Jinkins	John Jinkins						
Mar 29	Mary McDaniel					1	6	
Mar 29	Phillip Nash	Phillip Nash				1	2	
Mar 29	Winneford Ratliff			3	5	6	18	
Mar 29	Thomas Right	Thomas Right	1	3		5	15	
Mar 29	Gowry Right	Gowry Right						
Mar 29	Willis Edwards Sr.	Willis Edwards		1		1	3	
Mar 29	William Stark	William Stark	1	1		3	5	
Mar 29	William Stone	William Stone		5	9	7	20	
Mar 29	Savanah Womsly			1		3	6	
Mar 30	John Dillon	John Dillon				1	2	

Date	chargeable w/tax	white males over 21	" 16-21	/blks/ 16+	/blks/ -16	H/	C/	other
Mar 30	William Dorson	William Dorson				1	3	
Mar 30	Backer Edwards	Backer Edwards	1			2	8	
Mar 30	Joseph Franklin	Joseph Franklin						
Mar 30	Aron Garrison	Aron Garrison				1	2	
Mar 30	Isaac Gaskins	Isaac Gaskins				3	6	
Mar 30	James Hore	James Hore		1	2	2	11	
Mar 30	Jane Lunsford					1	4	
Mar 30	Benjamin Million	Benjamin Million	1			2	10	
Mar 30	Robert Smith	Robert Smith						
Mar 30	John Franklin Sr.	John Franklin				2	8	
Mar 30	James Cloe Sr.	tax free				4	10	
Mar 30	John Waters Sr.	levy free		2	2	4	12	
Mar 30	Josius Stone	Josius Stone		5	5	3	13	
Mar 30	John Stork	John Stork		4	7		6	stud 15.0
Mar 30	John Warren	John Warren	1			3	8	
Mar 30	William West	William West		1		3	10	
Mar 31	Jacob Bridwell	tax free		2		3	8	
Mar 31	Joseph Cooper	tax free				1	4	
Mar 31	Eliab Cooper	under 21		1	1	1		
Mar 31	Christopher Dorson	Christopher Dorson				1	1	
Mar 31	Reuben Franklin	Reuben Franklin				3	6	
Mar 31	Elizabeth Garrison					1	6	
Mar 31	John Johnston	John Johnston				1		
Mar 31	James Cloe Jr.	James Cloe				1		
Mar 31	Uriah Knight	Uriah Knight				3		
Mar 31	Richard Poats	Richard Poats				5	8	
Mar 31	John Poats	John Poats				1	4	
Mar 31	William Poats	William Poats		1		3	8	
Mar 31	Moses Poats	Moses Poats				2	4	
Mar 31	Benjamin Tolson	Benjamin Tolson			1	1		
Mar 31	John Tolson	John Tolson						
Mar 31	Elizabeth Tolson			4	6	8	36	
Mar 31	Ann Vaun					3	4	
Apr 3	Jonathan Bell	Jonathan Bell				1		
Apr 3	William Bradly	William Bradly	*[see next line]*					
Apr 3	*William Bradly*	Cha.ˢ Bradly				2	6	
Apr 3	Daniel Cane	Daniel Cane				2	1	

Date	chargeable w/tax	white males over 21	" 16-21/	/blks/ 16+	H/ -16	C/	other
Apr 3	Harris Carter	Harris Carter				1 5	
Apr 3	George Coats	George Coats	2	6	1		
Apr 3	Hesekiah Patterson	Hesekiah Patterson			2 1		
Apr 3	John Patterson	John Patterson	1		3 17		
Apr 3	Elizabeth Peyton	Thomas Peyton	[see next line]				
Apr 3	*Elizabeth Peyton*	Sam. H. Peyton	11 11	7 14			ord. lic.
Apr 3	Richard Stone	Richard Stone	2 4	3 5			
Apr 3	William Wilson	William Wilson	1		3 1		
Apr 4	Magdalin Betty				2 4		
Apr 4	Francis Brooks	Francis Brooks			2 7		
Apr 4	Hannah Dickenson	Anthony Latham	6 8	9 23			stud@1.4.0
Apr 4	Margaret Eaton				1		
Apr 4	William West Jr.	William West			1		
Apr 4	James More	James More			1 7		
Apr 4	Burdit Readish	Burdit Readish	[see next line]				
Apr 4	*Burdit Readish*	John Smith	1		2 6		
Apr 4	Thomas Sedden	T. Sedden	[see next line]				
Apr 4	*Thomas Sedden*	Richard Taylor	14 14	9 34			
Apr 4	William West Sr.	William West	1 1	2 4			
Apr 4	Thomas Sudduth	Thomas Sudduth			2 3		
Apr 4	Benjamin Wine	Benjamin Wine					
Apr 9	John Achison	John Achison	1		1		
Apr 9	Benjamin Adie	Benjamin Adie	5 2	4 0			
Apr 9	William Adie	William Adie	[see next line]				
Apr 9	*William Adie*	William Adie	9 14	6 14			2whl. carr.
Apr 9	Daniel Antrum	Daniel Antrum	[see next line]				
Apr 9	*Daniel Antrum*	Levy Antrum	1		4		
Apr 9	Nathan Atchison	Nathan Achison	2 2	2 2 8			
Apr 9	Enough Benson	Enough Benson	3 5	5 11			
Apr 9	John Botts	John Botts	1 5	2 6 11			
Apr 9	Aron Botts	Aron Botts	5 6	7 15			
Apr 9	William Botts	William Botts	3 5	4 9			
Apr 9	George Bridwell	George Bridwell			2 5		
Apr 9	Moses Bridwell	Moses Bridwell	1 4	3 3 7			
Apr 9	Walter Browne	Walter Browne			4 10		
Apr 9	John Browne	Jn.º Browne	[see next line]				
Apr 9	*John Browne*	Nathaniel Williams	12 13	6 19			

Date	chargeable w/tax	white males over 21	" 16-21	/blks/ 16+	-16	H/	C/	other
Apr 9	George Byrum	George Byrum	1				1	
Apr 9	Josua Carney	Josua Carney						[see next line]
Apr 9	*Josua Carney*	Benj.a Carnet	2	1	1	7	14	
Apr 9	Sarah Daniel			14	16	12	43	4-whl carr.
Apr 9	RawleighWmDownman	Nathaniel Elkins		9	16	4	16	
Apr 9	Thomas Edrington	Thomas Edrington		2	2	2	2	
Apr 9	Haden Edwards	Haden Edwards		5	4	5	20	2-whl carr.
Apr 9	Samuel Faunt	Samuel Faunt				4	11	
Apr 9	Anthony Ficklin	Anthony Ficklin	1	7	8	6	15	
Apr 9	John Finch	John Finch						
Apr 9	Joseph Franklin	tax free				5	5	
Apr 9	Richard Fristoe	do.		1		1	12	
Apr 9	William Fritter	William Fritter				2	3	
Apr 9	George Garrison	George Garrison	1			2	3	
Apr 9	John Grigsby	John Grigsby				1	5	
Apr 9	Thomas Harding	Thomas Harding			1	2	8	
Apr 9	William Honey	William Honey				2	7	
Apr 9	James Horton	James Horton				3	4	
Apr 9	Elijah Horton	Elijah Horton				1	6	
Apr 9	John Horton	John Horton		5	7	7	18	
Apr 9	Causom Horton	Causom Horton	1			3	4	
Apr 9	Gabril Jones	Gabril Jones						[see next line]
Apr 9	*Gabril Jones*	Fieldin Ficklin		4	6	4	4	
Apr 9	George Bridwell Jr.	George Bridwell				2	4	
Apr 9	Travers Daniel Jr.	Travers Daniel		5	1	5	3	
Apr 9	Henry Kendall	Henry Kendall		1	1	3	7	
Apr 9	Sarah Kirk					3	7	
Apr 9	James Kirk	James Kirk		2				
Apr 9	Snodon Latham	Snodon Latham				2	7	
Apr 9	Gavin Lawson	Gavin Lawson						[see next line]
Apr 9	*Gavin Lawson*	David Bridges						[see next line]
Apr 9	*Gavin Lawson*	Charles Duncanson		18	18	13	46	4whl. carr.
Apr 9	Chondrid Lewis	Chondrid Lewis				1	1	
Apr 9	Moses Lunsford	Moses Lunsford				3	9	
Apr 9	Lewis Mason	Lewis Mason				3	5	
Apr 9	Daniel Mason	Daniel Mason	2	1	1	6	16	

Date	chargeable w/tax	white males over 21	" 16-21/	/blks/ 16+	H/ -16	C/	other
Apr 9	John Mason	John Mason			*[see next line]*		
Apr 9	*John Mason*	Joel Mason	1	2	2	6 13	
Apr 9	Lettace Massey		1		1	4	
Apr 9	Robert Million	Robert Million	2		6	9	
Apr 9	James Nailer	James Nailer	1		7	9	
Apr 9	Robert Painter	Robert Painter	1		4	12	
Apr 9	Vallentine Peyton	Vallentine Peyton		9 15	4	17	4whl.carr.
Apr 9	*Vallentine Peyton*						physician's license
Apr 9	James Primm	James Primm		2	2	2 7	
Apr 9	William Randol	Wᵐ Randol			*[see next line]*		
Apr 9	George Randol	Thomas Gill			2	9	
Apr 9	*William Randol*	John Randol	1		4	7	
Apr 9	Charles Rauls	Charles Rauls			*[see next line]*		
Apr 9	*Charles Rauls*	George Williams	3	2 4	1	7	
Apr 9	Rawleigh Rawls	Rawleigh Rauls		3	3	3 12	stud .15.0
Apr 9	James Robeson	James Robeson			2	6	
Apr 9	William Rout	William Rout		1	3	3 11	
Apr 9	Wilson Shelton	Wilson Shelton			1	6	
Apr 9	James Sims	James Sims			3	4	
Apr 9	Nathaniel Smith	Nathaniel Smith	2		3	12	
Apr 9	Charles Porter Sr.	Charles Porter	4	9	5	11	
Apr 9	Moses Fritter Sr.	Moses Fritter Sr.	1		2	7	
Apr 9	Travers Daniel Sr.	Travers Daniel	1 16		6 14	41	2-whl carr.
Apr 9	Peter Knight Sr.	Peter Knight	2		4	12	
Apr 9	John Holloway Sr.	John Holloway			2	3	
Apr 9	Dennis Doyall Sr.	Dennis Doyall	1		4	6	
Apr 9	Richard Sims Sr.	Levy free			2	9	
Apr 9	Samuel Thompson	Samuel Thompson	2	1	3	5	
Apr 9	John Waters	John Waters			1	3	
Apr 9	Nathaniel Williams	Nathaniel Williams		6 10	5	7	
Apr 9	George Williams	George Williams		7 10	2	11	
Apr 9	Peter Wood	Peter Wood		1	2	3	
Apr 9	George Wort	George Wort	1		6	6	
Apr 14	Amus Atchison	Amus Atchison	1		3	13	
Apr 15	John Fr.ᵃ Mercer	Wᵐ Amrose Browne			*[see next line]*		
Apr 15	*John Fr.ᵃ Mercer*	Wᵐ More			*[see next line]*		
Apr 15	*John Fr.ᵃ Mercer*	David Habern		44 30	191	20	

Date	chargeable w/tax	white males over 21	" 16-21/	/blks/ 16+	H/ -16	C/	other
Apr 16 James Faunt	Ja.s Faunt			[see next line]			
Apr 16 *James Faunt*	William Faunt					4 12	
Apr 16 Benjamin Ficklin	Benjamin Ficklin	1	2	2	4	9	
Apr 16 James Henderson	James Henderson			1			
Apr 16 Daniel Kendall	Daniel Kendall				3	3	
Apr 16 Sarah Knight		1				2	
Apr 16 Ann Knight		1	2	2	3	5	
Apr 16 John Nicholson	John Nicholson				1	5	
Apr 16 William Waters	Wm Waters			[see next line]			
Apr 16 *William Waters*	James Waters	1			1	5	
Apr 16 Sarah Williams					2	6	
Apr 17 Thomas Beach	Thomas Beach			3			
Apr 17 John Green	John Green				2	4	
Apr 17 Isaac Holloway	Isaac Holloway	1			3	9	
Apr 17 Francis Mcentosh	Francis Mcentosh			1			
Apr 17 John Primm	John Primm		2	3	2	9	
Apr 17 Margaret Primm				1	3	10	
Apr 17 Jessey Stone	Jessey Stone	2				5	
Apr 18 James Kendall	James Kendall				1	7	
Apr 18 George Waters	George Waters				5	18	
Apr 19 Edward Bethel	Edward Bethel			1	2	1	
Apr 19 Joseph Browne	Joseph Browne			[see next line]			
Apr 19 *Joseph Browne*	Tho.s Browne	1	5	4	6	13	
Apr 19 Patterson Doyall	Patterson Doyall				3	1	
Apr 19 Dennis Doyall	Dennis Doyall	1			4	5	
Apr 19 John Gunn	John Gunn				2		
Apr 19 John Minton	John Minton			1	1	2	
Apr 19 William Pattin	William Pattin			1			
Apr 19 William Phillips	William Phillips		7	3	2	10	
Apr 19 John Rogers	John Rogers		1	1	3	1	
Apr 20 William Battoe	William Battoe				3	4	
Apr 20 Joseph Botts	Joseph Botts			[see next line]			
Apr 20 *Joseph Botts*	John Prince		3	3	7	11	
Apr 20 Samuel Bridwell	Samuel Bridwell				2	1	
Apr 20 William Eaton	William Eaton	1				1	
Apr 20 Vintsin Foxworthy	Vintsin Foxworthy				1	3	
Apr 20 Phillip Foxworthy	Phillip Foxworthy				1	2	

Date	chargeable w/tax	white males over 21	16-21	blks 16+	-16	H	C	other
Apr 20	Jemime Grigory					1	2	
Apr 20	Elizabeth Jones						1	
Apr 20	George Wells	George Wells		1	2	4	8	
Apr 20	Elizabeth Wells			3	7	3	11	
Apr 22	Thomas Mountjoy	Thomas Mountjoy		7	9	6	27	
Apr 25	Thomas Powell	Thomas Powell						
Apr 27	Edward Mountjoy	Edward Mountjoy	1			4	12	
Apr 27	John Richards	John Richards						
Apr 27	John Mountjoy Sr.	John Mountjoy			1	3	4	
Apr 27	George Thralekeld	George Thralekeld		1		2	1	
Apr 27	Thomas Wells	Thomas Wells				1		
Apr 28	James Bridges	James Bridges				1	2	
Apr 28	Perry Chinn	Perry Chinn				1	2	
Apr 28	Robert Green	Robert Green	*[see next line]*					
Apr 28	*Robert Green*	John Green				4	2	
Apr 28	James Holloway	James Holloway		1		2	4	stud 18.0
Apr 28	George Holloway	George Holloway				2		
Apr 28	Charles Kendall	Charles Kendall	1	1		2	4	
Apr 28	Allen Way	Allen Way				1	1	
May 3	William Holloday	William Holloday			1	3	2	
May 3	Elijah Thralekeld	Elijah Thralekeld		13	13	9	32	
May 4	William Branson	William Branson		2				
May 4	Wilkinson Chandler	Wilkinson Chandler		4	3			
May 4	Elizabeth Chissom		1			1	2	
May 4	Phillip Gardner	Phillip Gardner		3	3	3	12	
May 4	William Right	William Right				3	11	
May 4	Stacy Wilson	Stacy Wilson						
May 5	George Enzor	George Enzor					1	
May 5	Isaac Eustace	Isaac Eustace	1	10	5	7	14	2whl.carr.
May 5	Asey Holloway Jr.		1			1	1	
May 5	Josua Kendall	Josua Kendall					3	
May 5	John Kendall	Jn.o Kendall	*[see next line]*					
May 5	*John Kendall*	James Kee Kendall		3	3	5	22	
May 5	*John Kendall*	Moses Kendall	*[see next line]*					
May 5	Asey Holloway Sr.	Asey Holloway	*[see next line]*					
May 5	*Asey Holloway Sr.*	Rich.d Ketchen				2	9	
May 5	Charles Thornton	Charles Thornton				2	7	

Date	chargeable w/tax	white males over 21	16-21	blks/H 16+	C/ -16	other
May 10 Merryman Ketchen		Merryman Ketchen	2	5	2	3
May 11 Alexander Taylor		Alexander Taylor 1			1	4
May 12 George Mawzy		George Mawzy				1
May 14 Joseph Barby		Joseph Barby 1		1	3	4
May 14 Derk Benear		Derk Benear			2	4
May 14 Zachariah Benson		Zachariah Benson 1		1	4	5
May 14 John Bradly		John Bradly 1				1
May 14 Eleoner Brent		John Blake	20	20	11	48
May 14 Richard Brent		Richard Brent				3
May 14 George Brent		George Brent	*[see next line]*			
May 14 Ann Brent		Ann Brent		23	29	6
May 14 Daniel C. Brent		D. C. Brent	*[see next line]*			
May 14 Daniel C. Brent		Wm Fritter	30	24	13	6
May 14 George Brent		Izaah Corbin 1	15	9	10	46
May 14 Daniel C. Brent		Jones Garner	*[see next line]*			
May 14 Eleoner Brent						4-wheeled carriage
May 14 John Bridwell		John Bridwell 1			2	3
May 14 Benjamin Brock		Benjamin Brock			1	5
May 14 Mary Ann Bronaugh		1	10	10	9	6
May 14 Joseph Buchanon		tax free 1				2
May 14 George Burroughs		George Burroughs	2	2	2	6
May 14 George Bussel		George Bussel			2	9
May 14 Charles Carter		C. Carter	*[see next line]*			
May 14 Charles Carter		Able Holloway	20	17	16	32
May 14 Mary Chesshire		1			2	5
May 14 John Cook		John Cook	20	34	12	36
May 14 John Brent's estate		4				
May 14 Moses Fritter		M. Fritter	*[see next line]*			
May 14 Moses Fritter		John Latham			1	5
May 14 John Holloway		John Holloway 1			2	10
May 14 John Knight		John Knight			2	6
May 14 John McCullough		John McCullough				3
May 14 William Mountjoy		William Mountjoy	4	6	9	24
May 14 Richard Ratliff		Richard Ratliff	1	2	2	6
May 14 Ann Rogers		1			3	4
May 14 George Shelton		George Shelton			3	8
May 14 Ann Snoxall					1	3

Date	chargeable w/tax	white males over 21	" 16-21/	/blks/ 16+	H/ -16	C/	other
May 14	John Snoxall	John Snoxall			1	1 2	
May 14	Sarsfield Snoxall	Sarsfield Snoxall			1		
May 14	Josua Kendall Sr.	Josua Kendall		*[see next line]*			
May 14	*Josua Kendall Sr.*	Anthony Kendall		4 3	7 20		
May 14	Hannah Stark			3	2 9		
May 15	John Latham	John Latham			2 7		
May 15	Francis Linum	Francis Linum					
May 15	Rob.ᵗ B. Morton	Rob.ᵗ B. Morton		7 6	4 12		2whl. carr.
May 18	Robert Brent	in Maryland	1	2 3	5		stud 1.10.0
May 18	Joseph Burroughs	Joseph Burroughs			1 1		
May 18	John Markham	John Markham	1	5 9	3 4		2whl. carr.
May 18	Michal Maze	Michal Maze		1			ord. lic.
May 18	Jonathan Mountjoy	Jonathan Mountjoy	1		1 5		
May 18	Joannah Tolson				1 4		
May 18	T.S. Tyler	T.S. Tyler	1	1 3	4 9		
May 19	Simon Bridwell	Simon Bridwell			1 3		
May 19	Benjamin Bridwell	Benjamin Bridwell	1		1		
May 19	John Brooker	John Brooker					
May 19	John Chiverall	John Chiverall			1 4		
May 19	Seth Combs			1 9	8 8 34		
May 19	Jessey Cooper	Jessey Cooper			2 4		
May 19	William Fristoe	William Fristoe	1		5 10		
May 19	William George	William George			3		
May 19	Virgen Huse				1 5		
May 19	Jonathan Reid	Jonathan Reid			2		
May 19	Nicholis Riley				1		
May 19	William Watson	Wᵐ Watson		*[see next line]*			
May 19	*William Watson*	Ja.ˢ Watson	1		1 5		
May 19	Margaret Williams			2 4	3 5		
May 19	Henry Woodgerd	Henry Woodgerd	1		3 4		
May 19	Richard Woodgerd	Richard Woodgerd			2 2		
May 24	Rawleigh T. Browne	R. T. Browne		*[see next line]*			
May 24	*Rawleigh T. Browne*	Pearson Williams		16 20	12 15		
May 25	James Battoe	James Battoe Levy free			2 10		
May 25	Thomas Bridwell	Thomas Bridwell	2		1 2		
May 25	Cuthbert Byrum	Cuthbert Byrum			1		
May 25	Peter Byrum	Peter Byrum			1 4		

Date	chargeable w/tax	white males over 21	" 16-21/	/blks/ 16+	H/ -16	C/	other
May 25	William Chadwell	William Chadwell			1		
May 25	Archebald Douglis		1		6	10	
May 25	Hannah Gough		1	1	2	3	2
May 25	Moses Grigsby	Moses Grigsby			1	5	
May 25	Ledia Hansbrough				1	2	3
May 26	Jerremiah Fugate	Jerremiah Fugate			1	1	
May 26	John Mountjoy	John Mountjoy	1	5	5	10	18
n.d.	Peter Knight	Peter Knight			1	3	4

*   *   *   *   *
*   *   *
*

[End of date-arranged returns for William Mountjoy]

A List of Taxable property within the district of
William Alexander, Commissioner in the County of Stafford
for the year 1787

[arranged by date of tax enumeration]

Date	chargeable w/tax	white males	over 21	16-21	/blks/ 16+	-16	H	C/	other
Mar -	Bengey John	John Bengey	1					2	2
Mar 6	James John	John James	*[see next line]*						
Mar 6	*James John*	George James	2		13	7	10	35	*[next line]*
Mar 6	*James John*	4 wheeled stage wagon & 2 wheeled riding chair							
Mar 7	Alexander William	William Alexander			7	7	6	25	2whl.rid.chr
Mar 7	Casson Thomas	Thomas Casson			5	4	7	23	
Mar 7	Clark Ann						4	7	
Mar 7	Curtice George	George Curtice Jr.			0	1			
Mar 7	Curtice George	George Curtice Sr.			1	4		11	
Mar 7	Donathan Gerard	Gerard Donathan			4	7	5	25	
Mar 7	Lang Robert tax free	James Lang	1				3	2	
Mar 7	Stone Joseph	Joseph Stone					1	7	
Mar 17	Alexander Phillip Est.	Thomas Bowen			6	10	6	18	
Mar 17	Ball William	William Ball			3	4	6	8	
Mar 17	Bolling William	William Bolling							
Mar 17	Bowen Thomas	*[name struck through]*			1	2	5	2	
Mar 17	Pitcher Richard	Richard Pitcher	1				3	8	
Mar 17	Stone William	William Stone					2	3	
Mar 17	Strother Anthony	Anth.o Strother	*[see next line]*						
Mar 17	*Strother Anthony*	Geo&Anth.o Strother	1		4	6	6	12	
Mar 19	Bates Joseph tax free	Joseph Bates				1	1	2	
Mar 19	Berry Sarah				1	2	2	4	
Mar 19	Bruce William	William Bruce	2		3	5	4	8	
Mar 19	Burnett William	William Burnett	2			4	4	7	
Mar 19	Butler William	William Butler			1	3	2	4	
Mar 19	Carter Henry	Henry Carter							
Mar 19	Chilton William	William Chilton	1				2	2	
Mar 19	Curtice Aaron	Aaron Curtice	1				1	3	
Mar 19	Fletcher Rachal	Darby Souillivant			1		2	7	
Mar 19	Garner Jacob	Jacob Garner							

Date	chargeable w/tax	white males over 21	" 16-21/	/blks/ 16+	H/ -16	C/	other
Mar 19 Garner John	John Garner	1			1	1	
Mar 19 Green Sarah					1	1	
Mar 19 Jones John	John Jones				1		
Mar 19 Jones Thomas	Thomas Jones				3	5	
Mar 19 Kenny Thomas	Thomas Kenny		3		4	21	
Mar 19 Limbrick Lettice		1			2	7	
Mar 19 Miner Elizabeth			1	1	1	4	
Mar 19 Payn John	John Payn		[see next line]				
Mar 19 *Payn John*	Thomas Payn	1			2	6	
Mar 19 Pitcher Mildred			1	4	1	10	
Mar 19 Swillivant Gabriel	Gabriel Swillivant	1			4	10	
Mar 19 Swillivant Lettice					3	8	
Mar 19 Templeman Jane					1	4	
Mar 19 Thornton Thomas	John Bern		7	7	6	8	
Mar 19 Waugh McCagby	McCagby Waugh				3	7	
Mar 19 Wisharts Est[a]	John Rawling		4	5	3	7	
Mar 20 Bussell William	William Bussell	1		1	3	9	
Mar 20 Chinn Susannah	Joseph Chinn			1	3	7	
Mar 20 Clemmons John	John Clemmons				2		
Mar 20 Cox George	George Cox				3	3	
Mar 20 Cox Vincent Jr.	Vincent Cox				4	7	
Mar 20 Edwards Andrew	Andrew Edwards	1	7	7	10	24	
Mar 20 Ellwell George	George Ellwell				1		
Mar 20 Finnell Jonathan	Jonathan Finnell		5	13	6	22	
Mar 20 Fugett Benj[a]	Benjaman Fugett			1	2	1	
Mar 20 Fugett Daniel	Daniel Fugett				1		
Mar 20 Fugett Francis	Francis Fugett				2	4	
Mar 20 Fugett Frances Jr.	Frances Fugett				1		
Mar 20 Green Jesse	Jesse Green				2	2	
Mar 20 Hewitt Susanna			6	4	8	16	
Mar 20 Hooe Harris Dust. Est.			9	13	9	35	
Mar 20 Johnson Scarlott	Scarlott Johnson						
Mar 20 Limbrick William	William Limbrick				1	11	
Mar 20 Newton John	John Newton	1	5	7	5	14	
Mar 20 Pates Aaron	Aaron Pates			1	2	2	
Mar 20 Pitcher Charles	Cha.[s] Pitcher					1	
Mar 20 Simpson Elizabeth		1			2	4	

Date	chargeable w/tax	white males over 21	" 16-21/	/blks/ 16+	H/ -16	C/	other
Mar 20	Smith Samuel	Samuel Smith		4	3	3 16	
Mar 20	Snellings Enoch	Enoch Snellings	1		3	3	
Mar 20	Swillivant Benjaman	Benj.a Swillivant			3	7	
Mar 20	Swillivant Darby	Darby Swillivant Sr. tax free			1	6	
Mar 21	Gilpin Israel	Israel Gilpin	[see next line]				
Mar 21	*Gilpin Israel*	Joseph Gilpin			1		
Mar 21	Guttery Thomas	Thomas Guttery			1	3	
Mar 21	Lateman Daniel	Daniel Lateman			4	3	
Mar 21	Leach Andrew	Andrew Leach			1		
Mar 21	Musselman Chrisher	Christopher Musselman	[next line]				
Mar 21	*Musselman Chrisher*	Chris Musselman			4 10		
Mar 22	Beasley Phillips	Phillips Beasley			1		
Mar 22	Bolling Charles	Charles Bolling			1		
Mar 22	Bolling James	James Bolling	2		2	6	
Mar 22	Bolling Thomas	Thomas Bolling	1		1	2	
Mar 22	Conyers John	John Conyers	4 5	6	3 12		
Mar 22	Laverty Peggy		1	2	3 3		
Mar 22	Massey Benjaman tax free				1	1	
Mar 22	Massey Thomas	Thomas Massey		3 2	5 18		
Mar 22	Mellett John	John Mellett			2	4	
Mar 22	Oliver John	John Oliver Sr.	[see next line]				
Mar 22	*Oliver John*	John Oliver			3	8	
Mar 22	Rose William	William Rose			4	6	
Mar 22	Sharp Thomas Jr.	Thomas Sharp		1	1	2	
Mar 22	Sharp Thomas	Thomas Sharp Sr.	[see next line]				
Mar 22	*Sharp Thomas*	John Sharp		4 3	2 2		
Mar 22	Siblee Benson	Benson Siblee	1		2	2	
Mar 22	Smith John	John Smith		2 5	4 8		
Mar 22	Stringfellow Townshand	Tows.d Stringfellow			1		
Mar 22	Sutor John	John Sutor	[see next line]				
Mar 22	*Sutor John*	Jesse Sutor			2		
Mar 22	Webb Aaron	Aaron Webb	1		5 15		
Mar 22	White George	George White		1 4	4 8		
Mar 22	Wooderd Mary		1 2		2 11		
Mar 22	Young William	William Young	[see next line]				
Mar 22	*Young William*	Leonard Young		1	5 4		
Mar 23	Anderson John	John Anderson	1		3	5	

Date	chargeable w/tax	white males over 21	" 16-21	/blks/ 16+	-16	H/	C/	other
Mar 23	Benson James	James Benson		2	5	2	2	
Mar 23	Cook David	David Cook		*[see next line]*				
Mar 23	*Cook David*	James Cook				1	2	
Mar 23	Crop John	John Crop		*[see next line]*				
Mar 23	*Crop John*	James Green		8	6	8	39	
Mar 23	Ellison Thomas	Thomas Ellison		2	4	3	13	
Mar 23	Faunt George	George Faunt		3	1	2	15	
Mar 23	Hord James	James Hord		*[see next line]*				
Mar 23	*Hord James*	William Hord		8	2	8	22	
Mar 23	Hord Rody	Rody Hord		3	3	4	11	
Mar 23	Hord Thomas	Thomas Hord		1	1	7		
Mar 23	Leach James	James Leach		3	5	4	7	
Mar 23	Logee Alexander	Alex.r Logee		1		3	4	
Mar 23	McDonnell Daniel	Daniel McDonnell		2	2	1		
Mar 23	Murrow Daniel	Daniel Murrow		1	2	3	4	
Mar 23	Parmer Rawleigh	Rawley Parmer	1	1	4	3	7	
Mar 23	Turner Benjaman	Benj.a Turner	1			3	11	
Mar 23	West Edward Jr.	Edward West Jr.		2	1	3	4	
Mar 23	West Edward Sr.	Edward West & John	1	3		6	7	
Mar 23	White Thomas	Thomas White		1		4	8	
Mar 24	Cotney John	John Cotney		3	2	4	12	
Mar 24	Crop James	James Crop		5	5	6	21	
Mar 24	Crop James Sr.	James Crop Sr.		6	4	4	13	
Mar 24	Hord Jesse	Jesse Hord		4	3	6	18	
Mar 24	Hord Peter Jr.	Peter Hord Jr.		1	1	3	14	
Mar 24	Hord Killis	Killis Hord	1	4	3	3	10	
Mar 24	Hord Peter Sr.	Peter Hord	1	6	3	4	18	
Mar 24	Humpfries William	William Humpfries	1			5	20	
Mar 24	Jett William	William Jett	2	1		3	11	
Mar 24	Jones Charles	Charles Jones	1	1		4	7	
Mar 24	Jones George	George Jones				2	3	
Mar 24	Lanman Griffin	Griffin Lanman				1	2	
Mar 24	Norwood John	John Norwood		*[see next line]*				
Mar 24	*Norwood John*	George Robertson		3	1	5	2	
Mar 24	Pettet Benjamin	Benj.a Pettet	2	1		3	9	
Mar 24	Pitcher Masson	Masson Pitcher		6	4	6	27	
Mar 26	Downman Joseph Ball	Q[uar]t[er] Little faul						*[see next line]*

Date	chargeable w/tax	white males over 21	16-21	blks 16+	-16	H	C	other
Mar 26	*Downman Joseph Ball*			7	14	5	35	
Mar 26	Genl Washington George	Jesse Hill		7	4	4	23	
Mar 26	Hill Jesse		1	3	1	4	3	
Mar 26	Masson Henry	Henry Masson		1				
Mar 26	Newton Margrett			2	1	5	5	
Mar 26	Newton William	William Newton	[see next line]					
Mar 26	*Newton William*	Theodotia Curtice		10	10	9	11	
Mar 26	*Newton William*	Isaac & Thomas Newton						[see next line]
Mar 26	*Newton William*	James Dodd	[see next line]					
Mar 26	Pollard John	John Pollard		9	12	5	20	
Mar 26	Posey Thomas	Rodith White		12	10	25	41	
Mar 26	Rods Mary					1		
Mar 26	Slaven Jesse	Jesse Slaven	[see next line]					
Mar 26	*Slaven Jesse*	Alexander Lensey	1			3	4	
Mar 26	Threlkell Jesse	Jesse Threlkell		1				
Mar 26	Turner James	James Turner	[see next line]					
Mar 26	*Turner James*	William Turner				4	13	
Mar 26	White George	George White tax free				1	2	
Mar 27	Berry Richard	Richard Berry					2	
Mar 27	Black Margrett		1			4	6	
Mar 27	Cox Charnock	Charnock Cox		2		2	3	
Mar 27	Cox Presly	Presly Cox				1	4	
Mar 27	Fines Patrick	Patrick & James Fines	1			4	8	
Mar 27	Gollohorn John taxfree	Tho.s Gollohorn				3	9	
Mar 27	Gollohorn Sollomon	Sollomon Gollohorn				2	4	
Mar 27	Green James	James Green						
Mar 27	Jones William tax free		1			1	1	
Mar 27	Kenny John	John Kenny	1	1		2	9	
Mar 27	Kitchen James	James Kitchen	[see next line]					
Mar 27	*Kitchen James*	Charles Kitchen				4	8	
Mar 27	Leach Benjaman	Benj.a Leach		2				
Mar 27	Limbrick Francis	Francis Limbrick				3	10	
Mar 27	Limbrick George	George Limbrick						
Mar 27	McGuire Rachal		1			2	5	
Mar 27	Pitcher Moses	Moses Pitcher		2	1	2	10	
Mar 27	Porch Thomas	Thomas Porch		8	12	7	25	
Mar 27	Swillivant Ann	Aaron Nonday				1	3	

Date	chargeable w/tax	white males over 21	" 16-21	/blks/ 16+	H/ -16	C/	other
Mar 27	Swillivant Daniel	Daniel Swillivant		1		3 7	
Apr -	Bowen Burkett	Burkett Bowen		*[see next line]*			
Apr -	*Bowen Burkett*	John Read		3	6	5 10	stud 10.0
Apr 2	Banks Gerard	Gerard Banks		8	7	5 21	*see next ln*
Apr 2	*Banks Gerard*	4 wheeled stage wagon & 2 wheeled *[riding]* chair					
Apr 2	Berry Thomas	Thomas Berry		1	3	2 1	
Apr 2	Briant John	John Briant			1	2	
Apr 2	Brown James	James Brown				3 2	
Apr 2	Peyton Ann	Charles Peyton	2	1	1	3 10	
Apr 2	Rose Jesse	Jesse Rose					
Apr 2	Sharp Linsfield	Linsfield Sharp		*[see next line]*			
Apr 2	*Sharp Linsfield*	William Sharp		8	3	8 16	
Apr 2	Snipe Nathaniel	Nathaniel Snipe				2 5	
Apr 4	Ballard Thomas	Thomas Ballard		3	3	4 11	
Apr 4	Ballard William	William Ballard				1	
Apr 4	Bolling William Sen[r]	William Bolling				1 2	
Apr 4	Bolling Simon	Simon Bolling					
Apr 4	Buchannan Andrew	Andrew Buchannan		7	8	5 15	2whl.rid.chr
Apr 4	Carter Joseph	Joseph Carter		1	2	3 7	
Apr 4	Faunt John	John Faunt				2 10	
Apr 4	Graves Benjamin	Benj.[a] Graves				1 5	
Apr 4	Groves William Sr.	W[m] & W[m] Groves	2	1		7 13	
Apr 4	Heffertin Martin	Martin Heffertin				2	
Apr 4	Hord Edward	Edward Hord	1	2		8 28	
Apr 4	Jackson Robert	Robert Jackson		*[see next line]*			
Apr 4	*Jackson Robert*	William Jackson				4 5	
Apr 4	Jackson Rosanna	George Jackson				3 11	
Apr 4	Lathrum George	George Lathrum				1 2	
Apr 4	Lathrum John	John Lathrum	2			4 12	
Apr 4	Marquess Anthony	Anthony Marquess	1			1 3	
Apr 4	Martin Daniel	Daniel Martin				2 1	
Apr 4	Martin Thomas	Thomas Martin				1 2	
Apr 4	Massey Elizabeth					1 4	
Apr 4	Massey Tolliferro	Tolliferro Massey					
Apr 4	Mulbury John	John Mulbury				2 11	
Apr 4	Porch Esum	Esum Porch		1	4	3 10	
Apr 4	Stripling Elizabeth			1		5 2	

Date	chargeable w/tax	white males over 21	" /blks/ H/ C/ 16-21/ 16+ -16	other
Apr 4	Stripling Joell	Joell Stripling	1	
Apr 4	Sutor Andrew	Andrew Sutor	[see next line]	
Apr 4	*Sutor Andrew*	William Sutor	1 1 3 4 9	
Apr 4	West John	John West	5 2	
Apr 4	Wood William	William Wood	1 1 3 6 14	
Apr 5	Briggs David	David Briggs	[see next line]	
Apr 5	*Briggs David*	George Patterson	10 7 7 472whl.rid.chr	
Apr 5	Burton John	John Burton	1 1	
Apr 5	Bussell Vincent	Vincent Bussell		
Apr 5	Conner John	John Conner Con.	3 7	
Apr 5	Doudle James	James Doudle	[see next line]	
Apr 5	*Doudle James*	Brawner Doudle	3 3 3 4	
Apr 5	Hall Hannah		2 6	
Apr 5	Hudson David	David Hudson	1 1 3 13	
Apr 5	Patten Rachal		3 7	
Apr 5	Patterson Perry	Perry Patterson	1	
Apr 5	Patterson Thomas	Thomas Patterson	3 3	
Apr 5	Timmons William	William Timmons	3 6	
Apr 5	Walker Solomon	Solomon Walker	1 4	
Apr 6	Hall Benjaman	Benj.ª Hall	3 6	
Apr 6	Hall John	John Hall		
Apr 6	James George	George James	3 4 3 6	
Apr 6	Jones Evins	Evins Jones	[see next line]	
Apr 6	*Jones Evins*	James Phillips	1 1 3 8	
Apr 6	Jones James	James Jones	[see next line]	
Apr 6	*Jones James*	John Jones	3 6	
Apr 6	Mattocks Lazarus	Lazarus Mattocks	1 5 6	
Apr 6	McFarling Obediah	Obediah McFarling	[see next line]	
Apr 6	*McFarling Obediah*	John Pare	5 12	
Apr 6	Meal John	John Meal	[see next line]	
Apr 6	*Meal John*	Samuel Meal	3 3.	
Apr 6	Morson Arthur	Arthur Morson	[see next line]	
Apr 6	*Morson Arthur*	John Andrews	[see next line]	
Apr 6	*Morson Arthur*	George Paten	7 15 15 57	
Apr 6	Payn George over 16		1	
Apr 6	Simpson Alex.ʳ	Alex.ʳ Simpson tax free	2 6	
Apr 6	Simpson John	John Simpson	2	

Date	chargeable w/tax	white males over 21	16-21	/blks/ 16+	-16	H/	C/	other
Apr 6	Stringfellow James	James Stringfellow			2	3	10	
Apr 7	Arrosmith Thomas	Thomas Arrosmith	1	1		2	3	
Apr 7	Berry Anthony	Anthony Berry	1			3	9	
Apr 7	Cox Enoch	Enoch Cox						
Apr 7	England John	John England	*[see next line]*					
Apr 7	*England John*	John Froughner .	1	1		2	3	
Apr 7	Faunt Joseph	Joseph Faunt		3	1	4	15	
Apr 7	Harwood John	John Harwood	1	1		3	8	
Apr 7	Horner John	John Horner			1	5	2	
Apr 7	Hume Francis	*[name struck through]*	1	2				
Apr 7	Jones Henry	Henry Jones				5	10	
Apr 7	Kirby James	James Kirby	1					
Apr 7	McIntosh James	James McIntosh				2	6	
Apr 7	Miller John	John Miller				2		
Apr 7	Payne Daniel	Daniel Payne	1	1	3	1	1	
Apr 7	Puzey Stephen	Stephen Puzey	2			1	4	
Apr 7	Richard William	William Richard	*[see next line]*					
Apr 7	*Richard William*	& William Richard		6	8	3	5	
Apr 7	Simmons William	Will Simmons						
Apr 7	Sudtherd William	William Sudtherd				1	7	
Apr 7	Thompson James	James Thompson	1			6	14	
Apr 7	Triplett Daniel	Daniel Triplett	1	5	4	4	1	4wlstg wag
Apr 9	Alexander William	William Alexander	*[see next line]*					
Apr 9	*Alexander William*	John Alexander	1			3	9	
Apr 9	Brown William	William Brown				4	15	
Apr 9	Burgess Rubin	Rubin Burgess	1			2	7	
Apr 9	Burton Girard	Girard Burton				2		
Apr 9	Callender Phillip	Phillip Callender				2	7	
Apr 9	Cotney Elisha	Elisha Cotney				1		
Apr 9	Cox Vincent Sr.	Vincent & John Cox				3	5	
Apr 9	Curtice William	William Curtice				2	4	
Apr 9	Debaptist John	John Debaptist	*[see next line]*					
Apr 9	*Debaptist John*	John Faggott	1			1	4	
Apr 9	*Debaptist John*	John Lucas	*[see next line]*					
Apr 9	Fickling John	John Fickling		3	7	6	11	
Apr 9	Horton William	William Horton				3	6	
Apr 9	Jett George	George Jett						

Date	chargeable w/tax	white males over 21	" 16-21	/blks/ 16+	H/ -16	C/	other
Apr 9	Jett Presly	Presly Jett				3	
Apr 9	Kenyon James	James Kenyon	5	10	8	25	
Apr 9	Kirk Jeremiah	Jeremiah Kirk	3	2	2	2	
Apr 9	Martin Charles	Charles Martin					
Apr 9	Miller Samuel	Samuel Miller	[see next line]				
Apr 9	*Miller Samuel*	Lewis Martin			4	14	
Apr 9	Reavley William	William Reavley	[see next line]				
Apr 9	*Reavley William*	William Burton	5	11	4		132whl.rid.chr
Apr 9	Roch Robert	Robert Roach tax free	2		2	6	
Apr 9	Schooler Thomas	Thomas Schooler			1	7	
Apr 9	Selden Samuel	Samuel Selden	[see next line]				
Apr 9	*Selden Samuel*	Pearce Perry	32	35	17	91	4whl.char
Apr 9	Seydmore Joshua	Joshua Seydmore		1	1		
Apr 9	Skinker Thomas		5	9	6	33	
Apr 9	Swann Asa	Asa Swann					
Apr 9	Taylor Jesse	Jesse Taylor				1	
Apr 9	Thompson Zacha.[a]	Zachariah Thompson		1	2	4	
Apr 9	Troop Thomas	Thomas Troop		1	2		
Apr 9	Turner Absolum	Absolum Turner	1		3	6	
Apr 9	Turner Grif.[n] William	William G. Turner	1		3	7	
Apr 9	Walker James	James Walker				2	
Apr 9	Wallice James Doct.[r]		3	2	2	8	no phys lic
Apr 9	Wallice John	John Wallice	5	7	4	5	
Apr 9	Weaks Thomas	Thomas Weaks			2	4	
Apr 9	White Nancy					1	
Apr 10	Manning John	John Manning			3	3	
Apr 10	Roberts Griffin	Griffin Roberts					
Apr 11	Allentharp Jacob	Jacob Allentharp	1	1	5	9	
Apr 11	Bates John	John Bates					
Apr 11	Branson Isaac	Isaac Branson			2		
Apr 11	Burgess William	William Burgess			1	2	
Apr 11	Burton Rachel	Isaac Brimmer	1		3	10	
Apr 11	Carter Robert (Westm.)		[see next line]				
Apr 11	*Carter Robert(West.)*	Leonard Hill Overseer	15	10	6	37	
Apr 11	Fields Samuel	Samuel Fields			1		
Apr 11	Foster Seth	Seth Foster			3	5	
Apr 11	Hill Leonard	William Barber	3	3	5	12	

Date	chargeable w/tax	white males over 21	16-21	blks 16+	-16	H	C	other
Apr 11	Linn Simon given by C.L.				2	1	7	
Apr 11	Lunsford Joanah			1	3	4	6	
Apr 11	Munrow William taxfree	John Munrow				1	4	
Apr 11	Rankins John	John Rankings				1		
Apr 11	Scott Sarah		1			1	4	
Apr 11	Tate William	William Tate				1	5	
Apr 11	Underwood John	John Underwood						
Apr 12	Archiball David	David Archiball				1	4	
Apr 12	Brimmer John	John Brimmer	1			1	2	
Apr 12	Burton James	James Burton				3	7	
Apr 12	Caves Thomas	Thomas Caves		0	3	4	2	
Apr 12	Gollohorn John Jr.	John Gollohorn				1	2	
Apr 12	Limbrick John	John Limbrick				1	5	
Apr 12	Martin Ann	Charles Martin	1	1		3	13	
Apr 12	Persifull Allen	Allen Persifull				3		
Apr 12	Pitcher Peter	Peter Pitcher			1	1	4	
Apr 12	Smith Henry Sr.	Henry Smith	[see next line]					
Apr 12	*Smith Henry Sr.*	Joseph Smith		6	3	6	23	
Apr 12	Stripling Samuel	Sam.l Stripling						
Apr 12	White George	George White Jr.				1	2	
Apr 13	Fitzhugh Henry	Henry Fitzhugh	[see next line]					
Apr 13	*Fitzhugh Henry*	Lowry Henry		7	16	6	10	
Apr 13	Fitzhugh John	John Fitzhugh	[see next line]					
Apr 13	*Fitzhugh John*	Elijah Curtice	1	18	20	9	23	[next line]
Apr 13	*Fitzhugh John*		4 phaeton or stage wheels					
Apr 13	Groves Thomas	Thomas Groves	1			1	2	
Apr 13	Hewitt William	William Hewitt		14	14	8		202whl.rid.chr
Apr 13	Lowry James	James Lowry		1	1	3	2	
Apr 13	More Edward	Edward Moor [sic]		7	7	6	35	
Apr 13	Weathers Charles	Cha.s Weathers				2		
Apr 13	Weathers James	James Weathers	1	8	8	7	36	
Apr 14	Beach Thomas	Thomas Beach				3		
Apr 14	Day John	John Day	1	1		1	2	
Apr 14	Dunbar Robert	Robert Dunbar	[see next line]					
Apr 14	*Dunbar Robert*	Alexander Rankins	1	4	2	3	1	
Apr 14	Graves George	George Graves	1	1		3		
Apr 14	Howard John	John Howard						

Date	chargeable w/tax	white males over 21	" 16-21/	/blks/ 16+	H/ -16	C/	other
Apr 14	Mortimore Charles Sr.		3	1	3	4	
Apr 14	Robertson John	John Robertson			1		
Apr 14	Templeman Edward	Edward Templeman			3	11	
Apr 14	Travis Margrett		1	3		2	
Apr 16	Drake John	John Drake					
Apr 16	Fitzhugh Thomas	Thomas Fitzhugh	*[see next line]*				
Apr 16	*Fitzhugh Thomas*	John Curtice	25	19	13	27	4char.whls.
Apr 16	Fitzhugh William	William Fitzhugh	54	54	27	15	*[next line]*
Apr 16	*Fitzhugh William*	8 chariot wheels & 4 chair wheels					
Apr 16	Waugh Lee George	George Lee Waugh	21	12	7	23	
Apr 16	Waugh T. Robert	Robert T. Waugh	3	3	2	13	
Apr 17	Dalrymple John	John Dalrymple	*[see next line]*				
Apr 17	*Dalrymple John*	Joseph Darling	2	1		1	
Apr 17	Gordon Samuel	Samuel Gordon		1	1		
Apr 17	Sedden John	John Sedden	12	9	10	40	
Apr 17	Taylor Robert	Robert Taylor					
Apr 17	Walker William	William Walker	1	3	3	3	8
Apr 18	Middleton Thomas	Thomas Middleton	1	1			
Apr 19	Colquhoun Walter	Walter Colquhoun		3	2	1	
Apr 19	Haner William	William Haner	*[see next line]*				
Apr 19	*Haner William*	Will Sutherly		5	1	3	7
Apr 19	McKittrick Anthony	Anthony McKittrick	1	9	2	13	2 2wl.rid.chr
Apr 19	Newell Ann				1	2	
Apr 19	Nooe Zepheniah	Zepheniah Nooe		3	5	2	2 2wl.rid.chr
Apr 19	West Thomas	Thomas West			1		
Apr 19	Williams Kiziah	John Zyley	*[see next line]*				
Apr 19	*Williams Kiziah*	Joseph Cornuck	1		1		
Apr 19	Wilson William	Wm Wilson		2	2	1	1
Apr 19	Winlock William	Wm Winlock		3		3	3
Apr 20	Bell John	John Bell		3	2	5	2
Apr 20	Bower Michal	Michal Bower		1	6	3	2
Apr 20	Collins Thomas	Thomas Collins		2	2	4	2
Apr 20	Conyers Benjaman	Benj.a Conyers				1	
Apr 20	Lotspick William	William Lotspick			1	2	3

Date	chargeable w/tax	white males over 21	" 16-21	/blks/ 16+	-16	H/	C/	other
Apr 20	Lyon James	James Lyon	*[see next line]*					
Apr 20	*Lyon James*	Henry Hill	1	1	2	1	2	
Apr 20	*Lyon James*	Tunis Joue?	*[see next line]*					
Apr 20	McCloud James	James McCloud	*[see next line]*					
Apr 20	*McCloud James*	John McCloud	1		1			
Apr 20	McMillon William	William McMillon				1		
Apr 20	Morison Alexander	Alex.r Morison	1	2	2	1	2	
Apr 20	Mortimore Charles	Charles Mortimore Jr.		1	1			
Apr 20	Moss John	John Moss						
Apr 20	Stringfellow George	Geo. Stringfellow	*[see next line]*					
Apr 20	*Stringfellow George*	Henry Stringfellow	*[see next line]*					
Apr 20	*Stringfellow George*	Theodosia Wine			1	2	1	
Apr 20	Taylor William	William Taylor	*[see next line]*					
Apr 20	*Taylor William*	Richard Gatewood	1	6	7	3	3	
Apr 20	*Taylor William*	William Elkins	*[see next line]*					
Apr 20	Vowles Henry	Henry Vowles	*[see next line]*					
Apr 20	*Vowles Henry*	Zacha.h Vowles		6	8	4	5	2wl.rid.chr
Apr 20	*Vowles Henry*	Cha.s Vowles	*[see next line]*					
Apr 20	Vowles Thomas	Thomas Vowles	*[see next line]*					
Apr 20	*Vowles Thomas*	Andrew Chinn	*[see next line]*					
Apr 20	*Vowles Thomas*	James Doratha	*[see next line]*					
Apr 20	*Vowles Thomas*	Joseph Shepherd	*[see next line]*					
Apr 20	*Vowles Thomas*	Andrew McDonnell	3	2	2			
Apr 21	Hunter Adam @ forge	Abner Vernon	*[see next line]*					
Apr 21	*Hunter Adam forge*	Benj.a Bussell	*[see next line]*					
Apr 21	*Hunter Adam forge*	Joseph Lavender	*[see next line]*					
Apr 21	*Hunter Adam forge*	Robert Lavender	*[see next line]*					
Apr 21	*Hunter Adam forge*	John Rogers	3	43	10	25	23	2wl.rid.chr
Apr 24	Smith Joseph	Joseph Smith						
Apr 25	Cook Christian	George Cook				1	4	
Apr 25	Day Elizabeth					1	4	
Apr 25	Hinson Elijah	Elijah Hinson				3	2	
Apr 25	Hinson Sarah				2	6		
Apr 25	Jacobs William	William Jacobs		3	6	3	6	
Apr 25	Jett Francis	Francis Jett		2	2	3	15	
Apr 25	Jett John	John Jett				2	3	
Apr 25	Lathum John Sr.	John Lathum		1	3	3	11	

Date	chargeable w/tax	white males over 21	16-21/	" 16+	/blks/ -16	H/	C/	other
Apr 25	Lowry Jerry	Charg.d to Henry Fitzhugh						
Apr 25	Robertson Thomas	Thomas Robertson				3	7	
Apr 25	Stripling William	Will Stripling				1	2	
Apr 25	Sudtherd Moses	Moses Sudtherd				1	3	
Apr 25	Tinsley John	John Tinsley					1	
Apr 25	Tyler Alice	John Tyler	1	6	7	5	15	
Apr 25	Walton James					3	5	
Apr 27	Allison William	David Allison	1	2		1	2	
Apr 28	Chapman Phillip	Phillip Chapman		1	1	4	4	
Apr 28	Curtice John	John Curtice						
Apr 28	*Curtice John*	John Curtice Jr.				3	9	
Apr 28	McAuslands Humpries	Humpries McAuslandsl		1				
Apr 28	Wellford Robert			10	13	19	26	
Apr 30	Barrett Bartho^w	Bartholomew Barrett	1		1	2		
May	Carter Charles Col.^o	Simon Linn		11	22	4	4	
May 2	Curtice Richard	Richd Curtice				1	2	
May 3	Swillivant Francis	Fra.^s Swillivant		1	4	3	4	
May 6	Graves Martha			1		3	6	
May 6	Hunter Adam	Adam Hunter	*[see next line]*					
May 6	*Hunter Adam*	George Bane	3	40	35	20	76	2chr.whls.
May 6	*Hunter Adam*	Chitton Hansdell	*[see next line]*					
May 6	Read Margrett	William Read				4	9	
May 6	Sanders James	James Sanders					2	
May 6	Snelling John	John Snelling				3	2	
May 6	Snelling William	Will Snelling				3	6	
May 6	Swann Phillip	Phillip Swann		1				
May 14	Lee Thomas & Mary	Thomas S. Lee	*[see next line]*					
May 14	*Lee Thomas & Mary*	Enoch Masson		27	42	20	61	*[next line]*
May 14	*Lee Thomas & Mary*	4 wheeled stage wagon & stud horse @ 1.10.0						
Jun 21	Ann Lewis				1	1		
Jun 22	James Donavan		1	1	5	3	6	
n.d.	Follis Thomas	Thomas Follis	1			3	14	
n.d.	Fox Nathaniel	Nath.^a Fox		6	4	6	13	4 chr.wls
n.d.	Hughs McCagby	McCagby Hughs	1	1		1	2	
n.d.	McCullock John	John McCullock				1	2	
n.d.	Pollard Linsey	Linsey Pollard		1				
n.d.	Rawlings John	John Rawlings		2				

Date	chargeable w/tax	white males over 21	" /blks/ H/ C/ 16-21/ 16+ -16	other
n.d.	Wallice B. William	Wm B. Wallice	2 6 4	
n.d.	Young Joseph	Jos. Young	[see next line]	
n.d.	Young Joseph	John Andrew	8 6 10 12	
n.d.	Young Joseph	Wm Gimbo	[see next line]	

*   *   *   *   *
*   *   *
*

[End of date-arranged 1787 Personal Property Tax List]

Stafford County
Virginia

Personal Property
Tax List

1788

Source: Virginia State Library, Archives Division. County Records. Stafford County Tax lists.

Form of return of taxable property to be made by the commissioners

List No. 1.

A List of the Taxable property within the district of Wm Mountjoy, commissioner in the county of Stafford for the year 1788

[Categories]:

Date of receiving lists from individuals;
Persons names chargeable with the tax;
Names of white male tithables above 21;
[col. 1] - No. of white males above 16 and under 21;
[col. 2] - Blacks above 16;
[col. 3] - Blacks above 12 and under 16;
[col. 4] - Horses, mares, colts & mules;
[other] - carriage wheels;
Ordinary licence;
Billiard tables;
no. of stud horses;
Rates of covering pr season.
practicing physicians, Apothecaries & surgeons;

List No. 2.

A List of taxable property within the district of William Alexander, Commissioner Stafford County year 1788, Returned as P. vouchers

[Categories]:

Month;
Day;
Proprietor's Names;
[col. 1] - Whites from 16 upwards;
[col. 2] - Blacks from 16 years;
[col. 3] - D^o from 12 to 16 years;
[col. 4] - Horses;
[other] - Coach & Chariot wheels;
Phaeton, stage, waggon wheels;
Chairs wheels;
Ordinaries;
B*[illiard]* tables;
Stud Horses;
Rates pr season;
Doctors;

354

[folio 1]

A List of the taxable property within the district of William Mountjoy, Commissioner in the county of Stafford for the year 1788

Date	chargeable w/tax	white males over 21	" /blacks/ H/ 16-21/16+12+			other
Mar 11	George Abbett	George Abbett			2	
Mar 11	James Arrowsmith	James Arrowsmith			3	
Mar 11	Nathan Atchison	Nathan Atchison	1	2	3	
Mar 15	Robert Ashley	Robert Ashley			1	
Mar 22	John Atchison	John Atchison	1		3	
Mar 28	Elijah Abbet	Elijah Abbet			3	
Apr 12	Amus Atchison	Amus Atchison	1		4	
Apr 14	Daniel Antrum	Dan[l] Antrum	[see next line]			
Apr 14		Levi Antrum	1		5	
Apr 14	William Alexander	William Alexander	2		3	
Apr 14	John Abbet levy free				2	
Apr 14	James Abbet	James Abbet			1	
Apr 14	Sarah Ashby				1	
Apr 26	Thomas Ambler	Tho.[s] Ambler	[see next line]			
Apr 26		Ja.[s] Ambler	[see next line]			
Apr 26		W[m] Ambler			6	
May 5	William Anderson	William Anderson		1	1	
May 5	John Agin	Benjamin Adie	5	2	6	
May 5	William Adie Sr.	W[m] Adie	[see next line]			
May 5		W[m] Adie Jr.	9	1	5	
Mar 11	Francis Brooks levy free				2	
Mar 11	John Beagle Sr.	Jno. Beagle	[see next line]			
Mar 11		John Bing			3	
Mar 11	John Bridwell	John Bridwell	3		2	
Mar 14	Peter Byrum	Peter Byrum			1	
Mar 14	Jonathan Bell	Jonathan Bell			1	

[folio 2]

Date	chargeable w/tax	white males over 21				other
Mar 15	William Battoe	William Battoe			3	
Mar 15	Cuthbert Byrum	Cuthbert Byrum			1	
Mar 15	Joseph Beagle	Joseph Beagle	1		1	
Mar 15	James Bridges	James Bridges			3	

Date	chargeable w/tax	white males over 21	" 16-21	/blacks/ H/ 16+12+		other
Mar 15	Nimrod Byrum	Nimrod Byrum				
Mar 15	Edward Bethell	Edward Bethell			3	
Mar 15	Thomas Beach	Thomas Beach			1	
Mar 15	Joseph Barber			3		
Mar 22	William Baul	William Baul	2	1	6	
Mar 22	John Browne	John Browne	[faded]	1		
Mar 22	George Barns	George Barns				
Mar 28	Vintsin Bussell	Vintsin Bussell			1	
Mar 28	William Barby	William Barby			2	
Mar 28	Bassell Burroughs	Bassell Burroughs			3	
Mar 28	Joseph Burroughs	Joseph Burroughs	1		1	
Mar 28	John Bannister	John Bannister			2	
Mar 28	Charles Bell	Charles Bell			1	
Mar 28	James Billingslee	James Billingslee	2		3	
Mar 28	William Botts	William Botts	3		5	
Mar 28	Walter Brown	Walter Brown			4	
Mar 28	John Butler	John Butler	2		3	
Mar 28	John Bridges	John Bridges			1	
Mar 28	Moses Bussell	Moses Bussell			1	
Mar 28	Joseph Botts	Joseph Bott	[see next line]			
Mar 28		Jno. Prince	4	2	6	
Mar 28	Aaron Botts	Aaron Botts	5		7	
Mar 28	George Bridwell	George Bridwell			2	
[folio 3]						
Mar 28	William Barnot	William Barnot			1	
Mar 28	Spencer Bowlin	Spencer Bowlin			1	
Apr 12	George Byrum	George Byrum	1		1	
Apr 12	Joseph Brown	Joseph Brown	[see next line]			
Apr 12		Tho.s Brown	6	1	7	
Apr 14	Enough Benson	Enough Benson	[see next line]			
Apr 14		Prue Benson	1	4	1	6
Apr 14	William Brown				2	
Apr 14	William Bradley Sr.	William Bradley	[see next line]			
Apr 14		Wm Bradley	1		2	
Apr 14	Thomas Barley l. free				2	
Apr 10	Benjamin Bowlin	Benjamin Bowlin			1	
Apr 23	Fielding Bell	Fielding Bell			1	

Date	chargeable w/tax	white males over 21	16-21	/blacks/ 16+	12+	H/	other
Apr 23	Clement Billingslee	Clement Billingslee		1		2	
Apr 26	James Barnot	Ja.s Barnot	*[see next line]*				
Apr 26		Daniel Bessick		1		3	
Apr 26	Mary Ann Bronaugh		1	9	2	8	2whl.rid.chr.
Apr 26	William Branson	William Branson	1				
Apr 26	John Bruing	John Bruing	1			1	
Apr 26	Robert Buchan	Robert Buchan		5	1	8	
May 5	Mary Bell		1	3		3	
May 6	Thomas Bridwell	Thomas Bridwell	2			1	
May 6	Sarah Byrum		1				
May 9	Robert Brent			1		5	
May 12	George Burroughs	George Burroughs		1	1	2	
May 12	Derek Benear L.free					2	
May 12	Jacob Bridwell L.free					3	
May 12	William Byrum	William Byrum					
May 12	John Browne	John Browne	*[see next line]*				
May 12		Nath.n Williams		13	2	8	
May 14	William Boboe	William Boboe					
May 14	Jesey Bails	Jesey Bails					
[folio 4]							
May 14	George Bell Sr.	George Bell Sr.		1	1	3	
May 14	Nath.n Bannister	Nath.n Bannister	1			3	
May 20	Benjamin Bridwell	Benjamin Bridwell	1			1	
May 20	James Battoe L.free					2	
May 20	Elizabeth Bridwell					2	
May 20	William Bridwell	William Bridwell	2	3		4	
May 20	Moses Bridwell	Moses Bridwell	1	4	1	2	
May 22	John Bails	John Bails				1	
May 24	George Bridwell Jr.	George Bridwell Jr.				2	
May 29	Elijah Bell	Elijah Bell				2	
May 30	William Bridwell	William Bridwell	1				
May 30	Simon Bridwell	Simon Bridwell				1	
May 30	Rawleigh T. Browne	Pearson Williams		18	3	11	
May 30	John Brooker						
Jun 9	Daniel C. Brent	Daniel C. Brent	*[see next line]*				
Jun 9		Jonus Garner	*[see next line]*				
Jun 9		John Blake	*[see next line]*				

Date	chargeable w/tax	white males over 21	" 16-21/16+12+	/blacks/ H/		other
Jun 9		William Fritter	33	6	16	1 stud
Jun 9 Richard Brent	Richard Brent				3	2whl.rid.chr.
Jun 9 Eleanor Brent	Eleanor Brent		17	2	12	4whl.chariot
Jun 9 Ann Brent			22	4	7	
Jun 9 George Brent	Geo. Brent	*[see next line]*				
Jun 9	Henry Peyton		10	2	7	
Jun 9 John Brent		1	4		2	
Jun 9 Samuel Bridwell	Samuel Bridwell				2	
Jun 9 Zachariah Benson	Zachariah Benson				2	
Jun 10 Benjamin Brock	Benjamin Brock				2	
[folio 5]						
Jun 10 Enough Cocks	Enough Cocks					
Mar 15 Asey Cummins	Asey Cummins				5	
Mar 15 William Cummins	William Cummins				3	
Mar 28 John Clemmons	John Clemmons				2	
Mar 28 Perry Chinn	Perry Chinn				1	
Mar 28 Jedediah Carter	Jedediah Carter		1		2	
Mar 28 Henry Clifton	Henry Clifton	*[see next line]*				
Mar 28	Lawrence Butler		4	1	5	
Mar 28 Harris Carter	Harris Carter	1			1	
Mar 28 Briant Chadwell	Briant Chadwell	1	3	2	4	
Mar 28 Josua Carney	Josua Carney	*[see next line]*				
Mar 28	Benj.ª Carney		4	2	5	
Mar 28 Jessey Cooper	Jessey Cooper				1	
Apr 1 John Chiveral	John Chiveral				1	
Apr 1 Joseph Combs	Joseph Combs		3	2	3	
Apr 19 William Cole	William Cole					
Apr 23 Elizabeth Chissom					4	
Apr 26 Joseph Cooper L.free			1		2	
May 5 William Chandler	William Chandler		1	1	3	
May 5 Mary Chesshire					2	
Apr 9 Charles Carter	under 21	1	1		1	
May 13 Seth Combs	Fielding Combs		9	1	7	
May 13 George Coats	George Coats				1	
May 24 John Cooke	John Cooke		23	7	16	
May 30 Cuthbert Combs	Cuthbert Combs		6		5	
May 30 John Carter	John Carter				2	

Date	chargeable w/tax	white males over 21	*16-21	/blacks/ 16+	12+	H/	other
May 30	James Cloe L.free					3	
May 30	James Cloe Jr.	James Cloe				1	

[folio 6]
[text very faded at this point]

Date	chargeable w/tax	white males over 21	*16-21	/blacks/ 16+	12+	H/	other
Mar 11	Patterson Doyall	Patterson Doyall				3	
Mar 15	Dennis Doyall	Dennis Doyall				1	
Mar 28	William Dunaway	William Dunaway				1	
Mar 28	James Dent	James Dent					
Mar 28	John Dorson	John Dorson				4	
Mar 28	Christopher Dorson	Christopher Dorson				1	
Mar 28	Bradly Dent	Bradly Dent	1			2	
Apr 12	Raw.l Wm Downman	Benjamin Ficklin		10		3	
Apr 12	Archabeld Douglis L.free		1			6	
Apr 12	Dennis Doyall	Dennis Doyall		1		3	
May 5	Hannah Dickenson	Anthony Latham		6	2	6	
May 5	Charles Davis	Charles Davis				1	
May 5	Jeremiah Day	Jeremiah Day					
May 6	Moses Dick	Moses Dick				1	
May 12	Sarah Daniel			15	1	10	4whl. chair
May 12	Travers Daniel Sr.	Travers Daniel Sr.		16	2	13	2whl.rid.chr
May 12	Travers Daniel	Travers Daniel		6		6	
May 13	William Dorson	William Dorson				2	
May 13	Spencer Dorson	Spencer Dorson				1	
May 14	William Devene	William Devene				1	
May 24	John Dillion	John Dillion				1	
May 29	Elizabeth Dunaway		1			2	
May 29	John Dalgair	John Dalgair				2	

[folio 7]

Date	chargeable w/tax	white males over 21	*16-21	/blacks/ 16+	12+	H/	other
Mar 15	Thomas Edrington	Thomas Edrington		3		6	
Mar 18	William Edrington	William Edrington	2	3	1	6	
Mar 18	Willis Edwards	Willis Edwards				1	
Mar 18	John Esque	John Esque				1	
Mar 18	Jessey Edwards Sr.	Jessey Edwards	*[see next line]*				
Mar 18		Jessey Edwards				2	
Apr 14	William Edwards	William Edwards	1	1		1	
Apr 26	Isaac Eustace	Isaac Eustace	1	10	1	6	
Apr 26	William Eaton	William Eaton	2			1	

Date	chargeable w/tax	white males over 21	16-21	/blacks/ H/ 16-21	16+12+	other
May 5	Margaret Eaton				1	
May 15	Haden Edwards	Haden Edwards		6	6	
May 20	William Eusey	William Eusey		2	3	
May 28	Isaac Eavs	Isaac Eavs			2	
May 29	William Edwards	William Edwards		2	2	
Mar 14	John Fristoe	John Fristoe		3		
Mar 14	Moses Fritter Jr.	Moses Fritter Jr.			1	
Mar 14	Moses Fritter Sr.	Moses Fritter Sr.		1	2	
Mar 15	Samuel Faunt	Samuel Faunt			4	
Mar 22	John Fritter	John Fritter			2	
Mar 22	William Fritter Jr.	William Fritter Jr.			2	
Mar 22	Francis Foushee	Francis Foushee	1	3	3	
Mar 28	Jeremiah Fugate	Jeremiah Fugate			2	
	[folio 8]					
Mar 28	Wm Franklin	Wm Franklin			3	
Mar 28	Josiah Faning	Josiah Faning			2	
Mar 28	Joseph Franklin L.free				2	
Mar 28	James Faunt	James Faunt *[see next line]*				
Mar 28		Wm Faunt			4	
Apr 12	John Faunt	John Faunt				
Apr 14	Richard Fristoe L.free			1	1	
Apr 14	James Ford	James Ford	3	1	5	
Apr 23	Benjamin Ficklin	Benjamin Ficklin		1	4	
Apr 26	Anthony Ficklin	Anthony Ficklin	1	3	4	
Apr 26	William Fristoe	William Fristoe	2	1	4	
May 13	John Franklin Jr.	John Franklin Jr.		1	1	
May 14	John Franklin Sr.	Joseph Franklin			3	
May 20	Phillip Foxworthy	Phillip Foxworthy			2	
May 20	Vintsin Foxworthy	Vintsin Foxworthy			2	
May 20	William French	Wm French *[see next line]*				
May 20		Steaphen French	5	1	5	
May 30	Rheuben Franklin	Reuben Franklin			3	
Mar 11	William Gant	William Gant		2	2	
Mar 11	John Goldsmith	John Goldsmith		4	2	
Mar 15	Moses Grigsby Sr.	Moses Grigsby Sr.			1	
Mar 15	Moses Grigsby Jr.	Moses Grigsby Jr.				
Mar 15	John Garrison	John Garrison		1	1	

Date	chargeable w/tax	white males over 21	" /blacks/ H/ 16-21/16+12+	other
Mar 15 Benjamin Gregory	Benjamin Gregory		3	
Mar 15 Phillip Gardner	Phillip Gardner	3	4	
[folio 9]				
Mar 15 John Gun	John Gun		2	
Mar 15 John Gun	John Gun		2	
Mar 22 Elisha Grigsby	Elisha Grigsby		2	
Mar 22 William Gollohorn	William Gollohorn	1	5	
Mar 22 William George	William George			
Mar 22 Richard Griffes	Richard Griffes		1	
Apr 1 Robert Green	Robert Green	*[see next line]*		
Apr 1	John Green		4	
Apr 1 John Grigsby	John Grigsby		1	
Apr 1 George Garrison	George Garrison	1	3	
Apr 23 John Green	John Green		2	
Mar 26 John Grey	John Grey		2	
May 6 James Gough	James Gough	1	1	
May 6 Hannah Gough		1	2	
May 7 Sollomon Gollohorn	L.free		1	
May 7 Benjamin Green	Benjamin Green			
May 10 William Gee	William Gee	*[see next line]*		
May 10	Joseph Gee	1	5	
May 10 Benjamin Gee	Benjamin Gee		1	
May 10 Ann Gaddis		1 5 1	6	
May 10 William Garrard	William Garrard	7	5	
May 14 Aaron Garrison	Aaron Garrison		1	
May 14 Henry Griffin	Henry Griffin		1	
May 24 William Groves	William Groves	1	1	
May 28 Samuel Groves	Samuel Groves	1 1	3	
May 28 Keziah Gee			2	
May 30 Elizabeth Garrison			1	
[folio 10]				
May 30 Isaac Gaskins	Isaac Gaskins		3	
Mar 11 Samuel Hudson	Samuel Hudson	2	3	
Mar 11 William Holloday	William Holloday		2	
Mar 14 Peter Hansbrough	Peter Hansbrough		3	
Mar 14 Cuthbert Harding	Cuthbert Harding	1 1	2	
Mar 15 John Harding	John Harding		2	

362   Stafford Co., Va. personal property tax list - 1788

Date	chargeable w/tax	white males over 21	16-21	16+	12+	other
Mar 15 Henry Horton	Henry Horton				1	
Mar 15 Thomas Harding	Thomas Harding					
[text very faded at this point]						
Mar 15 James Harding	James Harding				1	
Mar 15 George Holloway	George Holloway					
Mar 28 Elijah Horton	Elijah Horton			2		
Mar 28 George Harding	George Harding			2		
Mar 28 John Scott Harding	John Scott Harding			3		
Mar 28 John Hore	John Hore			1	1	
Apr 12 Asey Holloway	Asey Holloway *[see next line]*					
Apr 12	Ruth Kitchen			2		
Apr 14 John Holloway	John Holloway			2		
Apr 14 William Harding	William Harding *[see next line]*					
Apr 14	Enough Harding		1	1	5	
Apr 14 Henry Hiden	Henry Hiden			2		
Apr 14 John Holloway Jr.	John Holloway *[see next line]*					
Apr 14	Thomas Holloway				5	
Apr 14 Isaac Holloway	Isaac Holloway			2		
Apr 14 Asie Holloway	Asie Holloway					
Apr 26 James Horton	James Horton			3		
[folio 11]						
May 7 Mary Holloway					1	
May 9 William Harrod	William Harrod *[see next line]*					
May 9	Edmund Lumsdil				3	
May 12 Thomas Hay L.free					• 3	
May 12 James Hore	James Hore			1	3	
May 12 John Horton	John Horton		6	1	6	
May 20 Virgin Hughs					1	
May 22 Lydia Hansbrough			1	1	1	
May 24 Elies Hore	Elies Hore		1		1	
May 24 Mary Hore			7	2		
May 24 William Hore	William Hore			1	1	
May 28 John Hardy	John Hardy		7	12		
May 29 Thomas Heth L.free			1			
May 29 James Henderson	James Henderson				1	
May 29 John Hedgman	John Hedgman		13	3	8	
Mar 11 William Innes	William Innes					

Date	chargeable w/tax	white males over 21	" /blacks/ H/ 16-21/16+12+			other
Mar 11	Wm Jones	Wm Jones	1		3	
Mar 11	John Jones	John Jones	1	.	5	
Mar 11	David Jones	David Jones	1		2	
Mar 28	John Jones	John Jones			1	
Mar 28	Gabril Jones	Gabril Jones	*[see next line]*			
Mar 28		Fielding Ficklin	5	2	4	
Apr 14	Alexander Jameson	Alexander Jameson	1		2	
May 14	Steaphen Johnston	Steaphen Johnston			2	
[folio 12]						
Mar 15	John Kendall	John Kendall	*[see next line]*			
Mar 15		Moses Kendall	*[see next line]*			
Mar 15		James Kendall	3	1	4	
Mar 15	Christopher Knight	Christopher Knight			3	
Mar 22	Jessey Kendall	Jessey Kendall			3	
Mar 22	Peter Kendall	Peter Kendall			3	
Mar 28	Charles Kendall	Charles Kendall			2	
Mar 28	John Knight	John Knight			2	
Mar 28	James Kirk .	James Kirk			2	
Mar 28	Merriman Ketchen	Merriman Ketchen *[see next line]*				
Mar 28		James Ketchen	2	1	3	
Apr 1	Peter Knight	Peter Knight	*[see next line]*			
Apr 1		Baily Knight			5	
Apr 1	Ephraim Knight	Ephraim Knight			2	
Apr 1	James Kendall	James Kendall			1	
Apr 1	Daniel Kendall	Daniel Kendall			3	
Apr 14	Jeremiah Knight	Jeremiah Knight	1	1	4	
Apr 23	Sarah Knight.		1			
Apr 23	Ann Knight		1	2	1	2
Apr 23	Josua Kendall Sr.	Josua Kendall	*[see next line]*			
Apr 23		Anthony Kendall	4	1	6	
Apr 23	Henry Kendall	Henry Kendall	2	1	3	
May 7	Josua Kendall	Josua Kendall			3	
May 14	Uriah Knight	Uriah Knight	2		3	
May 22	Aaron Kendall	Aaron Kendall			1	
May 22	Sarah Knight				3	
May 22	Peter Knight Jr.	Peter Knight	1		3	
[folio 13]						

Date	chargeable w/tax	white males over 21	" /blacks/ H/ 16-21	16+	12+	other
Mar 11	Francis Linum	Francis Linum			1	
Mar 15	John Latham(s/Snodon)	John Latham			2	
Mar 28	John Lunsford	John Lunsford			3	
Mar 28	John Lawlis	John Lawlis			2	
Mar 28	James Lowry	James Lowry	[see next line]			
Mar 28		Thomas Lowry	1		2	
Mar 28	John Latham	John Latham			1	
Apr 26	Moses Lunsford	Moses Lunsford			3	
May 7	Charles Latham	Charles Latham				
May 24	Snodon Latham	Snodon Latham	1		2	
May 30	George Latham	George Latham			1	
May 30	Gavin Lawson	Gavin Lawson	[see next line]			
May 30		David Bridges	[see next line]			
May 30		Charles Dunkinson	16	5	13	4wheels
May 30	Chondrid Lewis	Chondrid Lewis			1	
Mar 11	Richard Morton	Richard Morton	2		2	
Mar 14	William Mullin	William Mullin	1	5	4	2whl.rid.chr
Mar 14	Henry Mcentire	Henry Mcentire	1	1	2	
Mar 15	Richard Mason	Richard Mason			4	
Mar 15	John Mccullough	John Mccullough			2	
Mar 15	Lewis Mason	Lewis Mason		1	3	
Mar 28	Peter Mauzy (Fairfax)		3	1	3	
Mar 28	George Mauzy	George Mauzy		1		
Mar 28	John Mountjoy	John Mountjoy			3	
[folio 14]						
Mar 28	Alexander Mcentire	Alexander Mcentire		1	3	
Mar 28	James More	James More			1	
Mar 28	Thomas Mallery	Thomas Mallery				
Mar 28	Daniel Mason	Daniel Mason	1	1	1 6	
Apr 9	John Fr.a Mercer	David Hepbourn	[see next line]			
Apr 9		William More	[see next line]			
Apr 9		Johnston Smith	16	3	18	
Apr 9	Hugh McDaniel	Hugh McDaniel			1	
Apr 14	Robert Million	Robert Million	2 1		6	
Apr 14	William Mauzy	William Mauzy		1	2 3	
Apr 16	Thomas Mountjoy	Thomas Mountjoy	7	3	8	
Apr 19	Edward Mountjoy	Edward Mountjoy	1		5	

Date	chargeable w/tax	white males over 21	" /blacks/ H/ 16-21/16+12+			other
Apr 26 William Monroe	William Monroe	5	2			
May 5 Edward McKenzy	Edward McKenzy		1			
May 12 John Mason	John Mason	4	7			
May 13 Ursly Morton			2	2		
May 13 Mary McDaniel	John Johnston		1			
May 13 Charles Mifflin L.free			2			
May 14 Benjamin Million	Benjamin Million		2			
May 15 John Murray (Prince Wm.)		9	4			
May 21 Margaret Matthews		3	3	6		2whl.rid.chr
May 28 James Murphy	James Murphy	1	1			
May 28 Ann Moncure		11	1	5		
May 29 Allen Mountjoy	Allen Mountjoy	2	3			
May 29 Thomas Mountjoy	Thomas Mountjoy	1	1			
May 29 William Mountjoy	William Mountjoy	6	2	9		
[folio 15]						
May 29 Robert B. Morton	Robert B. Morton	10	2	14		
May 29 James McBride	James McBride	1	2			
Jun 10 Charles Martin	Charles Martin		1?			
Jun 10 Fielding Mason	Fielding Mason		1			
Jun 10 John Markham	John Markham	2	2	2		
Jun 10 John Mountjoy	John Mountjoy	6	1	9		
Jun 10 Michael Maze	Michael Maze	[see next line]				
Jun 10	Lanstet Maze	1	2			
Mar 28 Phillip Nash	Phillip Nash		1			
Mar 28 George Norman	George Norman		5			
Mar 28 John Nicholson	John Nicholson		1			
Apr 14 James Nailer	James Nailer	1	5			
May 7 Sarah Nelson		1	1			
May 10 Edward Norman	Edward Norman	4	3	1		
Mar 15 James Ocane	James Ocane	1	4			
Mar 28 James Oglesby	James Oglesby		2			
Mar 28 Elizabeth Overall		1	6	8		
Mar 11 Calvert Porter	Calvert Porter	[see next line]				
Mar 11	Thomas Porter	3	1	8		
Mar 11 Richard Poats	Richard Poats		3			
Mar 15 Hesekiah Patterson	Hesekiah Patterson		1			
Mar 15 John Primm	John Primm	1	3			

Date	chargeable w/tax	white males over 21	"	/blacks/H/ 16-21/16+12+		other
Mar 15	Margaret Primm		1	1	3	
Mar 15	John Pattin	John Pattin			2	
[folio 16]						
Mar 28	John Poats	John Poats			4?	
Mar 28	Moses Poats	Moses Poats			3	
Mar 28	Abraham Parker	Abraham Parker				
Mar 28	Charles Porter	Charles Porter			3	
Apr 1	Charles Porter Jr.	Charles Porter Jr.				
Apr 12	James Primm	James Primm			3	
Apr 14	Robert Painter	Robert Painter		1	4	
Apr 16	Thomas Powell	Thomas Powell				
Apr 19	Mary Ann Payn			3	4	
Apr 19	Ezekiel Payn	Ezekiel Payn				
Apr 19	Sarah Payn	James Payn			2	
Apr 19	Francis Payn	Francis Payn				
Apr 23	John Packstein	John Packstein			4	
Apr 26	Elizabeth Peyton	Thomas Peyton	[see next line]			
Apr 26		Sam Peyton		9 3	8	
Apr 26	William Pattin	William Pattin				
May 9	John R. Peyton	John R. Peyton	[see next line]			
May 9		Zachariah Griffis	[see next line]			
May 9		Francis Lucus		10 4	10	
May 12	Benjamin Pritchet	Benjamin Pritchet	1	5	6	
May 13	William Poats	William Poats		2	3	
May 14	James Peak	James Peak			1	
May 14	Edward Pearson	Edward Pearson				
May 22	William Phillips	William Phillips	[see next line]			
May 22		Zachariah Cummins		7 1	4	
May 23	Jessey Payn	Jessey Payn			1	
May 24	Wharton Philbert	Wharton Philbert			1	
Jun 9	Vallentine Peyton	Vallentine Peyton		9 1	6	4whl.phaeton
Jun 9	Samuel Parker	Samuel Parker			1	
[folio 17]						
Jun 9	Charles Porter	Charles Porter			3	
Mar 11	Charles Rawls(PrW^m)	John Faning		1	1	
Mar 11	Thomas Right	Thomas Right	1	3	5	

Date	chargeable w/tax	white males over 21	" /blacks/ H/ 16-21	16+	12+	other
Mar 11	William Rout	William Rout	1		3	
Mar 11	Richard Reid Sr.	Richard Reid Sr. [see next line]				
Mar 11		Richard Reid	2		4	
Mar 14	Thomas Rakestraw	Thomas Rakestraw				
Mar 15	John Rogers	John Rogers			3	
Mar 15	Kenez Rauls	Kenez Rauls			1	
Mar 15	Aaron Reid	Aaron Reid			3	
Mar 15	Jonathan Reid	Jonathan Reid	1		2	
Mar 15	Joel Readish	Joel Readish [see next line]				
Mar 15		John Minton [see next line]				
Mar 15		John Thorp	4	2	7	
Mar 15	Joseph Readish	Joseph Readish [see next line]				
Mar 15		Jno. Bradly	4		6	
Mar 22	Geo. Randol L.free	Thomas Gill			2	
Mar 28	Habern Rauls	under 21	1	1	2	
Mar 28	Baily Riley	Baily Riley			2	
Mar 28	Jessey Riley	Jessey Riley	1		1	
Apr 14	Rawleigh Rauls		1	2	3	
Apr 19	John Richards	John Richards				
Apr 26	James Riley	James Riley				
Apr 26	William Right	William Right			2	
May 6	William Robeson	William Robeson	1		3	
May 6	James Robeson	James Robeson			2	
May 6	Ann Rogers				2	
May 6	Richard Ratliff	Richard Ratliff		2	3	
[folio 18]						
May 11	William Ross	William Ross	1	1	4	
May 12	Butler Raimy	Butler Raimy			3	
May 17	William Randol	William Randol [see next line]				
May 17		John Randol			4	
May 20	Mary Ann Rauls			3	2	
May 23	Reuben Rogers	Reuben Rogers			1	
May 24	William Richards	William Richards	1		3	
Mar 11	Sarsfield Snoxall	Sarsfield Snoxall			2	
Mar 11	Charles Stern	Charles Stern	2	1	1	
Mar 11	Francis Stern	Francis Stern	4	2	4	
Mar 15	John Stark	John Stark			1	

Date	chargeable w/tax	white males over 21	" /blacks/ H/ 16-21/16+12+			other
Mar 15 Richard Sims	Richard Sims				3	
Mar 15 John Stern	John Stern		2	1	2	
Mar 15 Henry Smith	Henry Smith	[see next line]				
Mar 15	Joseph Smith		5		6	
Mar 22 Thomas Sedden	Thomas Sedden	[see next line]				
Mar 22	Dennis Linum		13	4	6	
Mar 22 Elisha Skinner	Elisha Skinner					
Mar 22 John Snoxall	John Snoxall				2	
Mar 22 Henry Sudduth	Henry Sudduth				2	
Mar 28 Nath.l Smith	Nath.l Smith		1		2	
Mar 28 Wilson Shelton	Wilson Shelton				2	
Mar 28 William Stark	William Stark		2		2	
Mar 28 William Shelton	William Shelton				6	
Mar 28 George Shelton	George Shelton				2	
[folio 19]						
Mar 28 Abigale Shelton					2	
Mar 28 James Sims	James Sims				3	
Apr 12 William Stark	William Stark	1			3	
Apr 14 John Stark	John Stark	1	1		3	
Apr 14 John Smith	John Smith				2	
Apr 19 John Shelkel	John Shelkel			1	4	
Apr 19 Elizabeth Spilman					1	
Apr 26 Craven Spiller	Craven Spiller				2	
Apr 26 Presly Sims	Presly Sims				1	
Apr 26 Jeremiah Stark	Jeremiah Stark	[see next line]				
Apr 26	William Stark				5	
Apr 26 Rhoadnum Sims	Rhoadnum Sims				2	
May 5 Thomas Sudduth	Thomas Sudduth				2	
May 6 William Stephens	William Stephens					
May 7 Hannah Stark		1	1		2	
May 7 Joseph Slaughter	Joseph Slaughter					
May 9 Rich.d Stone	Rich.d Stone				3	
May 9 Wm B. Stone	Wm B. Stone		6	1	7	
May 10 Hawkin Stone	Hawkin Stone		5	3	7	
May 10 Benjamin Shacklet	Benjamin Shacklet [see next line]					
May 10	William Shacklet				4	
May 14 Josia Stone	Josia Stone		5		3	2whl.rid.chr.

Date	chargeable w/tax	white males over 21	" /blacks/ H/ 16-21/16+12+				other
May 14	Jessey Stone	Jessey Stone	2			2	
May 20	Richard Sims L.free		1			2	
May 22	Samuel Striblin	Samuel Striblin				1	
May 22	Edward Snoxall	Edward Snoxall	[see next line]				
May 22		Tho.ˢ Beagle				4	
May 22	John Stark (Princ. Wᵐ)						
[folio 20]							
Mar 15	Charles Thornton	Charles Thornton				2	
Mar 15	Edward Templeman	Edward Templeman				3	
Mar 22	John Tolson	John Tolson				2	
Mar 28	Richard Taylor	Richard Taylor				2	
Apr 12	Thomas Tharp	Thomas Tharp				1	
Apr 12	John Tuttle	John Tuttle				1	
May 5	Alexander Taylor	Alexander Taylor	1			2	
May 13	Joanna Tolson	Joanna Tolson (sic)	1			1	
May 14	William Tolson	William Tolson		1		5	
May 14	Elizabeth Tolson		1	5	1	8	
May 14	Benjamin Tolson	Benjamin Tolson				2	
May 20	Thomas Tennant	Thomas Tennant [see next line]					
May 20		Anthony Long				2	
May 21	William Taylor	William Taylor	1	7	2	6	
May 24	Samuel Thompson	Samuel Thompson		2		5	
May 24	Elijah Thraelkeld	Elijah Thraelkeld	1	13	2	10	
May 24	George Thraelkeld	George Thraelkeld		2		1	
Jun 10	William Tungate	William Tungate				4	
Jun 10	Tho.ˢ S. Tyler	S. Tyler			3	4	
May 13	Ann Vaughan					2	
[folio 21]							
Mar 11	George Withers	George Withers		1	1	3	
Mar 11	Richard Walker	Richard Walker	1	1		3	
Mar 11	John Waters	John Waters				1	
Mar 14	Mary Waller			3	1	5	
Mar 15	Peter Wood	Peter Wood	1			4	
Mar 22	Benjamin Wine	Benjamin Wine					
Mar 22	Allen Way	Allen Way				2	
Mar 28	James Walker	James Walker				1	
Mar 28	John Warren	John Warren	1			3	

Date	chargeable w/tax	white males over 21	" /blacks/ H/ 16-21/16+12+	other
Mar 28	Charles Waters	Charles Waters	2	
Apr 1	Benjamin Willits	Benjamin Willits	2	
Apr 1	Wm Waller	Wm Waller	*[see next line]*	
Apr 1		Edward Waller	*[see next line]*	
Apr 1		William Waller	4 2 6	
Apr 14	Baily Washington Sr.	Baily Washington Sr.	10 1 7	4 wheels
Apr 14	Baily Washington Jr.	Baily Washington Jr.	10 2 4	
Apr 14	John Waters Sr. L.free		2 1 4	
Apr 14	George Wort	George Wort	1 5	
Apr 14	William Waters	William Waters	*[see next line]*	
Apr 14		James Waters	*[text faded]* 1?	
Apr 14	William West	William West	1 2	
Apr 23	George Walters	George Walters	3	
Apr 26	Henry Woodgerd	Henry Woodgerd	2	
Apr 26	George Wells	George Wells	1 4	
Apr 26	Elizabeth Wells		3 3	
Apr 26	Jessey Woodgerd	Jessey Woodgerd	1	
May 10	Peter Waters	Peter Waters	3	
[folio 22]				
May 12	John Withers Sr.	Jno. Withers	*[see next line]*	
May 12		Benj.a Withers	13 5 9	
May 13	William West	William West	1 3	
May 14	George Williams	George Williams	7? 2 3	
May 14	Margaret Williams	Wm Williams	*[see next line]*	
May 14		Lewis Williams	4	
May 14	Nathaniel Williams	Nathaniel Williams	6 2	
May 14	John Waters Jr.	Waters Jr.	3	
May 14	Mark Waters	Mark Waters	*[see next line]*	
May 14		Baily Waters	7?	
May 20	Rich.d Woodgerd	Rich.d Woodgerd	3	
May 20	Sarah Wigginton		1	
May 24	Barsheba Walter		2	
May 24	Augustin Weadon	Augustin Weadon	3	
May 29	William Watson	William Watson		
May 30	Susanah Wormsly		2	
May 30	John Withers	John Withers	1 1 1	

Date	chargeable w/tax	white males over 21	" /blacks/ H/ 16-21/16+12+	other
May 30	Thomas Wells	Thomas Wells	1	
Mar 28	William Young	William Young	1	
		[totals]	823 1426	
			176 44	

* * * * *

* * *

*

[End of Mountjoy's returns]

A List of taxable property within the district of William Alexander, Commissioner Stafford County year 1788, Returned as P. vouchers

[folio 23]

Mo.	day	Proprietor's names	whites 16+	blacks 16+	12+	H	other
Mar	20	Alexander William	1	7	2	6	
Mar	20	D.º for Casson Est.		5	1	6	
Mar	23	Allentharp Jacob	2			5	
Apr	14	Arrowsmith Thomas	3	1		5	
Apr	15	Alexander Phillip Lfree	1	6	8	5	
Apr	25	Thomas Allison	1	2		3	
May	9	Alliason David	2	2		1	
Mar	21	Barrett Bartholomew	2		1	2	
Mar	22	Bruce William	0	2	1	4	
Mar	26	Berry Sarah	1	1		3	
Mar	26	Butler William	1	1		2	
Mar	26	Burnett William	3	2	1	5	
Mar	28	Berry Thomas	2	1		2	
Mar	28	Berry Anthony	1			2	
Mar	28	Berry Richard	1			1	
Mar	28	Black Margrett	2			4	
Mar	28	Brown James	1			2	
Mar	28	Bates Thomas	1			2	
Mar	28	Brimmer John	1			1	
Mar	28	Brimmer Isaac	1				
Mar	28	Burton James	2			3	
Mar	28	Burton Rachal	2			2	
Mar	31	Briant John	1		1	1	
Mar	31	Brown William	2			4	
Apr	1	Bates Joseph tax free				2	
Apr	5	Burgess Ruben	3			3	
Apr	5	Ballard Thomas	1	3		3	
Apr	5	Ballard William Senr.	1			1	
Apr	5	Bolling Samuel	3	1	1	4	
Apr	5	Bolling Thomas	1			1	
Apr	5	Bolling James	3			3	

Mo.	day	Proprietor's names	whites 16+	blacks 16+	12+	H	other
Apr	5	Bussell William	2			2	
Apr	7	Bingy John	1			1	
Apr	13	Ball William	?	3	1	5	
[folio 24]							
Apr	14	Bolling William	1				
Apr	14	Bowen Burkett	1	2	1	7	
Apr	15	Bowen Thomas		1		3	
Apr	21	Ball Burgess		24	1	15	
Apr	24	Banks Frances		8	2	8	2chr wheels
Apr	24	Benson James	1	3	1	4	
Apr	24	Beasly Philip	1				
Apr	24	Baker Moses	1				
Apr	25	Briggs David	2	10		8	
Apr	25	Barber William	1				
Apr	26	Ball John	1			1	
Apr	28	Buchannan Andrew	1	7	2	6	4 phaet whls
May	6	Bell John	2	3		4	ord. license
May	9	Bowers Michal	1	3	2	4	
May	9	Boyer John	1				
Mar	22	Curtice George	1		1	5	
Mar	22	Curtice Aaron	2			1	
Mar	22	Cox George	1				
Mar	22	Carter Henry	1				
Mar	22	Chinn Joseph	1			3	
Mar	26	Cox Charnox	1		1	2	
Mar	26	Cox Vincent Junr.	1		1	4	
Mar	26	Cox Presly	1			1	
Mar	27	Curtice William	1			2	
Mar	28	Carter Joseph	1	2		3	
Mar	28	Curtice Richard	1			1	
Mar	28	Cortney John	1	3	1	6	
Mar	28	Cox Vincent Junr.	2			2	
Mar	28	Connor John	2			3	
Mar	28	Colney Elisha	1			1	
[folio 25]							
Mar	28	Colney Joseph	1			1	
Mar	28	Curtice John	3			3	
Apr	5	Chapman Philip	1		1	3	
Apr	10	Curtice Elijah	1		0	1	

Mo.	day	Proprietor's names	whites 16+	blacks 16+ 12+		H	other
Apr	21	Carter George	2		1	3	
Apr	24	Conyers John	5	3		4	
Apr	24	Crop James Senr.	1	6	1	4	
Apr	25	Crop John	1	8	2	8	
Apr	25	Crop James Junr.	1	5	2	5	
Apr	23	Carter Charles	3	31	4	14	
Apr	23	Carter Rob.t W.	1	15	2	6	
May	5	Calender Philip	1			3	
May	6	Conyers Benj.a	1				
May	7	Collins Thomas	2	3		4	
May	9	Colquahoon Walter	1	3		1	
May	9	Clerk William	1				
Mar	20	Donathan Gerard	1	2		4	stud @ 0.12
Mar	20	Downman B. Jos.	1	7	4	6	
Apr	14	Daffin Vincent	1			1	
Apr	14	Dowdle James	1	3		3	
Apr	23	Day Benjaman	1	1		1	
Apr	23	Day Elizabeth	1			1	
May	6	Donavan James	1	3		3	
May	7	Dunbar Rob.t	4	4		3	
May	9	Disher Lewis	1				
Apr	4	Edwards Andrew	1	7	1	11	
Apr	23	England John	3			3	
[folio 26]							
Mar	25	Fox Nathaniel	1	6	2	7	
Mar	22	Fowler Thomas				1	
Mar	22	Finnall Jonathan	1	8	2	7	
Mar	26	Fines Patrick	2	1		3	
Mar	26	Fletcher Rachall	2	1		5	
Mar	27	Fugitt Francis Junr.	1			1	
Mar	28	Faunt John	1			2	
Apr	1	Fugitt Benj.a	1		1	2	
Apr	1	Fugitt Francis Senr.	1			1	
Apr	1	Fugitt Daniel	1			2	
Apr	5	Foster Seth	1			4	
Apr	5	Faunt George	1	3	1	4	
Apr	10	Fitzhugh John	3	15	1	7	4 phaeton whls
Apr	10	Fitzhugh Henry	2	8	1	9	
Apr	14	Fitzhugh William	1	61	11	25	8ph,2chr wh.

Mo.	day	Proprietor's names	whites 16+	blacks 16+12+		H	other
Apr	14	Fields Samuel	1			1	
May	9	Faunt Joseph	1	3	1	3	
n.d.		Fitzhugh Thomas	2	25	3	10	4 phaet whls
Mar	26	Garner John	2			2	
Mar	26	Gollohorn Solomon	1			1	
Mar	28	Groves Thomas	1			1	
Mar	28	Graves Benj.a	1			1	
Mar	28	Gollohorn Tho.s	1			3	
Mar	28	Graves [no given name]	1				
Mar	28	Graves Wm	4	1		6	
Apr	14	Green Jesse	1			1	
Apr	19	Garner William	2			1	
Apr	23	Guthry Thomas	1			1	
May	6	Graves Martha				3	
May	6	Golohorn John	1				
[folio 27]							
May	9	Gorden Samuel	2		1	1	
May	9	Graves George	1			1	
Mar	26	Hunter Adam forge	3	46	2	18	
		"					2whls,stud@1.1.4
Mar	26	Hill Jesse	1	3		5	
Mar	28	Hall Benjaman	1			4	
Mar	28	Horton William	1			3	
Mar	28	Hord Thomas	1	1		5	
Apr	1	Henson Sarah				2	
Apr	1	Henson Elijah	1			3	
Apr	1	Hewett William	1	14	3	9	2chr.whls.
Apr	5	Hord Peter	1	2		3	
Apr	5	Hall Hannah	1			2	
Apr	5	Hord James	2	8	1	8	
Apr	5	Hord Jesse	1	6	1	6	
n.d		Hord Rhody	1	4		6	
n.d.		Hord Kellis	3	5	2	5	
n.d.		Hord Edward	2	2		7	
Apr	23	Humphry William	2		2	6	
Apr	23	Hewett Susanna		6		8	2chr.whls.
Apr	23	Hooe Harris Est.		10	2	7	
Apr	23	Humes Francis		1			
n.d.		Hudson David	1	1	1	2	

Mo.	day	Proprietor's names	whites 16+	blacks 16+ 12+		H	other
Apr	25	Humphry Daniel	1			1	
Apr	25	Horton James	1			4	
Apr	25	Hill Leonard		3	1	5	
Apr	26	Harwood Allice		2		2	
May	5	Howard W^m	1				
May	6	Hunter Adam	3	23	3	10	4phaeton whls.
n.d.		D.^o@ Hamsted? *[blurred]*	1	9		5	
[folio 28]							
May	9	Hayney William	1	4		4	
May	9	Humphry McCausland	2	1			
Mar	21	Jones Thomas	1	1		3	
Mar	24	Jones George	1				
Mar	28	Jones James	1			4	
Mar	28	Jett John	1			2	
Mar	28	Jackson Robert	3			4	
n.d.		Jackson Rosana	2			3	
n.d.		James George	1	2	1	5	
n.d.		Jones George	1			2	
n.d.		Jett William	3	1		5	
n.d.		Jones Evins	3	1		3	
Apr	1	Jones William	1			1	
Apr	10	Jacobs William	1	2	1	3	
n.d.		Jett Peter Presly	1			1	
n.d.		Jett George	1				
Apr	25	Jones Charles	2	2	1	6	
May	5	Jones Henry	2	1		4	
May	7	Jett Francis	1	2	2	3	
May	12	James John	4	14	2	13	
Mar	22	Kenny Thomas	1			3	
Mar	28	Kenny John	1			3	
Mar	28	Kitchen James	2			3?	
Apr	14	Kirk Jeremiah	1	0	2	2	
Apr	19	Kenyon James	1	6	2	7	
Apr	23	Kirby James	1				
[folio 29]							
Mar	26	Long Robt	1			2	
Mar	26	Limbrick William	1			2	
Mar	26	Leach Andrew	2			2	
Mar	28	Leach Benjaman	1			2	

Mo.	day	Proprietor's names	whites 16+	blacks 16+ 12+		H	other
Mar	28	Leach Thomas	1	4	1	4	
Mar	28	Limbrick John	2			2	
Mar	28	Lathrum George	1	1		1	
Mar	28	Lowry James	1	1	1	2	
Mar	28	Lunsford Joanah	1	1		3	
Apr	1	Limbrick Francis	2			2	
Apr	5	Logue Alexander	1	1		3	
Apr	5	Linn Simon	1			1	
Apr	5	Lathrum Anth.º	3		1	5	
Apr	23	Lewis Ann		1			
Apr	23	Lavender Joseph	2				
Apr	23	Lavender Rob.ᵗ	2	1		4	
Apr	25	Lanman Newman	1	1		2	
Apr	25	Lathrum John	1	2		3	
Apr	25	Lathrum George	2	1		4	
May	5	Latimer Daniel	2			3	
May	6	Lotspieck William	1	1		2	
May	9	Lucas John	1				
May	9	Lyon James	3			1	
May	13	Lee Tho.ˢ & Mary	2	30	7	20	4phaet whls.
n.d.		Morris Casper	1			2	
Mar	22	Miner Elizabeth		1		1	
Mar	25	Monday Aaron	1			1	
Mar	28	Martin Daniel	1			1	
Mar	28	McEntosh James	1			?	
[folio 30]							
n.d.		McGuire Rachell	1			3	
Mar	28	Musselman Christopher	2			1	
Mar	28	Martin Thomas	1			1	
Mar	28	Munrow Daniel	1	1		3	
Mar	28	Meels Samuel	1			1	
Mar	28	Martin Lewis	1			1	
Mar	28	Martin Charles	2	1		3	
Mar	28	McDonall Daniel	1	2		1	
Apr	1	McCullock John	1			1	
Apr	5	Marquiss Anth.º	1		1	2	
Apr	5	Martin Samuel	1			3	
Apr	5	Munrow William	1			1	
Apr	5	Mannon John	1			3	

Mo.	day	Proprietor's names	whites 16+	blacks 16+12+		H	other
Apr	14	McFarlin Ovid	1			4	stud/0.13.4
Apr	24	Massey Thomas	2	3		7	
Apr	24	Massey Benj.ᵃ				1	
Apr	24	Millett John	1			2	
Apr	24	Mattox Lazarus	1	1		5	
Apr	26	Morison Arthur	4	13	4	15	
Apr	26	Massey Toliferrow	1				
Apr	26	Massey Elizabeth				1	
Apr	26	More Edward	1	7	2	6	
Apr	26	Mulbury John	1	2		1	
May	7	Manson Alexander	2	3	1	1	
May	9	Moss John	1				
May	9	McKeterick Anth.ᵒ	3	9		12	2chr.whls.
May	9	McMillion Wᵐ	1			1	
May	9	McCloud James	3	1		1	
May	15	Mortimer Ch.ˢ		4?		2	
[folio 31]							
Mar	27	Newton John	1	5	2	4	
Mar	28	Newton Margret	1	2		7	
Mar	31	Newton William	5	10	3	8	
Apr	25	Nickles Elijah	1			1	
May	9	Nooe Zephaniah	1	3	1	2	
May	9	Norwood Joseph	1				
Mar	27	Oliver John	2			3	
Mar	26	Pilcher Mildred	1	1		2	
Mar	26	Pates Aaron	2		1	2	
Mar	26	Pilcher Richard	3			2	
Mar	26	Payn John	3			3	
Mar	26	Pilcher Charles	3			2	
Mar	28	Payton Ann	3	1	1	3	
Mar	28	Puzey Stephen	2			1	
Mar	28	Porch Esum	1	1	2	3	
Mar	28	Patterson Thomas	1			2	
Mar	31	Pollard John	1	9	1	5	
Mar	31	Pollard Linsey	1			1	
Mar	31	Posey Thomas	1	9	2	16	
Apr	1	Pilcher Moses	1	2		3	
Apr	1	Paterson Fanny	1				
Apr	5	Pilcher Mason	3	6	1	5	

Mo. day		Proprietor's names	whites 16+	blacks 16+ 12+		H	other
Apr	14	Pettit Benjamin	3	1		3	
Apr	24	Parmer Rawley	3	1		2	
Apr	25	Patterson Perry	1				
Apr	25	Pilcher Peter	1			1	
Apr	25	Patten Rachell	1	5		3	
May	5	Paxton John	1			3	
May	5	Peyton Thomas	1	2		2	
[folio 32]							
May	9	Peters William	1				
n.d.		Poarch Thomas	1	9	2	8	
n.d.		Payn Daniel	2	1	1	1	
Mar	26	Robertson John	1			1	
Mar	26	Raulins John	1			2	
Mar	28	Robertson Thomas	1			3	
Mar	28	Roach Robert	2		1	3	
Apr	1	Rowley Archibald	1	1		1	
Apr	23	Robertson George	1				
Apr	23	Reavley William	2	4	2	3	2chr.whls.
Apr	23	Rose Jesse	1				
May	5	Read John	1	1		3	
May	6	Rogers John	1	1		2	
May	9	Ransdell John	1				
May	9	Richards William	1	10	1	4	4phae.whls.
Mar	26	Stone William	2			2	
Mar	26	Swillivant Lettice				2	
Mar	26	Swillivant Gabriel	2			4	
Mar	26	Stone Joseph	1			1	
Mar	28	Snipe Natha.l	1			2	
Mar	28	Striplin Joel	1			1	
Mar	28	Sutor William	1				
Mar	28	Sutor Andrew	2				
Mar	31	Strother George	3	5	1	7	
n.d.		D.o the Est.a Ann Clerk				4	
Apr	1	Swilliv.t Darby Senr.	1			1	
Apr	1	Swillivant Benj.a	1			3	
Apr	1	Swillivant Daniel	1			3	
Apr	1	Swillivant Darby Junr.	2			2	
Apr	1	Snellens Enoch	1			3	
Apr	1	Snellens William	2			3	

Mo.	day	Proprietor's names	whites 16+	blacks 16+12+	H		other
Apr	1	Seidmore Josua	1		1	1	
[folio 33]							
Apr	1	Swillivant Francis	1	1		3	
Apr	3	Stephens Richard	1	2		2	
Apr	3	Spence William				2	
Apr	3	Scott Sarah	1			3	
Apr	3	Schooler Thomas	1			2	
Apr	3	Stringfellow James	2	1	1	3	
Apr	3	Sharp Thomas Senr.	2	4	1	1	
Apr	3	Sharp Thomas Junr.	1	1		2	
Apr	3	Striplin William	1			2	
Apr	5	Smith John	1	2		5	
Apr	5	Sharp Linsfield	2	7	2	7	
Apr	10	Sudtherd William	2			1	
Apr	7	Slaven Jesse	2	1		4	
Apr	24	Suton John	1	1		1	
Apr	24	Smith Samuel	2	4		3	
Apr	25	Simpson Alexander				2	
Apr	25	Skinker Thomas		5	1	6	
Apr	26	Striplin Elizabeth		1			
May	5	Sudden John	2	12	3	9	
May	5	Saunders James	1			1	
May	5	Stringfellow Towns.d	1			1	
May	9	Stringfellow George	2	2		3	
May	9	Sapington Samuel	1				
May	14	Simpson John	1				
n.d.		Selden Samuel	2	33	11	15	4phaeton whls.
May	15	Smith & Young & Hyde					1 stud @ L3
Mar	22	Thornton Tho.s	1	4	1	4	
Mar	22	Templeman Jane				2	
Mar	27	Terrier John	1	1		3	
Mar	27	Troop Thomas	1			2	
Mar	28	Tompson John	1			1	
Mar	28	Timmons John	1			3	
[folio 34]							
Mar	28	Turner James	2			3	
Apr	1	Tisley John	2			3	
Apr	5	Turner Griffin	3			4	
Apr	5	Turner Absolum	3			2	

Mo.	day	Proprietor's names	whites 16+	blacks 16+	12+	H	other
Apr	7	Thompson James	3			6	
Apr	10	Tyler Allice	1	8		6	
Apr	19	Threlkill Jesse	1			1	
Apr	24	Turner Benj.ª	1			1	
n.d.		Trussell Rhodum	1				
May	7	Travis Margrett		1			
May	9	Tayler William	2	6		3	2chr.whls.
May	9	Triplett Daniel					
Mar	9	Vowles Chaveles [sic]	1				
n.d.		Vowles Richard	2	1		1	
n.d.		Vowles Henry	1	6		3	2chr.whls.
Mar	20	Waugh George	2	7		9	
Mar	20	Washington Gen.ˡ George	1	7		3	
Mar	26	Whitt George Senr.				2	
Mar	26	Wallace Michall		3	1	4	
Mar	26	Waugh McCagby	2			4	
Mar	28	White? George [blurred]	2			4?	
Mar	28	Weak George	1			2	
Mar	28	Webb Aaron	2			6	
Mar	28	Webb Moses	1			1	
Mar	28	Wine Dotia	1				
Mar	28	Walker Solomon	1			1	
Mar	28	Wallace John	1	4		5	
n.d.		Wallace James		4		2	
[folio 35]							
Apr	1	Walker William	3	3	1	3	
Apr	5	White Thomas	1	1		4	
Apr	5	White Ann		1		1	
Apr	5	West John	1	1		1	
Apr	5	Weaks Thomas	1			2	
Apr	5	West John Senr.	1			5	
Apr	7	Wellford Robert		10	1	10	1 stud
Apr	10	Warton James				2	
Apr	14	Wallace William	1	5	2	3	
Apr	23	Wooderd Mary	1	1		1	
Apr	24	White George	1	2		4	
Apr	24	West Edward Senr.	4	1		7	
May	7	Winlock William	3	4		3	
May	9	Weathers James	2	8	3	5	

Mo.	day	Proprietor's names	whites 16+	blacks 16+12+	H	other
May	9	Williams Leonard	1	1		
May	9	West Thomas	1			
May	9	Weaks Benjaman	1			
May	15	Young William	2	3		
		[totals]	506	160		
			291	1150		

Excepted. *[sic]*

William Alexander Comm.[r]

[folio 36]
Stafford Sct. 9 June 1788

     I certify the aforegoing List to be a true Copy of the List returned to me by William Alexander Gent. one of the Commissioners of Taxation in this County.

Tho.[s] Tyler

* * * * *
* * *
*

[End of 1788 personal property tax returns]

Stafford County
Virginia

Personal Property
Tax List

1788

[Arranged by date of tax enumeration]

Source: Virginia State Library, Archives Division. County Records. Stafford County Tax lists.

Form of return of taxable property to be made by the commissioners

List No. 1.

A List of the Taxable property within the district of Wm Mountjoy, commissioner in the county of Stafford for the year 1788

[Categories]:

    Date of receiving lists from individuals;
    Persons names chargeable with the tax;
    Names of white male tithables above 21;
    [col. 1] - No. of white males above 16 and under 21;
    [col. 2] - Blacks above 16;
    [col. 3] - Blacks above 12 and under 16;
    [col. 4]- Horses, mares, colts & mules;
    [other]- carriage wheels;
        Ordinary licence;
        Billiard tables;
        no. of stud horses;
        Rates of covering pr season.
        practicing physicians, Apothecaries & surgeons;

List No. 2.

A List of taxable property within the district of William Alexander, Commissioner Stafford County year 1788, Returned as P. vouchers

[Categories]:

    Month;
    Day;
    Proprietor's Names;
    [col. 1] - Whites from 16 upwards;
    [col. 2] - Blacks from 16 years;
    [col. 3] - D^O from 12 to 16 years;
    [col. 4] - Horses;
    [other] - Coach & Chariot wheels; Phaeton, stage, waggon wheels; Chairs wheels; Ordinaries; B*[illiard]* tables; Stud Horses; Rates pr season; Doctors;

A List of the taxable property within the district of William Mountjoy, Commissioner in the county of Stafford for the year 1788

[Arranged by date of tax enumeration]

Date	chargeable w/tax	white males over 21	* /blacks/ H/ 16-21	16+	12+	other
Mar 11	George Abbett	George Abbett			2	
Mar 11	James Arrowsmith	James Arrowsmith			3	
Mar 11	Nathan Atchison	Nathan Atchison	1	2	3	
Mar 11	John Bridwell	John Bridwell	3		2	
Mar 11	Patterson Doyall	Patterson Doyall			3	
Mar 11	Francis Brooks	levy free			2	
Mar 11	William Gant	William Gant	2		2	
Mar 11	John Goldsmith	John Goldsmith	4		2	
Mar 11	William Holloday	William Holloday			2	
Mar 11	Samuel Hudson	Samuel Hudson	2		3	
Mar 11	William Innes	William Innes				
Mar 11	John Jones	John Jones	1		5	
Mar 11	Wm Jones	Wm Jones	1		3	
Mar 11	David Jones	David Jones	1		2	
Mar 11	Francis Linum	Francis Linum			1	
Mar 11	Richard Morton	Richard Morton	2		2	
Mar 11	Richard Poats	Richard Poats			3	
Mar 11	Calvert Porter	Calvert Porter	[see next line]			
Mar 11	*Calvert Porter*	Thomas Porter	3	1	8	
Mar 11	Charles Rawls(PrWm)	John Faning		·1	1	
Mar 11	Thomas Right	Thomas Right	1	3	5	
Mar 11	William Rout	William Rout	1		3	
Mar 11	Sarsfield Snoxall	Sarsfield Snoxall			2	
Mar 11	John Beagle Sr.	Jno. Beagle	[see next line]			
Mar 11	*John Beagle Sr.*	John Bing			3	
Mar 11	Richard Reid Sr.	Richard Reid Sr.	[see next line]			
Mar 11	*Richard Reid Sr.*	Richard Reid	2		4	
Mar 11	Charles Stern	Charles Stern	2	1	1	
Mar 11	Francis Stern	Francis Stern	4	2	4	
Mar 11	Richard Walker	Richard Walker	1	1	3	
Mar 11	John Waters	John Waters			1	

Stafford Co., Va. personal property tax list - 1788

[arranged by date of tax enumeration]

Date	chargeable w/tax	white males over 21	" 16-21	/blacks/ 16+	H/ 12+	other
Mar 11	George Withers	George Withers	1	1	3	
Mar 14	Jonathan Bell	Jonathan Bell			1	
Mar 14	Peter Byrum	Peter Byrum			1	
Mar 14	John Fristoe	John Fristoe	3			
Mar 14	Peter Hansbrough	Peter Hansbrough			3	
Mar 14	Cuthbert Harding	Cuthbert Harding	1	1	2	
Mar 14	Moses Fritter Jr.	Moses Fritter Jr.			1	
Mar 14	Henry Mcentire	Henry Mcentire	1	1	2	
Mar 14	William Mullin	William Mullin	1	5	4	2whl.rid.chr
Mar 14	Thomas Rakestraw	Thomas Rakestraw				
Mar 14	Moses Fritter Sr.	Moses Fritter Sr.		1	2	
Mar 14	Mary Waller		3	1	5	
Mar 15	Robert Ashley	Robert Ashley			1	
Mar 15	Joseph Barber			3		
Mar 15	William Battoe	William Battoe			3	
Mar 15	Thomas Beach	Thomas Beach			1	
Mar 15	Joseph Beagle	Joseph Beagle	1		1	
Mar 15	Edward Bethell	Edward Bethell			3	
Mar 15	James Bridges	James Bridges			3	
Mar 15	Nimrod Byrum	Nimrod Byrum				
Mar 15	Cuthbert Byrum	Cuthbert Byrum			1	
Mar 15	William Cummins	William Cummins			3	
Mar 15	Asey Cummins	Asey Cummins			5	
Mar 15	Dennis Doyall	Dennis Doyall			1	
Mar 15	Thomas Edrington	Thomas Edrington		3	6	
Mar 15	Samuel Faunt	Samuel Faunt			4	
Mar 15	Phillip Gardner	Phillip Gardner		3	4	
Mar 15	John Garrison	John Garrison	1		1	
Mar 15	Benjamin Gregory	Benjamin Gregory			3	
Mar 15	John Gun	John Gun			2	
Mar 15	John Gun	John Gun			2	
Mar 15	John Harding	John Harding			2	
Mar 15	James Harding	James Harding			1	
Mar 15	Thomas Harding	Thomas Harding				
Mar 15	George Holloway	George Holloway				
Mar 15	Henry Horton	Henry Horton			1	

[arranged by date of tax enumeration]

Date	chargeable w/tax	white males over 21	"	/blacks/ H/ 16-21/16+12+		other
Mar 15	Moses Grigsby Jr.	Moses Grigsby Jr.				
Mar 15	John Kendall	John Kendall	*[see next line]*			
Mar 15	*John Kendall*	Moses Kendall	*[see next line]*			
Mar 15	*John Kendall*	James Kendall		3	1	4
Mar 15	Christopher Knight	Christopher Knight				3
Mar 15	Richard Mason	Richard Mason				4
Mar 15	Lewis Mason	Lewis Mason			1	3
Mar 15	John Mccullough	John Mccullough				2
Mar 15	James Ocane	James Ocane		1		4
Mar 15	Hesekiah Patterson	Hesekiah Patterson				1
Mar 15	John Pattin	John Pattin				2
Mar 15	Margaret Primm		1	1		3
Mar 15	John Primm	John Primm		1		3
Mar 15	Kenez Rauls	Kenez Rauls				1
Mar 15	Joel Readish	Joel Readish	*[see next line]*			
Mar 15	*Joel Readish*	John Minton	*[see next line]*			
Mar 15	*Joel Readish*	John Thorp		4	2	7
Mar 15	Joseph Readish	Joseph Readish	*[see next line]*			
Mar 15	*Joseph Readish*	Jno. Bradly		4		6
Mar 15	Jonathan Reid	Jonathan Reid	1			2
Mar 15	Aaron Reid	Aaron Reid				3
Mar 15	John Rogers	John Rogers				3
Mar 15	Richard Sims	Richard Sims				3
Mar 15	Henry Smith	Henry Smith	*[see next line]*			
Mar 15	*Henry Smith*	Joseph Smith		5		6
Mar 15	John Latham(s/Snodon)	John Latham				2
Mar 15	Moses Grigsby Sr.	Moses Grigsby Sr.				1
Mar 15	John Stark	John Stark				1
Mar 15	John Stern	John Stern		2	1	2
Mar 15	Edward Templeman	Edward Templeman				3
Mar 15	Charles Thornton	Charles Thornton				2
Mar 15	Peter Wood	Peter Wood	1			4
Mar 18	William Edrington	William Edrington	2	3	1	6
Mar 18	Willis Edwards	Willis Edwards				1
Mar 18	John Esque	John Esque				1
Mar 18	Jessey Edwards Sr.	Jessey Edwards	*[see next line]*			

Stafford Co., Va. personal property tax list - 1788

[arranged by date of tax enumeration]

Date	chargeable w/tax	white males over 21	16-21	16+	12+	other
Mar 18	*Jessey Edwards Sr.*	Jessey Edwards			2	
Mar 22	John Atchison	John Atchison	1		3	
Mar 22	George Barns	George Barns				
Mar 22	William Baul	William Baul		2 1	6	
Mar 22	John Browne	John Browne		[faded]	1	
Mar 22	Francis Foushee	Francis Foushee	1	3	3	
Mar 22	John Fritter	John Fritter			2	
Mar 22	William George	William George				
Mar 22	William Gollohorn	William Gollohorn		1	5	
Mar 22	Richard Griffes	Richard Griffes			1	
Mar 22	Elisha Grigsby	Elisha Grigsby			2	
Mar 22	William Fritter Jr.	William Fritter Jr.			2	
Mar 22	Peter Kendall	Peter Kendall			3	
Mar 22	Jessey Kendall	Jessey Kendall			3	
Mar 22	Geo. Randol L.free	Thomas Gill			2	
Mar 22	Thomas Sedden	Thomas Sedden	*[see next line]*			
Mar 22	*Thomas Sedden*	Dennis Linum	13	4	6	
Mar 22	Elisha Skinner	Elisha Skinner				
Mar 22	John Snoxall	John Snoxall			2	
Mar 22	Henry Sudduth	Henry Sudduth			2	
Mar 22	John Tolson	John Tolson			2	
Mar 22	Allen Way	Allen Way			2	
Mar 22	Benjamin Wine	Benjamin Wine				
Mar 26	John Grey	John Grey			2	
Mar 28	Peter Mauzy (Fairfax)		3	1	3	
Mar 28	Elijah Abbet	Elijah Abbet			3	
Mar 28	John Bannister	John Bannister			2	
Mar 28	William Barby	William Barby			2	
Mar 28	William Barnot	William Barnot			1	
Mar 28	Charles Bell	Charles Bell			1	
Mar 28	James Billingslee	James Billingslee	2		3	
Mar 28	William Botts	William Botts	3		5	
Mar 28	Joseph Botts	Joseph Botts	*[see next line]*			
Mar 28	*Joseph Botts*	Jno. Prince	4	2	6	
Mar 28	Aaron Botts	Aaron Botts	5		7	
Mar 28	Spencer Bowlin	Spencer Bowlin			1	

[arranged by date of tax enumeration]

Date	chargeable w/tax	white males over 21	" 16-21/16+12+	/blacks/ H/	other
Mar 28	John Bridges	John Bridges		1	
Mar 28	George Bridwell	George Bridwell		2	
Mar 28	Walter Brown	Walter Brown		4	
Mar 28	Bassell Burroughs	Bassell Burroughs		3	
Mar 28	Joseph Burroughs	Joseph Burroughs	1	1	
Mar 28	Vintsin Bussell	Vintsin Bussell		1	
Mar 28	Moses Bussell	Moses Bussell		1	
Mar 28	John Butler	John Butler	2	3	
Mar 28	Josua Carney	Josua Carney	[see next line]		
Mar 28	*Josua Carney*	Benj.ᵃ Carney	4 2 5		
Mar 28	Jedediah Carter	Jedediah Carter	1	2	
Mar 28	Harris Carter	Harris Carter	1	1	
Mar 28	Briant Chadwell	Briant Chadwell	1 3 2 4		
Mar 28	Perry Chinn	Perry Chinn		1	
Mar 28	John Clemmons	John Clemmons		2	
Mar 28	Henry Clifton	Henry Clifton	[see next line]		
Mar 28	*Henry Clifton*	Lawrence Butler	4 1 5		
Mar 28	Jessey Cooper	Jessey Cooper		1	
Mar 28	Bradly Dent	Bradly Dent	1	2	
Mar 28	James Dent	James Dent			
Mar 28	Christopher Dorson	Christopher Dorson		1	
Mar 28	John Dorson	John Dorson		4	
Mar 28	William Dunaway	William Dunaway		1	
Mar 28	Josiah Faning	Josiah Faning		2	
Mar 28	James Faunt	James Faunt	[see next line]		
Mar 28	*James Faunt*	Wᵐ Faunt		4	
Mar 28	Wᵐ Franklin	Wᵐ Franklin		3	
Mar 28	Jeremiah Fugate	Jeremiah Fugate		2	
Mar 28	John Scott Harding	John Scott Harding		3	
Mar 28	George Harding	George Harding		2	
Mar 28	John Hore	John Hore	1	1	
Mar 28	Elijah Horton	Elijah Horton		2	
Mar 28	John Jones	John Jones		1	
Mar 28	Gabril Jones	Gabril Jones	[see next line]		
Mar 28	*Gabril Jones*	Fielding Ficklin	5 2 4		
Mar 28	Charles Kendall	Charles Kendall		2	

[arranged by date of tax enumeration]

Date	chargeable w/tax	white males over 21	" /blacks/ 16-21	16+	H/ 12+	other
Mar 28	Merriman Ketchen	Merriman Ketchen[see next line]				
Mar 28	*Merriman Ketchen*	James Ketchen	2	1	3	
Mar 28	James Kirk	James Kirk			2	
Mar 28	John Knight	John Knight			2	
Mar 28	Joseph Franklin L.free				2	
Mar 28	John Latham	John Latham			1	
Mar 28	John Lawlis	John Lawlis			2	
Mar 28	James Lowry	James Lowry		[see next line]		
Mar 28	*James Lowry*	Thomas Lowry	1		2	
Mar 28	John Lunsford	John Lunsford			3	
Mar 28	Thomas Mallery	Thomas Mallery				
Mar 28	Daniel Mason	Daniel Mason	1	1	1	6
Mar 28	George Mauzy	George Mauzy		1		
Mar 28	Alexander Mcentire	Alexander Mcentire		1	3	
Mar 28	James More	James More			1	
Mar 28	John Mountjoy	John Mountjoy			3	
Mar 28	Phillip Nash	Phillip Nash			1	
Mar 28	John Nicholson	John Nicholson			1	
Mar 28	George Norman	George Norman			5	
Mar 28	James Oglesby	James Oglesby			2	
Mar 28	Elizabeth Overall		1	6		8
Mar 28	Abraham Parker	Abraham Parker				
Mar 28	Moses Poats	Moses Poats			3	
Mar 28	John Poats	John Poats			4?	
Mar 28	Charles Porter	Charles Porter			3	
Mar 28	Habern Rauls	under 21	1	1	2	
Mar 28	Jessey Riley	Jessey Riley	1		1	
Mar 28	Baily Riley	Baily Riley			2	
Mar 28	Abigale Shelton				2	
Mar 28	William Shelton	William Shelton			6	
Mar 28	Wilson Shelton	Wilson Shelton			2	
Mar 28	George Shelton	George Shelton			2	
Mar 28	James Sims	James Sims			3	
Mar 28	Nath.l Smith	Nath.l Smith		1	2	
Mar 28	William Stark	William Stark		2	2	
Mar 28	Richard Taylor	Richard Taylor			2	

[arranged by date of tax enumeration]

Date	chargeable w/tax	white males over 21	"	/blacks/ H/ 16-21/16+12+	other
Mar 28	James Walker	James Walker		1	
Mar 28	John Warren	John Warren	1	3	
Mar 28	Charles Waters	Charles Waters		2	
Mar 28	William Young	William Young		1	
Apr 1	John Chiveral	John Chiveral		1	
Apr 1	Joseph Combs	Joseph Combs		3 2 3	
Apr 1	George Garrison	George Garrison	1	3	
Apr 1	Robert Green	Robert Green	[see next line]		
Apr 1	*Robert Green*	John Green		4	
Apr 1	John Grigsby	John Grigsby		1	
Apr 1	Charles Porter Jr.	Charles Porter Jr.			
Apr 1	Daniel Kendall	Daniel Kendall		3	
Apr 1	James Kendall	James Kendall		1	
Apr 1	Peter Knight	Peter Knight	[see next line]		
Apr 1	*Peter Knight*	Baily Knight		5	
Apr 1	Ephraim Knight	Ephraim Knight		2	
Apr 1	Wm Waller	Wm Waller	[see next line]		
Apr 1	*Wm Waller*	Edward Waller	[see next line]		
Apr 1	*Wm Waller*	William Waller		4 2 6	
Apr 1	Benjamin Willits	Benjamin Willits		2	
Apr 9	Charles Carter	under 21	1 1	1	
Apr 9	Hugh McDaniel	Hugh McDaniel		1	
Apr 9	John Fr.^a Mercer	David Hepbourn	[see next line]		
Apr 9	*John Fr.^a Mercer*	William More	[see next line]		
Apr 9	*John Fr.^a Mercer*	Johnston Smith		16 3 18	
Apr 10	Benjamin Bowlin	Benjamin Bowlin		1	
Apr 12	Amus Atchison	Amus Atchison	1	4	
Apr 12	Joseph Brown	Joseph Brown	[see next line]		
Apr 12	*Joseph Brown*	Thos Brown		6 1 7	
Apr 12	George Byrum	George Byrum	1	1	
Apr 12	Raw.^l Wm Downman	Benjamin Ficklin		10 3	
Apr 12	Dennis Doyall	Dennis Doyall	1	3	
Apr 12	John Faunt	John Faunt			
Apr 12	Asey Holloway	Asey Holloway	[see next line]		
Apr 12	*Asey Holloway*	Ruth Kitchen		2	
Apr 12	Archabeld Douglis L.free	.	1	6	

[arranged by date of tax enumeration]

Date	chargeable w/tax	white males over 21	" 16-21/16+12+	/blacks/ H/	other
Apr 12 James Primm	James Primm			3	
Apr 12 William Stark	William Stark	1		3	
Apr 12 Thomas Tharp	Thomas Tharp			1	
Apr 12 John Tuttle	John Tuttle			1	
Apr 14 James Abbet	James Abbet			1	
Apr 14 William Alexander	William Alexander	2		3	
Apr 14 Daniel Antrum	Dan¹ Antrum	[see next line]			
Apr 14 *Daniel Antrum*	Levi Antrum	1		5	
Apr 14 Sarah Ashby				1	
Apr 14 Enough Benson	Enough Benson	[see next line]			
Apr 14 *Enough Benson*	Prue Benson	1	4 1	6	
Apr 14 William Brown				2	
Apr 14 William Edwards	William Edwards	1	1	1	
Apr 14 James Ford	James Ford		3 1	5	
Apr 14 Thomas Barley l. free				2	
Apr 14 John Abbet levy free				2	
Apr 14 William Harding	William Harding	[see next line]			
Apr 14 *William Harding*	Enough Harding		1 1	5	
Apr 14 Henry Hiden	Henry Hiden			2	
Apr 14 Asie Holloway	Asie Holloway				
Apr 14 Isaac Holloway	Isaac Holloway			2	
Apr 14 John Holloway	John Holloway			2	
Apr 14 Alexander Jameson	Alexander Jameson	1		2	
Apr 14 John Holloway Jr.	John Holloway	[see next line]			
Apr 14 *John Holloway Jr.*	Thomas Holloway			5	
Apr 14 Baily Washington Jr.	Baily Washington Jr.		10 2	4	
Apr 14 Jeremiah Knight	Jeremiah Knight	1	1	4	
Apr 14 Richard Fristoe L.free			1	1	
Apr 14 John Waters Sr. L.free			2 1	4	
Apr 14 William Mauzy	William Mauzy		1	2 3	
Apr 14 Robert Million	Robert Million	2	1	6	
Apr 14 James Nailer	James Nailer	1		5	
Apr 14 Robert Painter	Robert Painter	1		4	
Apr 14 Rawleigh Rauls			1	2 3	
Apr 14 John Smith	John Smith			2	
Apr 14 William Bradley Sr.	William Bradley	[see next line]			

[arranged by date of tax enumeration]

Date	chargeable w/tax	white males over 21	" /blacks/ H/ 16-21/16+12+			other
Apr 14	*William Bradley Sr.*	Wm Bradley	1		2	
Apr 14	Baily Washington Sr.	Baily Washington Sr.	10	1	7	4 wheels
Apr 14	John Stark	John Stark	1 1		3	
Apr 14	William Waters	William Waters	[see next line]			
Apr 14	*William Waters*	James Waters	[text faded] 1?			
Apr 14	William West	William West	1		2	
Apr 14	George Wort	George Wort	1		5	
Apr 16	Thomas Mountjoy	Thomas Mountjoy	7	3	8	
Apr 16	Thomas Powell	Thomas Powell				
Apr 19	William Cole	William Cole				
Apr 19	Edward Mountjoy	Edward Mountjoy	1		5	
Apr 19	Mary Ann Payn		3		4	
Apr 19	Sarah Payn	James Payn			2	
Apr 19	Francis Payn	Francis Payn				
Apr 19	Ezekiel Payn	Ezekiel Payn				
Apr 19	John Richards	John Richards				
Apr 19	John Shelkel	John Shelkel		1	4	
Apr 19	Elizabeth Spilman				1	
Apr 23	Fielding Bell	Fielding Bell			1	
Apr 23	Clement Billingslee	Clement Billingslee	1		2	
Apr 23	Elizabeth Chissom				4	
Apr 23	Benjamin Ficklin	Benjamin Ficklin	1		4	
Apr 23	John Green	John Green			2	
Apr 23	Henry Kendall	Henry Kendall	2	1	3	
Apr 23	Sarah Knight		1			
Apr 23	Ann Knight		1	2 1	2	
Apr 23	John Packstein	John Packstein			4	
Apr 23	Josua Kendall Sr.	Josua Kendall	[see next line]			
Apr 23	*Josua Kendall Sr.*	Anthony Kendall	4	1	6	
Apr 23	George Walters	George Walters			3	
Apr 26	Thomas Ambler	Tho.s Ambler	[see next line]			
Apr 26	*Thomas Ambler*	Ja.s Ambler	[see next line]			
Apr 26	*Thomas Ambler*	Wm Ambler			6	
Apr 26	James Barnot	Ja.s Barnot	[see next line]			
Apr 26	*James Barnot*	Daniel Bessick	1		3	
Apr 26	William Branson	William Branson	1			

[arranged by date of tax enumeration]

Date	chargeable w/tax	white males over 21	" 16-21	/blacks/ 16	H/ 12+		other
Apr 26	Mary Ann Bronaugh		1	9	2	8	2whl.rid.chr.
Apr 26	John Bruing	John Bruing	1			1	
Apr 26	Robert Buchan	Robert Buchan		5	1	8	
Apr 26	William Eaton	William Eaton	2			1	
Apr 26	Isaac Eustace	Isaac Eustace	1	10	1	6	
Apr 26	Anthony Ficklin	Anthony Ficklin	1	3		4	
Apr 26	William Fristoe	William Fristoe	2	1		4	
Apr 26	James Horton	James Horton				3	
Apr 26	Joseph Cooper L.free			1		2	
Apr 26	Moses Lunsford	Moses Lunsford				3	
Apr 26	William Monroe	William Monroe		5		2	
Apr 26	William Pattin	William Pattin					
Apr 26	Elizabeth Peyton	Thomas Peyton	[see next line]				
Apr 26	*Elizabeth Peyton*	Sam Peyton .		9	3	8	
Apr 26	William Right	William Right				2	
Apr 26	James Riley	James Riley					
Apr 26	Presly Sims	Presly Sims				1	
Apr 26	Rhoadnum Sims	Rhoadnum Sims				2	
Apr 26	Craven Spiller	Craven Spiller				2	
Apr 26	Jeremiah Stark	Jeremiah Stark	[see next line]				
Apr 26	*Jeremiah Stark*	William Stark				5	
Apr 26	George Wells	George Wells	1			4	
Apr 26	Elizabeth Wells			3		3	
Apr 26	Henry Woodgerd	Henry Woodgerd				2	
Apr 26	Jessey Woodgerd	Jessey Woodgerd				1	
May 5	John Agin	Benjamin Adie		5	2	6	
May 5	William Anderson	William Anderson			1	1	
May 5	Mary Bell		1	3		3	
May 5	William Chandler	William Chandler		1	1	3	
May 5	Mary Chesshire					2	
May 5	Charles Davis	Charles Davis				1	
May 5	Jeremiah Day	Jeremiah Day					
May 5	Hannah Dickenson	Anthony Latham		6	2	6	
May 5	Margaret Eaton					1	
May 5	Edward McKenzy	Edward McKenzy				1	
May 5	William Adie Sr.	Wm Adie	[see next line]				

[arranged by date of tax enumeration]

Date	chargeable w/tax	white males over 21	" 16-21/16+	/blacks/ 12+	H/	other
May 5	*William Adie Sr.*	Wm. Adie Jr.	9	1	5	
May 5	Thomas Sudduth	Thomas Sudduth			2	
May 5	Alexander Taylor	Alexander Taylor	1		2	
May 6	Thomas Bridwell	Thomas Bridwell	2		1	
May 6	Sarah Byrum		1			
May 6	Moses Dick	Moses Dick			1	
May 6	James Gough	James Gough		1	1	
May 6	Hannah Gough		1		2	
May 6	Richard Ratliff	Richard Ratliff	2		3	
May 6	William Robeson	William Robeson	1		3	
May 6	James Robeson	James Robeson			2	
May 6	Ann Rogers				2	
May 6	William Stephens	William Stephens				
May 7	Benjamin Green	Benjamin Green				
May 7	Mary Holloway				1	
May 7	Josua Kendall	Josua Kendall			3	
May 7	Sollomon Gollohorn	L.free			1	
May 7	Charles Latham	Charles Latham				
May 7	Sarah Nelson		1		1	
May 7	Joseph Slaughter	Joseph Slaughter				
May 7	Hannah Stark		1	1	2	
May 9	Robert Brent		1		5	
May 9	William Harrod	William Harrod	[see next line]			
May 9	*William Harrod*	Edmund Lumsdil			3	
May 9	John R. Peyton	John R. Peyton	[see next line]			
May 9	*John R. Peyton*	Zachariah Griffis	[see next line]			
May 9	*John R. Peyton*	Francis Lucus	10	4	10	
May 9	Rich.d Stone	Rich.d Stone			3	
May 9	Wm B. Stone	Wm B. Stone	6	1	7	
May 10	Ann Gaddis		1 5	1	6	
May 10	William Garrard	William Garrard	7		5	
May 10	Benjamin Gee	Benjamin Gee			1	
May 10	William Gee	William Gee	[see next line]			
May 10	*William Gee*	Joseph Gee	1		5	
May 10	Edward Norman	Edward Norman	4	3	1	
May 10	Benjamin Shacklet	Benjamin Shacklet	[see next line]			

[arranged by date of tax enumeration]

Date	chargeable w/tax	white males over 21	" 16-21	/blacks/ /16+	H/ 12+	other
May 10	*Benjamin Shacklet*	William Shacklet			4	
May 10	Hawkin Stone	Hawkin Stone	5	3	7	
May 10	Peter Waters	Peter Waters			3	
May 11	William Ross	William Ross	1	1	4	
May 12	John Browne	John Browne	*[see next line]*			
May 12	*John Browne*	Nath.ⁿ Williams	13	2	8	
May 12	George Burroughs	George Burroughs	1	1	2	
May 12	William Byrum	William Byrum				
May 12	Travers Daniel	Travers Daniel	6		6	
May 12	Sarah Daniel		15	1	10	4whl. chair
May 12	James Hore	James Hore		1	3	
May 12	John Horton	John Horton	6	1	6	
May 12	Jacob Bridwell L.free				3	
May 12	Thomas Hay L.free				3	
May 12	Derek Benear L.free				2	
May 12	John Mason	John Mason	4		7	
May 12	Benjamin Pritchet	Benjamin Pritchet	1	5	6	
May 12	Butler Raimy	Butler Raimy			3	
May 12	Travers Daniel Sr.	Travers Daniel Sr.	16	2	13	2whl.rid.chr
May 12	John Withers Sr.	Jno. Withers	*[see next line]*			
May 12	*John Withers Sr.*	Benj.ᵃ Withers	13	5	9	
May 13	George Coats	George Coats			1	
May 13	Seth Combs	Fielding Combs	9	1	7	
May 13	William Dorson	William Dorson			2	
May 13	Spencer Dorson	Spencer Dorson			1	
May 13	John Franklin Jr.	John Franklin Jr.		1	1	
May 13	Charles Mifflin L.free				2	
May 13	Mary McDaniel	John Johnston			1	
May 13	Ursly Morton			2	2	
May 13	William Poats	William Poats		2	3	
May 13	Joanna Tolson	Joanna Tolson *(sic)*	1		1	
May 13	Ann Vaughan				2	
May 13	William West	William West	1		3	
May 14	Jesey Bails	Jesey Bails				
May 14	Nath.ⁿ Bannister	Nath.ⁿ Bannister	1		3	
May 14	William Boboe	William Boboe				

[arranged by date of tax enumeration]

Date	chargeable w/tax	white males over 21	" 16-21	/blacks/ 16+	H/	12+	other
May 14	William Devene	William Devene				1	
May 14	Aaron Garrison	Aaron Garrison				1	
May 14	Henry Griffin	Henry Griffin				1	
May 14	Steaphen Johnston	Steaphen Johnston				2	
May 14	John Waters Jr.	Waters Jr.				3	
May 14	Uriah Knight	Uriah Knight		2		3	
May 14	Benjamin Million	Benjamin Million				2	
May 14	James Peak	James Peak				1	
May 14	Edward Pearson	Edward Pearson					
May 14	George Bell Sr.	George Bell Sr.		1	1	3	
May 14	John Franklin Sr.	Joseph Franklin				3	
May 14	Josia Stone	Josia Stone		5		3	2whl.rid.chr.
May 14	Jessey Stone	Jessey Stone	2			2	
May 14	Benjamin Tolson	Benjamin Tolson				2	
May 14	Elizabeth Tolson		1	5	1	8	
May 14	William Tolson	William Tolson		1		5	
May 14	Mark Waters	Mark Waters	*[see next line]*				
May 14	*Mark Waters*	Baily Waters				7?	
May 14	Nathaniel Williams	Nathaniel Williams		6		2	
May 14	Margaret Williams	Wm Williams	*[see next line]*				
May 14	*Margaret Williams*	Lewis Williams				4	
May 14	George Williams	George Williams		7?	2	3	
May 15	Haden Edwards	Haden Edwards		6		6	
May 15	John Murray (Prince Wm.)			9		4	
May 17	William Randol	William Randol	*[see next line]*				
May 17	*William Randol*	John Randol				4	
May 20	Benjamin Bridwell	Benjamin Bridwell	1			1	
May 20	Moses Bridwell	Moses Bridwell	1	4	1	2	
May 20	Elizabeth Bridwell					2	
May 20	William Bridwell	William Bridwell	2	3		4	
May 20	William Eusey	William Eusey		2		3	
May 20	Vintsin Foxworthy	Vintsin Foxworthy				2	
May 20	Phillip Foxworthy	Phillip Foxworthy				2	
May 20	William French	Wm French	*[see next line]*				
May 20	*William French*	Steaphen French		5	1	5	
May 20	Virgin Hughs					1	

Stafford Co., Va. personal property tax list - 1788

[arranged by date of tax enumeration]

Date	chargeable w/tax	white males over 21	"	/blacks/ 16-21	H/ 16+	12+	other
May 20	James Battoe L.free					2	
May 20	Richard Sims L.free		1			2	
May 20	Mary Ann Rauls			3		2	
May 20	Thomas Tennant	Thomas Tennant [see next line]					
May 20	*Thomas Tennant*	Anthony Long				2	
May 20	Sarah Wigginton					1	
May 20	Rich.d Woodgerd	Rich.d Woodgerd				3	
May 21	Margaret Matthews			3	3	6	2whl.rid.chr
May 21	William Taylor	William Taylor	1	7	2	6	
May 22	John Stark (Princ. Wm)						
May 22	John Bails	John Bails				1	
May 22	Lydia Hansbrough			1	1	1	
May 22	Peter Knight Jr.	Peter Knight			1	3	
May 22	Aaron Kendall	Aaron Kendall				1	
May 22	Sarah Knight					3	
May 22	William Phillips	William Phillips [see next line]					
May 22	*William Phillips*	Zachariah Cummins		7	1	4	
May 22	Edward Snoxall	Edward Snoxall [see next line]					
May 22	*Edward Snoxall*	Tho.s Beagle				4	
May 22	Samuel Striblin	Samuel Striblin				1	
May 23	Jessey Payn	Jessey Payn				1	
May 23	Reuben Rogers	Reuben Rogers				1	
May 24	John Cooke	John Cooke		23	7	16	
May 24	John Dillion	John Dillion				1	
May 24	William Groves	William Groves			1	1	
May 24	William Hore	William Hore			1	1	
May 24	Mary Hore			7		2	
May 24	Elies Hore	Elies Hore		1		1	
May 24	George Bridwell Jr.	George Bridwell Jr.				2	
May 24	Snodon Latham	Snodon Latham	1			2	
May 24	Wharton Philbert	Wharton Philbert				1	
May 24	William Richards	William Richards		1		3	
May 24	Samuel Thompson	Samuel Thompson		2		5	
May 24	Elijah Thraelkeld	Elijah Thraelkeld	1	13	2	10	
May 24	George Thraelkeld	George Thraelkeld		2		1	
May 24	Barsheba Walter					2	

[arranged by date of tax enumeration]

Date	chargeable w/tax	white males over 21	" 16-21	/blacks/ 16+	H/ 12+	other
May 24	Augustin Weadon	Augustin Weadon			3	
May 28	Isaac Eavs	Isaac Eavs			2	
May 28	Keziah Gee				2	
May 28	Samuel Groves	Samuel Groves	1	1	3	
May 28	John Hardy	John Hardy		7	12	
May 28	Ann Moncure			11	1 5	
May 28	James Murphy	James Murphy		1	1	
May 29	Elijah Bell	Elijah Bell			2	
May 29	John Dalgair	John Dalgair			2	
May 29	Elizabeth Dunaway		1		2	
May 29	William Edwards	William Edwards		2	2	
May 29	John Hedgman	John Hedgman		13	3 8	
May 29	James Henderson	James Henderson			1	
May 29	Thomas Heth L.free			1		
May 29	James McBride	James McBride	1		2	
May 29	Robert B. Morton	Robert B. Morton		10	2 14	
May 29	William Mountjoy	William Mountjoy		6	2 9	
May 29	Allen Mountjoy	Allen Mountjoy	2		3	
May 29	Thomas Mountjoy	Thomas Mountjoy	1		1	
May 29	William Watson	William Watson				
May 30	Simon Bridwell	Simon Bridwell			1	
May 30	William Bridwell	William Bridwell		1		
May 30	John Brooker					
May 30	Rawleigh T. Browne	Pearson Williams		18	3 11	
May 30	John Carter	John Carter			2	
May 30	Cuthbert Combs	Cuthbert Combs		6	5	
May 30	Rheuben Franklin	Reuben Franklin			3	
May 30	Elizabeth Garrison				1	
May 30	Isaac Gaskins	Isaac Gaskins			3	
May 30	James Cloe Jr.	James Cloe			1	
May 30	James Cloe L.free				3	
May 30	George Latham	George Latham			1	
May 30	Gavin Lawson	Gavin Lawson	[see next line]			
May 30	*Gavin Lawson*	David Bridges	[see next line]			
May 30	*Gavin Lawson*	Charles Dunkinson		16	5 13	4wheels
May 30	Chondrid Lewis	Chondrid Lewis			1	

Stafford Co., Va. personal property tax list - 1788

[arranged by date of tax enumeration]

Date	chargeable w/tax	white males over 21	" /blacks/ H/ 16-21/16+12+	other
May 30	Thomas Wells	Thomas Wells	1	
May 30	John Withers	John Withers	1 1 1	
May 30	Susanah Wormsly		2	
Jun 9	Zachariah Benson	Zachariah Benson	2	
Jun 9	Ann Brent		22 4 7	
Jun 9	Daniel C. Brent	Daniel C. Brent	[see next line]	
Jun 9	*Daniel C. Brent*	Jonus Garner	[see next line]	
Jun 9	*Daniel C. Brent*	John Blake	[see next line]	
Jun 9	*Daniel C. Brent*	William Fritter	33 6 16	1 stud
Jun 9	Richard Brent	Richard Brent	3	2whl.rid.chr.
Jun 9	George Brent	Geo. Brent	[see next line]	
Jun 9	*George Brent*	Henry Peyton	10 2 7	
Jun 9	Eleanor Brent	Eleanor Brent	17 2 12	4whl.chariot
Jun 9	John Brent		1 4 2	
Jun 9	Samuel Bridwell	Samuel Bridwell	2	
Jun 9	Samuel Parker	Samuel Parker	1	
Jun 9	Vallentine Peyton	Vallentine Peyton	9 1 6	4whl.phaeton
Jun 9	Charles Porter	Charles Porter	3	
Jun 10	Benjamin Brock	Benjamin Brock	2	
Jun 10	Enough Cocks	Enough Cocks		
Jun 10	John Markham	John Markham	2 2 2	
Jun 10	Charles Martin	Charles Martin	1?	
Jun 10	Fielding Mason	Fielding Mason	1	
Jun 10	Michael Maze	Michael Maze	[see next line]	
Jun 10	*Michael Maze*	Lanstet Maze	1 2	
Jun 10	John Mountjoy	John Mountjoy	6 1 9	
Jun 10	William Tungate	William Tungate	4	
Jun 10	Thos S. Tyler	S. Tyler	3 4	

[End of date-arranged returns for William Mountjoy]

A List of taxable property within the district of William Alexander, Commissioner Stafford County year 1788, Returned as P. vouchers

Mo.	day	Proprietor's names	whites 16+	blacks 16+	blacks 12+	H	other
Mar	9	Vowles Chaveles [sic]	1				
Mar	20	Alexander William	1	7	2	6	
Mar	20	D°. for Casson Est.		5	1	6	
Mar	20	Donathan Gerard	1	2		4	1 stud @ 0.12
Mar	20	Downman B. Jos.	1	7	4	6	
Mar	20	Washington Gen.l George	1	7		3	
Mar	20	Waugh George	2	7		9	
Mar	21	Barrett Bartholomew	2		1	2	
Mar	21	Jones Thomas	1	1		3	
Mar	22	Bruce William	0	2	1	4	
Mar	22	Carter Henry	1				
Mar	22	Chinn Joseph	1			3	
Mar	22	Cox George	1				
Mar	22	Curtice Aaron	2			1	
Mar	22	Curtice George	1		1	5	
Mar	22	Finnall Jonathan	1	8	2	7	
Mar	22	Fowler Thomas				1	
Mar	22	Kenny Thomas	1			3	
Mar	22	Miner Elizabeth		1		1	
Mar	22	Templeman Jane				2	
Mar	22	Thornton Tho.s	1	4	1	4	
Mar	23	Allentharp Jacob	2			5	
Mar	24	Jones George	1				
Mar	25	Fox Nathaniel	1	6	2	7	
Mar	25	Monday Aaron	1			1	
Mar	26	Berry Sarah	1	1		3	
Mar	26	Burnett William	3	2	1	5	
Mar	26	Butler William	1	1		2	
Mar	26	Cox Presly	1			1	
Mar	26	Cox Charnox	1		1	2	
Mar	26	Cox Vincent Junr.	1		1	4	
Mar	26	Fines Patrick	2	1		3	
Mar	26	Fletcher Rachall	2	1		5	

[arranged by date of tax enumeration]

Mo.	day	Proprietor's names	whites 16+	blacks 16+ 12+		H	other
Mar	26	Garner John	2			2	
Mar	26	Gollohorn Solomon	1			1	
Mar	26	Hill Jesse	1	3		5	
Mar	26	Hunter Adam forge	3	46	2	18	*[see next line]*
Mar	26	*Hunter Adam forge*				2 chair wheels & stud @ £1.1.4	
Mar	26	Leach Andrew	2			2	
Mar	26	Limbrick William	1			2	
Mar	26	Long Robt	1			2	
Mar	26	Pates Aaron	2		1	2	
Mar	26	Payn John	3			3	
Mar	26	Pilcher Richard	3			2	
Mar	26	Pilcher Mildred	1	1		2	
Mar	26	Pilcher Charles	3			2	
Mar	26	Raulins John	1			2	
Mar	26	Robertson John	1			1	
Mar	26	Stone William	2			2	
Mar	26	Stone Joseph	1			1	
Mar	26	Swillivant Gabriel	2			4	
Mar	26	Swillivant Lettice				2	
Mar	26	Wallace Michall		3	1	4	
Mar	26	Waugh McCagby	2			4	
Mar	26	Whitt George Senr.				2	
Mar	27	Curtice William	1			2	
Mar	27	Fugitt Francis Junr.	1			1	
Mar	27	Newton John	1	5	2	4	
Mar	27	Oliver John	2			3	
Mar	27	Terrier John	1	1		3	
Mar	27	Troop Thomas	1			2	
Mar	28	Bates Thomas	1			2	
Mar	28	Berry Anthony	1			2	
Mar	28	Berry Richard	1			1	
Mar	28	Berry Thomas	2	1		2	
Mar	28	Black Margrett	2			4	
Mar	28	Brimmer John	1			1	
Mar	28	Brimmer Isaac	1				
Mar	28	Brown James	1			2	
Mar	28	Burton James	2			3	

[arranged by date of tax enumeration]

Mo.	day	Proprietor's names	whites 16+	blacks 16+12+		H	other
Mar	28	Burton Rachal	2			2	
Mar	28	Carter Joseph	1	2		3	
Mar	28	Colney Joseph	1			1	
Mar	28	Colney Elisha	1			1	
Mar	28	Connor John	2			3	
Mar	28	Cortney John	1	3	1	6	
Mar	28	Cox Vincent Junr.	2			2	
Mar	28	Curtice John	3			3	
Mar	28	Curtice Richard	1			1	
Mar	28	Faunt John	1			2	
Mar	28	Gollohorn Tho.s	1			3	
Mar	28	Graves Wm	4	1		6	
Mar	28	Graves Benj.a	1			1	
Mar	28	Graves [no given name]	1				
Mar	28	Groves Thomas	1			1	
Mar	28	Hall Benjaman	1			4	
Mar	28	Hord Thomas	1	1		5	
Mar	28	Horton William	1			3	
Mar	28	Jackson Robert	3			4	
Mar	28	Jett John	1			2	
Mar	28	Jones James	1			4	
Mar	28	Kenny John	1			3	
Mar	28	Kitchen James	2			3?	
Mar	28	Lathrum George	1	1		1	
Mar	28	Leach Benjaman	1			2	
Mar	28	Leach Thomas	1	4	1	4	
Mar	28	Limbrick John	2			2	
Mar	28	Lowry James	1	1	1	2	
Mar	28	Lunsford Joanah	1	1		3	
Mar	28	Martin Lewis	1			1	
Mar	28	Martin Thomas	1			1	
Mar	28	Martin Charles	2	1		3	
Mar	28	Martin Daniel	1			1	
Mar	28	McDonall Daniel	1	2		1	
Mar	28	McEntosh James	1			?	
Mar	28	Meels Samuel	1			1	
Mar	28	Munrow Daniel	1	1		3	

[arranged by date of tax enumeration]

Mo.	day	Proprietor's names	whites 16+	blacks 16+ 12+		H	other
Mar	28	Musselman Christopher	2			1	
Mar	28	Newton Margret	1	2		7	
Mar	28	Patterson Thomas	1			2	
Mar	28	Payton Ann	3	1	1	3	
Mar	28	Porch Esum	1	1	2	3	
Mar	28	Puzey Stephen	2			1	
Mar	28	Roach Robert	2		1	3	
Mar	28	Robertson Thomas	1			3	
Mar	28	Snipe Natha.[l]	1			2	
Mar	28	Striplin Joel	1			1	
Mar	28	Sutor William	1				
Mar	28	Sutor Andrew	2				
Mar	28	Timmons John	1			3	
Mar	28	Tompson John	1			1	
Mar	28	Turner James	2			3	
Mar	28	Walker Solomon	1			1	
Mar	28	Wallace John	1	4		5	
Mar	28	Weak George	1			2	
Mar	28	Webb Aaron	2			6	
Mar	28	Webb Moses	1			1	
Mar	28	White? George *[blurred]*	2			4?	
Mar	28	Wine Dotia	1				
Mar	31	Briant John	1		1	1	
Mar	31	Brown William	2			4	
Mar	31	Newton William	5	10	3	8	
Mar	31	Pollard Linsey	1			1	
Mar	31	Pollard John	1	9	1	5	
Mar	31	Posey Thomas	1	9	2	16	
Mar	31	Strother George	3	5	1	7	
Apr	1	Bates Joseph tax free				2	
Apr	1	Fugitt Francis Senr.	1			1	
Apr	1	Fugitt Daniel	1			2	
Apr	1	Fugitt Benj.[a]	1		1	2	
Apr	1	Henson Sarah				2	
Apr	1	Henson Elijah	1			3	
Apr	1	Hewett William	1	14	3	9	2chr.whls.
Apr	1	Jones William	1			1	

[arranged by date of tax enumeration]

Mo.	day	Proprietor's names	whites 16+	blacks 16+	12+	H	other
Apr	1	Limbrick Francis	2			2	
Apr	1	McCullock John	1			1	
Apr	1	Paterson Fanny	1				
Apr	1	Pilcher Moses	1	2		3	
Apr	1	Rowley Archibald	1	1		1	
Apr	1	Seidmore Josua	1		1	1	
Apr	1	Snellens William	2			3	
Apr	1	Snellens Enoch	1			3	
Apr	1	Swilliv.ᵗ Darby Senr.	1			1	
Apr	1	Swillivant Francis	1	1		3	
Apr	1	Swillivant Darby Junr.	2			2	
Apr	1	Swillivant Benj.ᵃ	1			3	
Apr	1	Swillivant Daniel	1			3	
Apr	1	Tisley John	2			3	
Apr	1	Walker William	3	3	1	3	
Apr	3	Schooler Thomas	1			2	
Apr	3	Scott Sarah	1			3	
Apr	3	Sharp Thomas Senr.	2	4	1	1	
Apr	3	Sharp Thomas Junr.	1	1		2	
Apr	3	Spence William				2	
Apr	3	Stephens Richard	1	2		2	
Apr	3	Stringfellow James	2	1	1	3	
Apr	3	Striplin William	1			2	
Apr	4	Edwards Andrew	1	7	1	11	
Apr	5	Ballard Thomas	1	3		3	
Apr	5	Ballard William Senr.	1			1	
Apr	5	Bolling Thomas	1			1	
Apr	5	Bolling James	3			3	
Apr	5	Bolling Samuel	3	1	1	4	
Apr	5	Burgess Ruben	3			3	
Apr	5	Bussell William	2			2	
Apr	5	Chapman Philip	1		1	3	
Apr	5	Faunt George	1	3	1	4	
Apr	5	Foster Seth	1			4	
Apr	5	Hall Hannah	1			2	
Apr	5	Hord Jesse	1	6	1	6	
Apr	5	Hord James	2	8	1	8	

[arranged by date of tax enumeration]

Mo.	day	Proprietor's names	whites 16+	blacks 16+ 12+		H	other
Apr	5	Hord Peter	1	2		3	
Apr	5	Lathrum Anth.º	3		1	5	
Apr	5	Linn Simon	1			1	
Apr	5	Logue Alexander	1	1		3	
Apr	5	Mannon John	1			3	
Apr	5	Marquiss Anth.º	1		1	2	
Apr	5	Martin Samuel	1			3	
Apr	5	Munrow William	1			1	
Apr	5	Pilcher Mason	3	6	1	5	
Apr	5	Sharp Linsfield	2	7	2	7	
Apr	5	Smith John	1	2		5	
Apr	5	Turner Absolum	3			2	
Apr	5	Turner Griffin	3			4	
Apr	5	Weaks Thomas	1			2	
Apr	5	West John	1	1		1	
Apr	5	West John Senr.	1			5	
Apr	5	White Ann		1		1	
Apr	5	White Thomas	1	1		4	
Apr	7	Bingy John	1			1	
Apr	7	Slaven Jesse	2	1		4	
Apr	7	Thompson James	3			6	
Apr	7	Wellford Robert		10	1	10	1 stud
Apr	10	Curtice Elijah	1		0	1	
Apr	10	Fitzhugh Henry	2	8	1	9	
Apr	10	Fitzhugh John	3	15	1	7	4 phaeton whls
Apr	10	Jacobs William	1	2	1	3	
Apr	10	Sudtherd William	2			1	
Apr	10	Tyler Allice	1	8		6	
Apr	10	Warton James				2	
Apr	13	Ball William	?	3	1	5	
Apr	14	Arrowsmith Thomas	3	1		5	
Apr	14	Bolling William	1				
Apr	14	Bowen Burkett	1	2	1	7	
Apr	14	Daffin Vincent	1			1	
Apr	14	Dowdle James	1	3		3	
Apr	14	Fields Samuel	1			1	

[arranged by date of tax enumeration]

Mo.	day	Proprietor's names	whites 16+	blacks 16+12+		H	other
Apr	14	Fitzhugh William	1	61	11	25	
		"			8 phaeton + 2 chair whls.		
Apr	14	Green Jesse	1			1	
Apr	14	Kirk Jeremiah	1	0	2	2	
Apr	14	McFarlin Ovid	1				41 stud @ 0.13.4
Apr	14	Pettit Benjamin	3	1		3	
Apr	14	Wallace William	1	5	2	3	
Apr	15	Alexander Phillip Lfree	1	6	8	5	
Apr	15	Bowen Thomas		1		3	
Apr	19	Garner William	2			1	
Apr	19	Kenyon James	1	6	2	7	
Apr	19	Threlkill Jesse	1			1	
Apr	21	Ball Burgess		24	1	15	
Apr	21	Carter George	2		1	3	
Apr	23	Carter Charles	3	31	4	14	
Apr	23	Carter Rob.t W.	1	15	2	6	
Apr	23	Day Benjaman	1	1		1	
Apr	23	Day Elizabeth	1			1	
Apr	23	England John	3			3	
Apr	23	Guthry Thomas	1			1	
Apr	23	Hewett Susanna		6		8	2chr.whls.
Apr	23	Hooe Harris Est.		10	2	7	
Apr	23	Humes Francis		1			
Apr	23	Humphry William	2		2	6	
Apr	23	Kirby James	1				
Apr	23	Lavender Rob.t	2	1		4	
Apr	23	Lavender Joseph	2				
Apr	23	Lewis Ann		1			
Apr	23	Reavley William	2	4	2	3	2chr.whls.
Apr	23	Robertson George	1				
Apr	23	Rose Jesse	1				
Apr	23	Wooderd Mary	1	1		1	
Apr	24	Baker Moses	1				
Apr	24	Banks Frances		8	2	8	2chair wheels
Apr	24	Beasly Philip	1				
Apr	24	Benson James	1	3	1	4	
Apr	24	Conyers John	5	3		4	

Stafford Co., Va. personal property tax list - 1788

[arranged by date of tax enumeration]

Mo. day	Proprietor's names	whites 16+	blacks 16+ 12+		H	other
Apr 24	Crop James Senr.	1	6	1	4	
Apr 24	Massey Benj.a				1	
Apr 24	Massey Thomas	2	3		7	
Apr 24	Mattox Lazarus	1	1		5	
Apr 24	Millett John	1			2	
Apr 24	Parmer Rawley	3	1		2	
Apr 24	Smith Samuel	2	4		3	
Apr 24	Suton John	1	1		1	
Apr 24	Turner Benj.a	1			1	
Apr 24	West Edward Senr.	4	1		7	
Apr 24	White George	1	2		4	
Apr 25	Barber William	1				
Apr 25	Briggs David	2	10		8	
Apr 25	Crop James Junr.	1	5	2	5	
Apr 25	Crop John	1	8	2	8	
Apr 25	Hill Leonard		3	1	5	
Apr 25	Horton James	1			4	
Apr 25	Humphry Daniel	1			1	
Apr 25	Jones Charles	2	2	1	6	
Apr 25	Lanman Newman	1	1		2	
Apr 25	Lathrum John	1	2		3	
Apr 25	Lathrum George	2	1		4	
Apr 25	Nickles Elijah	1			1	
Apr 25	Patten Rachell	1	5		3	
Apr 25	Patterson Perry	1				
Apr 25	Pilcher Peter	1			1	
Apr 25	Simpson Alexander				2	
Apr 25	Skinker Thomas		5	1	6	
Apr 25	Thomas Allison	1	2		3	
Apr 26	Ball John	1			1	
Apr 26	Harwood Allice		2		2	
Apr 26	Massey Elizabeth				1	
Apr 26	Massey Toliferrow	1				
Apr 26	More Edward	1	7	2	6	
Apr 26	Morison Arthur	4	13	4	15	
Apr 26	Mulbury John	1	2		1	
Apr 26	Striplin Elizabeth		1			

[arranged by date of tax enumeration]

Mo.	day	Proprietor's names	whites 16+	blacks 16+	12+	H	other
Apr	28	Buchannan Andrew	1	7	2	6	4 phae. wheels
May	5	Calender Philip	1			3	
May	5	Howard W^m	1				
May	5	Jones Henry	2	1		4	
May	5	Latimer Daniel	2			3	
May	5	Paxton John	1			3	
May	5	Peyton Thomas	1	2		2	
May	5	Read John	1	1		3	
May	5	Saunders James	1			1	
May	5	Stringfellow Towns.^d	1			1	
May	5	Sudden John	2	12	3	9	
May	6	Bell John	2	3		4	ord's license
May	6	Conyers Benj.^a	1				
May	6	Donavan James	1	3		3	
May	6	Golohorn John	1				
May	6	Graves Martha				3	
May	6	Hunter Adam	3	23	3	10	4phaet.whls.
n.d.		D.^o@ Hamsted? [blurred]	1	9		5	
May	6	Lotspieck William	1	1		2	
May	6	Rogers John	1	1		2	
May	7	Collins Thomas	2	3		4	
May	7	Dunbar Robt	4	4		3	
May	7	Jett Francis	1	2	2	3	
May	7	Manson Alexander	2	3	1	1	
May	7	Travis Margrett		1			
May	7	Winlock William	3	4		3	
May	9	Alliason David	2	2		1	
May	9	Bowers Michal	1	3	2	4	
May	9	Boyer John	1				
May	9	Clerk William	1				
n.d.		D.^o the Est.^a Ann Clerk				4	
May	9	Colquahoon Walter	1	3		1	
May	9	Disher Lewis	1				
May	9	Faunt Joseph	1	3	1	3	
May	9	Gorden Samuel	2		1	1	
May	9	Graves George	1	1			
May	9	Hayney William	1	4		4	

[arranged by date of tax enumeration]

Mo.	day	Proprietor's names	whites 16+	blacks 16+ 12+		H	other
May	9	Humphry McCausland	2	1			
May	9	Lucas John	1				
May	9	Lyon James	3			1	
May	9	McCloud James	3	1		1	
May	9	McKeterick Anth.ᵒ	3	9		12	2 chr.whls.
May	9	McMillion Wᵐ	1			1	
May	9	Moss John	1				
May	9	Nooe Zephaniah	1	3	1	2	
May	9	Norwood Joseph	1				
May	9	Peters William	1				
May	9	Ransdell John	1				
May	9	Richards William	1	10	1	4	4phaeton whls.
May	9	Sapington Samuel	1				
May	9	Stringfellow George	2	2		3	
May	9	Tayler William	2	6		3	2 chr.whls.
May	9	Triplett Daniel					
May	9	Weaks Benjamin	1				
May	9	Weathers James	2	8	3	5	
May	9	West Thomas	1				
May	9	Williams Leonard	1			1	
May	12	James John	4	14	2	13	
May	13	Lee Tho.ˢ & Mary	2	30	7	20	4phaeton whls.
May	14	Simpson John	1				
May	15	Mortimer Ch.ˢ		4?		2	
May	15	Smith & Young & Hyde					1 stud @ £3
May	15	Young William	2			3	
n.d		Hord Rhody	1	4		6	
n.d.		Fitzhugh Thomas	2	25	3	10	4 phaeton whls
n.d.		Hord Edward	2	2		7	
n.d.		Hord Kellis	3	5	2	5	
n.d.		Hudson David	1	1	1	2	
n.d.		Jackson Rosana	2			3	
n.d.		James George	1	2	1	5	
n.d.		Jett William	3	1		5	
n.d.		Jett Peter Presly	1			1	
n.d.		Jett George	1				
n.d.		Jones Evins	3	1		3	

[arranged by date of tax enumeration]

Mo. day	Proprietor's names	whites 16+	blacks 16+ 12+		H	other
n.d.	Jones George	1			2	
n.d.	McGuire Rachell	1			3	
n.d.	Morris Casper	1			2	
n.d.	Payn Daniel	2	1	1	1	
n.d.	Poarch Thomas	1	9	2	8	
n.d.	Selden Samuel	2	33	11	15	4phaeton whls.
n.d.	Trussell Rhodum	1				
n.d.	Vowles Henry	1	6		3	2chr.whls.
n.d.	Vowles Richard	2	1		1	
n.d.	Wallace James		4		2	

*   *   *   *   *
    *   *   *
        *

[End of date-arranged 1788 personal property tax returns]

[This page blank]

Stafford County
Virginia

Personal Property
Tax List

1789

Source: Virginia State Library, Archives Division. County Records. Stafford County Tax lists.

Form of return of taxable property to be made by the commissioners

List No. 1.
A List of the Taxable property within the district of Wᵐ Mountjoy, commissioner in the county of Stafford for the year 1789
[Categories]:
Date of receiving lists from individuals;
Persons names chargeable with the tax;
[col. 1] - White males above 16 years;
[col. 2] - Blacks above 16 years;
[col. 3] - Blacks above 12 & under 16;
[col. 4] - Horses mares colts & mules;
[other]-Coach & chariot wheels;
   Phaeton & stage wagons;
   Chair wheels;
   Ordinaries;
   Stud horses;
   Rates of covering pr season;
   Doctors *[dropped after the first page]*.

List No. 2.
A List of Taxable Property continued Viz.
[Categories]:
Months;
Days;
Proprietor's Names;
[col. 1] - White tythes;
[col. 2] - Neg.o tythes;
[col. 3] - Young Negros 12 to 16;
[col. 4] - Horses;
[other] - Coach & Char Wheels;
   Pha & stage wheels;
   Chairs;
   Studs;
   Rates pr season;
   O*[rdinary]*. licences;
   B*[illiard]*Tables;
   Doctors;

[folio 1]

A List of the taxable property within the district of
Wᵐ Mountjoy, commissioner in the county of Stafford for the year 1789

Mo. day chargeable w/tax		white males 16+	/blacks 16+	12+	H	other
Mar	10	William Anderson	1	1		1	
Mar	21	John Atchison	1			2	
Mar	21	Elijah Abbet	1			2	
Mar	21	Robert Ashby	2			4	
Mar	21	Nath.ⁿ Atchison	1	2		3	
Mar	28	Halifax Ashby	1			1	
Mar	30	Ja.ˢ Arrowsmith	1			3	
Apr	13	Ja.ˢ Abbet	1			1	
Apr	13	George Abbet	1			1	
Apr	13	Daniel Antrum	3			7	
Apr	13	Amus Atchison	2			4	
May	23	William Adie	1	9		7	
May	23	John Agin	1			1	
Jul	10	Joseph Amblee	1			1	
Jul	10	Tho.ˢ Amblee	2			5	
Sep	8	John Abbet Sen.ʳ	1			2	
Sep	8	Benjamin Adie	2	5	2	6	
n.d.		George Bussell	1			2	
n.d.		John Brooker	1			1	
Mar	10	George Barns	1				
Mar	10	John Beagle	1			3	
Mar	10	George Burroughs	1	2	1	4	
Mar	14	William Barnot	1			1	
Mar	14	James Barnot	1	2		1	
Mar	20	Cuthbert Byrum	1			1	

[folio 2]

Mar	21	Joseph Barber	1			3	
Mar	21	Joel Beagle	1			2	
Mar	21	George Byrum	2			1	

Mo. day chargeable w/tax	white males 16+	/blacks 16+	12+	H	other
Mar 21 William Barbee	1			3	
Mar 21 Edward Bethel	1			3	
Mar 21 James Bridges	1			3	
Mar 21 William Bradly	1			3	
Mar 21 John Bridwell s/T.B	1				
Mar 21 Byrum Bowlin	1			1	
Mar 28 George Bell Junr	1			2	
Mar 28 John Banister	2			2	
Mar 28 Bazel Burroughs	1			2	
Mar 28 Elijah Bell	1			2	
Mar 28 John Bridges	1			2	
Mar 28 Jonathan Bell	1			2	
Mar 28 George Bell Senr	1			2	
Mar 30 John Butler	2	2		5	
Mar 30 William Brown	1			2	
Mar 30 John Browne	1		1	1	
Mar 30 Clem. Billingslee	1	1		2	
Mar 30 Charles Bell	1			1	
Mar 30 George Bridwell Junr	1			3	
Mar 30 Simon Bridwell	1			2	
Mar 30 Mary Bell	1	1		3	
Mar 30 Fielding Bell	1	2		3	
Mar 30 George Bridwell	1			2	
Mar 30 William Bant	1	1	1	6	
[folio 3]					
Mar 30 Philomon Bramel	3			2	
Mar 30 Thomas Barber	1			1	
Mar 30 James Billingslee	2	2		2	
Mar 30 Joseph Buchanan L.free				1	
Mar 30 Sam. Bridwell	1			2	
Mar 30 Dederick Benear (exempt)				2	
Mar 30 William Byrum	1				
Mar 30 John Bradly	1			1	
Apr 13 Nath.^{n} Banister	1			4	
Apr 13 Daniel C. Brent	4	36	11	25	

Mo. day	chargeable w/tax	white males 16+	blacks 16+	blacks 12+	H	other
Apr 13	Eleanor Brent		2	1	9	4 coach&char whls.
Apr 13	Jacob Bridwell L.free				3	
Apr 13	Moses Bridwell	3	4	1	3	
Apr 13	Joseph Botts	2	6	1	5	
Apr 13	John Bridwell	2			2	
Apr 13	William Botts	2	3		4	
Apr 13	Enough Benson	2	3	2	5	
Apr 13	William Branson	1				
Apr 13	Benjamin Brock	1			1	
Apr 13	Henry Bridwell	1			1	
Apr 24	Robert Buchan		5	1	8	
Apr 26	John Browne	2	13	3	8	
May 11	Mary Ann Bronaugh	1	12	1	6	2 chair whls.
May 16	William Bridwell	3	3		4	
May 16	Edward Barber	1			2	
May 16	Thomas Bridwell	2			1	
May 16	George Brent	3	39	5	12	
May 16	John Brent		4?	1	1	
[folio 4]						
Jun 8	Aaron Botts	1	4	1	7	
Jun 8	Daniel Bell	1				
Jun 17	T. Browne	1	18	3	11	
Jun 17	Thomas Barbee L.free				2	
Jun 17	Uriah Bradshaw	2			4	
Jun 17	William Bruce	1		1	2	
Jun 17	Robert Brent	1		1	8	
Jul 8	Benjamin Bowlin	1			1	
Jul 8	Jessey Bails	1			1	
Jul 8	Benjamin Bridwell	1			1	
Jul 8	James Battoe L.free				2	
Jul 8	William Battow	1			3	
Jul 10	William Bridwell	1			1	
Jul 10	Peter Byrum	1			1	
Jul 10	Sarah Byrum	1				
Jul 10	Joseph Brown	2	4	1	6	

Mo.	day	chargeable w/tax	white males 16+	/blacks 16+	12+	H	other
Jul	10	Isaac Branson	1			1	
Jul	10	Nimrod Byrum	1				
Jul	16	Thomas Beach	1			1	
Jul	16	Spencer Bowlin	1			1	
Jul	17	John Bruing	1			1	
Aug	24	Wm Bobs	1				
Aug	25	John Bails	1			2	
Mar	10	George Coats	1			2	
Mar	10	William Carl	1			1	
Mar	10	Elizabeth Chissom	1			2	
Mar	28	James Carter	1	1		2	
Mar	28	Harris Carter	2			1	
[folio 5]							
Mar	23	John Carter	1			1	
Mar	23	Henry Clifton	2	4	1	6	
Mar	23	Jessey Cooper	1			1	
Mar	23	Jedediah Carter	1			3	
Mar	30	Brian Chadwell	2	3	1	4	
Mar	30	John Clemmons	1			2	
Mar	30	Perry Chinn	1			1	
Mar	30	James Cumberford L.free				1	
Apr	13	Joseph Combs	2	4	1	3	
Apr	13	Seth Combs	1	9		7	
Apr	13	Josua Carney	3	1	2	8	
Apr	13	Joseph Cooper L.free				2	
Apr	13	William Cummins	2			3	
Apr	24	Williamson Chandler	2	2	1	2	
Apr	25	Catharine Conaway		3		4	
Apr	25	Peter Cash	1			1	
May	11	Charles Carter	1	23	4	13	
May	11	John Cash	2	29	6	14	
May	16	Cuthbert Combs	2	6		7	
Aug	24	John Chiverault	1				
Aug	24	Ja.^s Cloe Senr L.free				4	
Aug	25	Ja.^s Cloe Junr	1			1	

Mo. day	chargeable w/tax	white males 16+	/blacks 16+	12+	H	other
Aug 25	Asie Cummins	3			4	
Mar 10	Archibild Douglis L.free	1			5	
Mar 10	Dennis Doyall	1	1		3	
Mar 10	Patterson Doyall	1			2	
[folio 6]						
Mar 10	Dennis Doyall Jun.r	1			2	
Mar 10	Bradly Dent	2			2	
Mar 10	Thomas Dunaway	1			1	
Mar 10	Joseph Dunaway	1				
Mar 14	Jerremiah Day	1				
Mar 21	Shadrick Davis	1				
Mar 28	William Dunaway	1			1	
Mar 28	William Devene	1				
Mar 28	John Dillon				1	
Mar 30	Wiliiam Dorson	2			2	
Mar 30	John Delgair	1				
Mar 30	Moses Dick	1			1	
Mar 30	John Dorson	2			3	
Mar 30	Christopher Dorson	1			1	
Mar 30	Mashack Davis	1			1	
Mar 30	RawleighWmDownman	1	10	3	4	
Apr 13	Charles Davis	2			1	
Apr 13	Lewis Disher	1				
Apr 24	Hannah Dickenson	1	6	3	9	
Jun 8	Travers Daniel Sen.r	2	21	3	17	2 chair wheels
Jun 26	Elizabeth Dunaway				1	
Aug 22	John Dunbar	1	1	1	2	
Aug 24	John Dilley	1			3	
Aug 24	Travers Daniel Jun.r	1	12	3	11	
Mar 11	Willis Edwards	1			1	
Mar 11	William Edrington	2	2	1	6	
Mar 30	Backer Edwards	1			3	
[folio 7]						
Mar 30	Jessey Edwards	2	1		3	
Mar 30	Isaac Eustace	2	10	1	7	2 chair wheels

Mo. day chargeable w/tax	white males 16+	/blacks 16+	12+	H	other
Apr	25	William Edwards Sen.r	1	1		3	
Apr	25	William Edwards Jun.ʳ	1	2		1	
Jun	8	Jane Eavs *[name struck through]*					
Jun	13	John Esque	1			1	
Jun	27	Haden Edwards	1	5	1	4	2 chair wheels
Jun	27	Isaac Eavs	1			1	
Aug	24	William Eaton	3			2	
Mar	10	John Fritter	1			2	
Mar	21	Samuel Faunt	1			3	
Mar	21	John Faning	1	1		2	
Mar	21	Josiah Faning	1		1	2	
Mar	21	William French	2	5	1	8	
Mar	28	William Fritter	1			2	
Mar	28	William Franklin	1	1		2	
Mar	30	John Franklin Jun.ʳ	1			1	
Mar	30	Reuben Franklen	1		1	2	
Mar	30	Moses Fritter	2			2	
Mar	30	James Faunt	3			5	
Mar	30	Moses Fritter Jun.ʳ	1			1	
Mar	30	John Franklin Sen.ʳLF	1			3	
Apr	13	Anthony Ficklin	2	5		6	
Apr	13	Joseph Franklin Sr LF			4		
[folio 8]							
Apr	13	Richard Fristoe LF		1		1	
May	11	Phillip Foxworthy	1			2	
May	11	Vintsin Foxworthy	1			2	
May	13	John Fitzgerald	1				
May	16	James Ford	1	3	1	6	
May	16	Thomas Fristoe	1	1		2	
Jun	27	William Fristoe	3			4	
Jun	28	Francis Foushee	3	3		3	
Jun	28	Benjamin Ficklin	1	2		5	
Aug	28	John Faunt	1			1	
Aug	28	Walter Greyham	1	3		7	ordinary license

Mo. day	chargeable w/tax	white males 16+	/blacks 16+	/blacks 12+	H	other
Mar 14	Elisha Green	1			1	
Mar 21	John Grigsby	1			1	
Mar 21	John Garrison	1			2	
Mar 21	Benjamin Grigory	1			3	
Mar 21	Phillip Gardner	1	3		4	
Mar 21	John Goldsmith	1	4		2	
Mar 28	William Groves	1		1	2	
Mar 28	Samuel Groves	3	1		4	
Mar 28	John Gie	1			4	
Mar 28	Benjamin Gie	1			1	
Mar 28	George Garrison	3			2	
Mar 30	Richard Griffis	1			2	
Mar 30	Elisha Grigsby	1		1	1	
Mar 30	James Gough	1		1	2	
Mar 30	Hannah Gough		1		3	
Mar 30	William Gant	1	1		2	
[folio 9]						
Apr 13	William Garrard	1	9		3	
Apr 13	Moses Grigsby Sen.r	2			1	
Apr 25	William Gie	2			7	
Apr 25	Ann Gaddis	1	5		5	
May 16	Robert Green	3			3	
May 16	Joseph Gie	1				
Jun 13	Benjamin Green	1			1	
Jun 28	John Green	2			3	
Jun 28	Walter Greyham	1	8	2	7	ordinary license
	[Walter Greyham's line struck through]					
Aug 22	Isaac Gaskins	1			3	
Aug 24	Solomon Gollohorn	1			1	
Aug 24	John Gun	1			2	
Aug 25	*[no name]* Green	1			1	
Aug 25	Moses Grigsby Jun.r	1				
Aug 25	William Gollohorn	1			5	
Aug 27	William George	1				
Aug 27	John Grey	1			2	

Mo. day chargeable w/tax	white males 16+	/blacks 16+	/blacks 12+	H	other
Aug 27	Aaron Garrison	1			1	
Mar 10	Able Holloway	1	1		2	
Mar 10	Thomas Hay L.free	2			3	
Mar 10	John Hore	1	1	1	1	
Mar 14	William Hallowday	1			2	
Mar 21	Peter Hansbrough	1	1		3	
Mar 21	John Harding	1			3	
Mar 21	Cuthbert Harding	1	1		2	
Mar 22	Frances Hereford	1				
Mar 22	James Hore	1	1	1	3	
[folio 10]						
Mar 28	William Hore	1		1	1	
Mar 28	Elias Hore	1			1	
Mar 28	Mary Hore		7		3	
Mar 28	George Harding	1	1		2	
Mar 30	Thomas Harding	1		1	3	
Mar 30	John Scott Harding	2			4	
Mar 30	Ledia Hansbrough		1	1	2	
Mar 31	Samuel Hudson	1	2		3	
Apr 13	Asie Holloway	2			3	
Apr 13	Isaac Holloway	1			1	
Apr 13	John Holloway	2			3	
Apr 13	William Harding	3	1	1	7	
Apr 24	Elizabeth Hollowday				1	
May 16	Mary Holloway				1	
May 16	George Holloway	1				
May 16	Henry Hiden	1			2	
Jun 8	Causom Horton	2			2	
Jun 26	William Harrod	2			3	
Jun 26	Thomas Heth L.free		1			
Jun 29	Wm Harding	1				*[of]* Chapawamsick
Jun 29	John Hedgman	1	17	4	6	
Jun 29	John Hardy	1	6	2	8	
Aug 22	Michal Houson	1			1	
Aug 22	Asie Holloway Junr	1			2	

Mo. day chargeable w/tax	white males 16+	/blacks 16+ 12+		H	other
Aug 27 John Holloway	2			4	
Aug 28 James Horton	1			3	
Aug 28 John Horton	2	6	1	6	
[folio 11]					
Mar 10 John Jones	2			4	
Mar 10 William Jones	2			3	1 stud horse
Mar 30 John Jones Jun.ʳ	2			1	
Mar 30 John Johnston	1			1	
Mar 30 William Innis	1				
Apr 13 Gabril Jones	2	4	2	2	
Apr 13 Alexander Jameson	2	1		2	
May 11 David Jones	2			2	
May 11 Richard Johnston Sen.ʳ	1	1		4	2 chair wheels
May 16 Steaphen Johnston	1			3	
Mar 21 Henry Kendall	1	1	1	3	
Mar 21 Josua Kendall	1			3	
Mar 30 Merryman Kitchen	1	1		3	
Mar 30 Charles Kendall	1	2		2	
Mar 30 Anthony Kendall	2	?		2	
Mar 30 Christopher Knight	1			5	
Mar 30 Ann Knight	1	3		1	
Mar 30 James Kirk	1			2	
Mar 30 Daniel Kendall	1			4	
Mar 30 Sarah Kirk	1			2	
Mar 30 Josua Kendall	1	4		4	
Apr 13 John Knight	1			1	
Apr 13 Jerremiah Knight	2	1		4	
[folio 12]					
Apr 30 James Kendall	1		1	1	
Apr 30 Uriah Knight	1			2	
Apr 30 John Kendall	3	2	3	5	
Apr 30 Peter Knight Sen.ʳ	3			4	
May 11 Peter Knight Jun.ʳ	1		1	2	
May 16 Wordon Kendall	1			2	
Jun 8 Aron Kendall	1	1		1	

Mo. day chargeable w/tax	white males 16+	/blacks 16+	12+	H	other
Jun 8 Jessey Kendall	1			3	
Aug 27 Epraim Knight	1			2	

[The following two names are struck through on the list:]

~~James Murphy~~	1			6	
~~Charles Mifflin L.free~~				2	

Mo. day chargeable w/tax	white males 16+	/blacks 16+	12+	H	other
Mar 10 Thomas Loury	1				
Mar 10 Charles Latham	1				
Mar 10 John Latham	1			2	
Mar 21 John Latham(s/Snodon)	1			3	
Mar 30 Francis Linum	1				
Mar 30 John Lawlis	2			3	
Mar 30 John Lunsford	1			3	
Apr 13 Chandrid Lewis	1			1	
Apr 13 Moses Lunsford	1			3	
May 16 James Lee	1			2	
May 29 Snodon Latham	1			2	
Jun 30 Gavin Lawson	2	19	5	13	4 phaeton wheels
Mar 10 John Miller	1			1	
Mar 10 William Monroe	1	2	1	2	

[folio 13]

Mo. day chargeable w/tax	white males 16+	/blacks 16+	12+	H	other
Mar 14 Peter Mauzy	1	1		4	
Mar 14 George Mauzy	1		1		
Mar 14 Peter Mauzy (Fairfax)		2	1	3	
Mar 14 William Mauzy	1	2		2	
Mar 21 Lewis Mason	1	1		2	
Mar 21 Henry McEntire	1	1	1	2	
Mar 21 John McCullough	1			2	
Mar 21 James McBride	2			2	
Mar 28 Allen Mountjoy	3			3	
Mar 30 Benjamin Million	3			2	
Mar 30 James More	1			1	
Mar 30 Richard Morton	1	1		1	
Mar 30 Daniel Mason	3	1	1	6	

Mo. day chargeable w/tax	white males 16+	/blacks 16+	12+	H	other
Mar 30 Robert Million	3	1		5	
Mar 30 Richard Mason	1	1		4	
Mar 30 Fielding Mason	1			2	
Mar 30 Charles Martin	1			1	
Apr 24 Thomas Mallery	1			1	
Apr 26 John Murray	1	7		4	
Apr 26 John Markham	1	6	1	2	
Apr 26 William Mountjoy	1	5	1	6	
May 11 Alexander McEntire	1	3		3	
May 11 William Mullin	3	5		6	
May 16 John Mason	1	4		5	
May 16 Mary McDaniel				1	
May 16 Thomas Mountjoy	1	10		7	
May 23 John Francis Mercer	2	37	4	14	
[folio 14]					
Jun 3 John Mountjoy	1		1	3	
Jun 26 Ann Moncure		11	2	5	
Jun 26 Ursly Morton		1	2	2	
Jun 26 Margaret Matthews		6	1	4	2 chair wheels
Aug 27 James Murphy	1			1	
Aug 27 Charles Mifflin L.free				2	
Aug 28 Edward Mountjoy	2			6	
Aug 28 Robert B. Morton	1	8	1	3	2 chair wheels
Aug 28 John Mountjoy	1	6	1	9	1 stud horse
Mar 14 George Normon	1	3		6	
Mar 28 Phillip Nash	1			2	
Mar 28 Charles Nixon	1			1	
Mar 30 John Nicholson	1			1	
Apr 13 James Nailer	1			5	
Apr 13 Edward Normon	1	5	3	7	
Aug 29 Mary Nelson		1		1	
Aug 27 Elizabeth Overall		5		6	
Aug 27 Hezekiah Olover *[sic]*	1			3	
Aug 27 James Ocain	1	1		4	
Aug 28 James Oglesby	1			2	

Mo. day	chargeable w/tax	white males 16+	/blacks 16+	12+	H	other
[folio 15]						
Mar 11	Francis Payn	1				
Mar 11	James Payn	1			2	
Mar 11	Ezekiel Payn	1			1	
Mar 11	William Payn	1			1	
Mar 11	John Payn	1			1	
Mar 21	Charles Porter	1	2		2	
Mar 21	John Primm	1	1		3	
Mar 21	Margaret Primm		1		4	
Mar 21	William Patton	1				
Mar 28	Colvert Porter Jun.ʳ	1			1	
Mar 28	Colvert Porter	2	3	1	5	
Mar 28	Elizabeth Peyton	2	10	3	6	
Mar 28	Richard Poats	1	1		4	
Mar 28	Wharton Philbert	1				
Mar 30	Kelly Payn	1			1	
Mar 30	Moses Poats	1	2		5	
Mar 30	John Poats	1			2	
Mar 30	Jesse Payn	1			1	
Mar 30	James Primm	1	2		3	
Apr 13	Robert Painter	2			4	
Apr 13	Benjamin Pritchet	1	4		8	1 stud horse
Apr 13	Mary Ann Payn				1	
May 11	Vallentine Peyton	1	9	2	5	4 phaeton wheels
May 16	James Peak	1			1	
Jun 8	William Phillips	2	7	1	5	
Jun 8	Lynzey Pollard	1				
Jun 13	John R. Peyton	2	11	3	10	
[folio 16]						
Aug 28	William Poats	1		1	4	
Aug 28	Edward Pearson	2			3	
Aug 29	Thomas Powell	1				
Aug 29	Samuel Parker	1			1	
Aug 29	John Rankings	1				
Mar 10	Joel Readish	2	4	2	8	

Mo. day	chargeable w/tax	white males 16+	/blacks 16+	12+	H	other
Mar 14	James Robinson	1			1	
Mar 14	William Robinson	1			2	
Mar 14	John Richards	1			1	
Mar 21	Joseph Rogers	1				
Mar 21	Rawleigh Ralls	1	2	1	3	
Mar 21	Hepborn Ralls	1			2	
Mar 21	Kenez Ralls	1		1	1	
Mar 21	John Rogers	1		1	3	
Mar 21	John Read	1			1	
Mar 21	Jonathan Read	1			3	
Mar 28	Jessey Riley	1	1		2	
Mar 28	Baily Riley	1			2	
Mar 28	James Riley	1			1	
Mar 28	William Richards	1	1		3	
Mar 28	Richard Ratliff	1			4	
Mar 30	Butler Ramey	1			2	
Mar 30	William Rising	1				
Mar 30	Thomas Right	3	2		6	
Mar 30	Aaron Read	1			3	
Mar 30	Benjamin Rogers	1			2	
[folio 17]						
Mar 30	William Ross	2	1		5	
Mar 31	George Randol	2			2	
Apr 13	William Right	2			2	
May 11	Joseph Readish	2	4		3	
Jun 18	Richard Reid	1		1	4	
Jun 18	Mary Ann Ralls		3		2	
Jun 18	Thomas Rakestraw	1				
Aug 22	Reuben Rogers	1			1	
Aug 22	William Rout	1	2		3	
Aug 25	Ann Rogers				2	
Aug 25	William Randol	3			4	
Mar 10	Charles Stern	1	1	1	1	
Mar 10	Thomas Striblin	1			1	
Mar 10	Joel Striblin	1			1	

Mo. day chargeable w/tax	white males 16+	/blacks 16+	12+	H	other
Mar 14 Sarsfield Snoxall	1			3	
Mar 14 Edward Snoxall	1			3	
Mar 14 John Snoxall	1			1	
Mar 14 Moses Sudduth	1			1	
Mar 14 Henry Sudduth	1			3	
Mar 14 Thomas Sudduth	1			1	
Mar 14 John Shelket	2			4	
Mar 21 Rhoadnum Sims	1			3	
Mar 21 Wilson Shelton	1			3	
Mar 21 George Shelton	1			2	
Mar 21 Abigale Shelton				3	
Mar 21 William Stark	1	1		3	
Mar 28 John Smith	2			1	
[folio 18]					
Mar 28 William B. Stone	2	5	1	7	
Mar 28 Hawkin Stone	1	5	2	6	
Mar 28 Joseph Slaughter	1				
Mar 28 Richard Stone	1	3	1	4	
Mar 28 Charles Stuart	1	6	1	6	
Mar 28 William Stark	1	1	1	3	
Mar 28 William Shacklet	1	1		4	
Mar 30 Richard Sims	2			3	
Mar 30 William Shelton	2			6	
Mar 30 James Sims	1			3	
Apr 13 John Stork		3		2	
Apr 13 Nathaniel Smith	1	1		3	
Apr 13 Jerremiah Stark	2	2		5	
Apr 13 Francis Steen	1	5		4	
Apr 13 Presly Sims	1			2	
Apr 13 John Stern	1	3		2	
Apr 13 John Stark Sen.ʳ	1			1	
Apr 24 Gabrel Sullaven	2			3	
May 11 Thomas Sedden	2	13	4	9	
May 11 John Stark	2	1		4	
May 16 Richard Sims Sen.ʳ L.free				2	

Mo. day	chargeable w/tax	white males 16+	/blacks 16+	12+	H	other
Jun 8	Jane Silvey	1			2	
Jun 8	Jessey Stone	3			3	
Aug 24	Hannah Stark	1		1	2	
Aug 27	Josia Stone	1	5		4	2 chair wheels
Aug 27	Samuel Striblin	1			1	
[folio 19]						
Mar 10	Charles Thornton	1			1	
Mar 21	Thomas Tharp	1			1	
Mar 21	Edward Templeman	1			4	
Mar 30	John Tuttle	1			1	
Mar 30	Thomas Tolson	1			2	
Mar 30	Richard Taylor	1			2	
Mar 30	George Thorn	1			1	
Apr 13	Alexander Taylor	2			2	
Apr 13	Benjamin Tolson	1			2	
Apr 13	Elizabeth Tolson		3	1	5	
Apr 13	William Taylor	2	8	1	5	2 chair wheels
Apr 25	William Tolson	1	1		3	
May 16	Joanna Tolson	1			1	
Jun 4	Elijah Threlkeld	1	11	1	12	
Jun 27	Samuel Thompson	1	1		6	
Jun 27	Elijah Thompson	1			3	
Aug 28	Thomas Tennant	1			3	
Aug 28	William Tunzgate	1			3	
Aug 28	Tho.s G. Tyler	1	2	3	5	1 stud horse @ 15/
May 16	Ann Vaun				1	
Mar 10	George West	1	1		5	
Mar 10	Richard Walker	1	1	1	3	
Mar 10	Mark Walters L.free		1	1	3	1 stud horse @ 10/
[folio 20]						
Mar 28	Henry Woodgerd	1			2	
Mar 28	William Watson	1				
Mar 28	John Walters(Peacenck)	1	1		1	
Mar 28	John Walters Jun.r	2	1		4	
Mar 30	William West	2			3	

Mo. day chargeable w/tax	white males 16+	/blacks 16+	12+	H	other
Mar 30	Allen Way	1			1	
Mar 30	Peter Walters	1			3	
Mar 30	Jessey Woodgerd	1			1	
Apr 13	Nathaniel Williams	1	5			
Apr 13	Charles Walters	1		1	3	
Apr 13	John Walters	1	2	1	4	
Apr 13	George Wells	2	3		4	
Apr 13	William West	1	1		4	
Apr 13	Benjamin Willits	1			1	
Apr 24	George Withers	1	2		2	
May 11	Baily Washington Jun.ʳ	1	10	2	5	
May 11	Baily Washington Sen.ʳ	1	12	1	7	4 coach wheels
May 11	William Williams	1			1	
May 16	Margaret Williams	1	3		3	
Apr 23	Bathsheba Waller				2	
Apr 23	Mary Waller		2	1	5	
Jun 1	John Withers	2	12	2	11	
Jun 1	Benjamin Withers				4	
Jun 12	William Waller	3	3	3	6	
Jun 19	Susanah Wormsly		1		2	
Jun 27	George Williams	1	7	1	3	
[folio 21]						
Aug 22	John Warren	1			2	
Aug 22	Augustin Weadon	1			2	
Aug 25	George Walters	1			3	
Aug 28	James Walker	1			1	
Aug 28	Thomas Wells	1			1	
Mar 10	William Young	1			1	
	[totals]	614	175			
			842	1480		

Stafford 12ᵗh of Oct.ʳ 1789 I certify the aforegoing as agreeing with other returns made to me.

Wm. Garrard CK

Mo. day chargeable w/tax		white males 16+	/blacks 16+ 12+	H		other

To	842	Blacks above 16 years	10/	£ 421	
	175	d.º . . . d.º 12	10/	87	10
	1480	Horses	2/	148	
	8	Chariot wheels	36/	14	8
	8	Phaeton's d.º	24/	9	12
	18	Chair d.º	12/	10	16
	1	Ordinary licence		5	
	5	Stud horses		3	3
		Billiard tables none			
		Practising physician's none			
				£ 699	9

W.ᵐ Mountjoy Comm.ʳ

* * * * *
* * *
*

[End of Mountjoy's returns]

432

[folio 22]

A List of Property continued Viz.

Mo. day	chargeable w/tax	white males 16+	/blacks 16+	12+	H	other
Mar 11	Alexander William	1	15	2	9 4	phaet & stge whls
Mar 11	Ditto Tho.S Casson		4	1	6	
Mar 23	Allison Henry	1			1	
Mar 28	Anderson John	2			4	
Mar 30	Allentharp Jacob	2			4	
Apr 8	Alexander Phillip	1	8	3	4	
Apr 11	Allison Thomas	1	3		3	
Apr 13	Arrowsmith Thomas	2	1		4	
Apr 25	Allison David	2	2	1	1	
Mar 13	Bruce William	3	2	1	4	
Mar 14	Barnett William	3	3		5	
Mar 14	Black Margrett	2			5	
Mar 18	Brooks Thomas	1			1	
Mar 18	Ball William	3	2	1	6	[line badly faded]
Mar 19	Bryant John	1		2	3	
Mar 20	Butler William	1	1		3	
Mar 20	Berry Sarah	1	1		3	
Mar 23	Brown William	1			2	
Mar 23	Brown James	1			2	
Mar 23	Barrett Barth.O	1		1	3	
Mar 23	Berry Richard	1			1	
Mar 26	Bowen Burkett	1	3	2	5	1 stud @ 10/
Mar 28	Briggs David	2	12	5	8	
Mar 30	Berry Thomas	2	1	1	2	
Mar 30	Berry Anth.O	1			3	
Mar 30	Beasly Phillip	1			2	

Mo. day chargeable w/tax	white males 16+	/blacks 16+	12+	H	other
Mar 30 Brimmer John	1			1	
Mar 30 Burton Natha.¹	1			3	
Mar 30 Burton James	1			4	
Mar 30 Brown Walter	1			3	
Mar 30 Brimmer Isaac	1				
Apr 4 Buchanan Andrew	2	8	1	7	4phaet,2chr whls
Apr 8 Burton Gerrard	1			3	
[folio 23]					
Apr 8 Bowen Thomas		1		3	
Apr 8 Burton William	1			1	
Apr 10 Ballard Thomas	1	3		2	
Apr 11 Burton Samuel	2	1		1	
Apr 11 Bolling Charles	1			1	
Apr 11 Bolling James	3			1	
Apr 11 Benson James	2	3	1	5	
Apr 11 Barbee John	1			1	
Apr 11 Bolling Thomas	2			1	
Apr 11 Benson Zachariah	1				
Apr 25 Brauder William	2	3	1	3	
Apr 27 Ball John	1			1	
Apr 28 Banks Francis		8	2	5	
Apr 28 Bolling William	1			1	
Apr 29 Barber William	1			1	
May 1 Buckner Richard	1	4		2	
May 2 Barrett Jacob	1				
May 2 Ballard William	1			1	
May 2 Bowers Michal	2	3	2	4	
May 2 Bell John	2	4		4	
May 2 Bates Joseph Tax free				2	
May 9 Ball Burgess		23	1	12	
Mar 16 Chinon Joseph	1		1	5	
Mar 16 Cox George	1			3	
Mar 16 Curtice Aaron	2			1	

Mo. day	chargeable w/tax	white males 16+	/blacks 16+	12+	H	other
Mar 16	Carter Henry	1			1	
Mar 17	Cox Vincent Jun.ʳ	1		1	3	
Mar 18	Chelkett William	1			3	
Mar 18	Curtice George	2			3	
Mar 19	Carter George	1			1	
Mar 20	Cox Presly	1			1	
Mar 20	Cox Charnox	1		1	3	
Mar 21	Colney Elisha	1			1	
Mar 23	Cox Vincent Sen.ʳ	2			2	
Mar 23	Curtice Theodocius	1				
Mar 23	Curtice William	1			2	
Mar 23	Curtice Richard	1			1	
[folio 24]						
Mar 23	Curtice John	2			4	
Mar 30	Conner John	1			3	
Mar 30	Cahal James	1			1	
Apr 13	Crop John	1	9	1	6	
Apr 13	Carter Joseph	1	2	1	3	
Apr 13	Crop James Jn.ʳ	1	4		6	
Apr 13	Crop James Sen.ʳ	1	3	1	3	
Apr 23	Conyers John	4	3	0	3	
Apr 25	Colquohound Walter	1	3		1	
May 1	Carter Charles		6	1	2	
May 1	Conyers Benjamin	1				
May 1	Cotney John	1	4		4	
May 1	Carter Robert Wor	1	17		6	
May 2	Critchett James	1				
May 5	Collins Thomas	1	4		5	
Mar 14	Day John	2	1			
Mar 14	Day Elizabeth		1		1	
Mar 18	Donathan Gerrard	1	1	1	3	
Mar 19	Downman B Joseph	1	8	3	6	
Apr 4	Donavan Joseph	1	2	1	2	

Mo. day	chargeable w/tax	white males 16+	/blacks 16+	12+	H	other
Apr 13	Dowdle James	1	5		3	
Apr 30	Devenport William	1	2		1	
May 2	Dunbar Robert	3	4		8	
Mar 17	Edmonds William	1	2	1	1	
Mar 20	Edwards Andrew	1	6	1	8	
Apr 4	England John	3	1		2	
Mar 17	Fox Natha.ˡ	2	8	3	8	2 chair wheels
Mar 17	Fugett Frances	1			1	
Mar 17	Fugett Daniel	1			1	
Mar 17	Fugitt Benjᵃ	1		2	3	
Mar 17	Fines Patrick	2	1		3	
[folio 25]						
Mar 20	Fletcher Rachel	1	1		4	
Mar 21	Fitzhugh Henry	2	10	2	5	
Mar 30	Faunt John	1			4	
Mar 30	Faunt George	1	3	1	4	
Apr 10	Fitzhugh William	1	54	8	20	4 phae&2 chr whls
Apr 11	Foster Seth	1			3	
Apr 11	Fitzhugh Thomas	2	25	1	14	4 phaeton whls
Apr 25	Faunt Joseph	1	3	1	3	2 chair whls
Apr 25	Fugett Frances Junʳ	1			2	
Apr 27	Fennal Jonathan	2	5	1	5	
Apr 28	Fickling Fielding	1				
May 2	Fenton John	1				
Mar 13	Garner John	1			2	
Mar 14	Guttery Thomas	1			1	
Mar 16	Garner William	1			1	
Mar 20	Gollehorn Solomon	1			2	
Mar 23	Gollehorn Thomas	1			2	
Mar 27	Groves Thomas	1			2	
Apr 25	Gordon Bazell	2	1		1	
May 5	Graves George	1	1	1		
May 5	Graves Polly	.			3	

Mo. day	chargeable w/tax	white males 16+	/blacks 16+	12+	H	other
May 5	Graves Daniel	1				
May 5	Graves George	1				
May 5	Graves William	3	1		6	
Mar 14	Hord James	1	7	1	6	
Mar 14	Hord Jesse	1	6		6	
Mar 19	Hill Jesse	2	3		5	
Mar 19	Hooe Harris Est.	2	7	3	5	
Mar 19	Henson Elijah	2			3	
Apr 27	Hewitt William	1	13	3	8	
Apr 27	Henson Sarah				3	
[folio 26]						
Mar 30	Horton William	1			3	
Apr 4	Hunter Adam forge	3	47	2	14	
Apr 11	Hudson David	1	1		3	
Apr 11	Hall John	1			2	
Apr 11	Hefferlin Martin	1			1	
Apr 11	Hord Rhoden	2	4		6	
Apr 11	Hord Peter	1	2		3	
Apr 11	Hord Killis	4	5		5	
Apr 13	Humphrys William	3	1	1	6	
Apr 25	Hunter Adam @ home	3	16	6	9	4 phaeton whls
Apr 25	Ditto Hanstead	1	7	2	5	
Apr 27	Harwood Allice	1	1		3	
Apr 27	Hewitt Susannah		7	1	3	
Apr 27	Hore Edward	2	3		6	
Apr 28	Hord Thomas	2	2		5	
Apr 29	Humphrys Daniel	1			1	
Apr 29	Hall Benjamin	1			2	
Apr 29	Horton Charles	1				
Apr 29	Hill Leonard	1	5		4	
May 2	Hany William	2	5		4	
May 5	Hill Henry	1				
Mar 16	Jones George	1				

Mo. day	chargeable w/tax	white males 16+	/blacks 16+	12+	H	other
Mar 21	Jett George	1				
Mar 21	Jett Presly	1			1	
Mar 27	Jacobs William	2	3	1	3	
Mar 28	Jones Henry	2	2		3	
Mar 30	Jett William	3			4	
Apr 10	Jackson William	1			2	
Apr 11	Jackson Robert	1			4	
Apr 11	Jackson Rosanah	1			3	
Apr 27	Jett Frances	1	2	2	4	
Apr 29	Jones Charles	2	2	1	5	
Apr 29	Jones Evins	3	1		4	
[folio 27]						
Apr 29	Jones George	1			3	
Apr 29	Jones James	1			4	
Apr 29	James George	2	6		5	
May 5	James John	3	14	5	16	
Mar 23	Kenny John	2	1		3	
Mar 23	Ketchen William	1				
Mar 30	Kerk Jeremiah	1	3	1	3	
Mar 30	Ketchen James	1			4	
Apr 8	Kenyon James Est.		6	2	8	
Apr 13	Kerk Jesse	1	1		1	
Mar 16	Lang James	1	1		1	
Mar 18	Limbrick William	1			2	
Mar 18	Lang Robert	1			2	
Mar 19	Limbrick George	1				
Mar 19	Limbrick Frances	2			3	
Mar 21	Lowry James Jun.r	2	1		2	
Mar 21	Lowry James Sen.r	1			3	
Mar 21	Lathrum George	3	1		5	
Mar 23	Leach Andrew	1			1	
Mar 23	Leach Benj.a	4			2	
Mar 28	Logy Alexander	1	1		4	

Mo. day chargeable w/tax	white males 16+	/blacks 16+	12+	H	other
Mar 28 Lathrum John	2	1	1	3	
Mar 30 Limbrick John	1			1	
Mar 30 Leach James	1	2	1	3	
Apr 4 Lavender John Ju.ʳ	1				
Apr 4 Lavender Robʳt	1			4	
Apr 4 Lavender Joseph	1				
Apr 11 Lathrum Anth.º	2			3	
Apr 11 Lathrum George	1			2	
Apr 13 Linn Simon	1			1	
Apr 13 Laitman Daniel	1	1		4	
Apr 13 Lewis Conyard	1			1	
Apr 25 Lewis Ann		1			
Apr 25 Lucus Leonard	1			1	
[folio 28]					
Apr 28 Lavender Robert Junʳ	1			1	
Apr 28 Lathrum John	1			1	
Apr 29 Lee James	1			2	
May 2 Lyon James	1				
May 5 Lathrum John Sen.ʳ	1	2		4	
May 5 Lunsford Joanah		1		4	
May 5 Lee Thomas	2	32	7	20	
May 5 Lotspeak William	2	1		2	
Mar 13 McFarlin Alexander Revᵈ				1	
Mar 16 McDonol Hew	1			1	
Mar 16 Miner Elizabeth		1		1	
Mar 23 McGuire Rachel	1			3	
Mar 24 Monday Aaron	1			2	
Mar 24 McFarlen Obed	1			5	1 stud horse
Mar 30 Martin Charles	2	1		3	
Mar 30 Martin Thomas	1			1	
Apr 10 Martin Daniel	1			1	
Apr 10 Massey Thomas	1	3		6	
Apr 10 Marquiss Antho	1			2	

Mo. day	chargeable w/tax	white males 16+	/blacks 16+ 12+		H	other
Apr 11	Munrow Daniel	2	2		6	
Apr 11	Munrow William tax free				1	
Apr 11	Musselman Henry	1				
Apr 11	Mattox Lazarus	2	1		5	
Apr 11	Martin Samuel	2			3	
Apr 13	Mortimore Charles		4		2	
Apr 13	More Edward	1	6	2	5	
Apr 13	Mulbury John	2			2	
Apr 13	Musselman Christian	2			2	
Apr 25	McFarlin Walter	1				
Apr 28	Mannoa (sic) John	1			3	
Apr 28	Massey Elizabeth				1	
Apr 28	Massey Taliaferrow	1				
Apr 28	Manson Auther	4	14	2	14	
Apr 28	Martin Lewis	1			1	
Apr 28	Meal Samuel	1			1	
May 2	Manson Alexander	2	2	1	2	
[folio 29]						
May 2	McCloud James	1				
May 5	McKetterick Anthony	2	10	1	10	2 chair whls
May 5	McMillon William	1				
May 5	McCloud John	1				
Mar 13	Nooe Zepheniah	1	5	2	3	2 chair whls
Mar 18	Newton Thomas	2	2	1	4	
Mar 19	Newton Margrett		2		6	
Mar 30	Newton John	1	5	2	6	
Apr 4	Newton William	2	9	1	6	
May 2	Norwood Joseph	2		1		
Mar 11	Pilcher Moses	2	2		3	
Mar 14	Pettet Benjamin	3	1		3	
Mar 16	Payn Thomas	1	1		1	
Mar 17	Pilcher Mildred	2	2		2	
Mar 18	Pates Aaron	2			2	

Mo. day chargeable w/tax	white males 16+	/blacks 16+	12+	H	other
Mar 19 Perry Thomas Est.e	1	12	2	12	
Mar 20 Pilcher Richard	3			3	
Mar 20 Puzey Stephen	3			1	
Mar 20 Pilcher Daniel	1			1	
Mar 20 Payn John	2	1		3	
Mar 23 Payton James	2			2	
Mar 23 Payton Ann	2			3	
Mar 27 Porch Thomas	1	9	3	8	
Mar 28 Patterson Perry	1				
Mar 28 Patterson Thomas	1			1	
Mar 30 Parmer Rawley	2	1	1	2	
Mar 30 Porch Esum	1	1	2	3	
Apr 11 Payne Daniel	2	1	1	1	
Apr 11 Patterson George	1				
Apr 11 Payton John	2			3	
Apr 13 Pollard John Est.e	2	7	2	5	
[folio 30]					
Apr 19 Patterson Hezekiah	1			1	
Apr 19 Pow Elizabeth				1	
Apr 30 Patten Rachel	1	3		2	
May 1 Pilcher John tax free				4	
May 2 Pilcher Mason	2	6	1	5	
May 2 Payton Thomas	1	2		2	
May 2 Puzey Olden	1				
May 2 Payn John Jun.r	1				
Mar 16 Rawlins John	1			3	
Mar 18 Robertson Thomas					
Mar 23 Robertson John	1	1	1	1	
Mar 18 Row John	1			1	
Mar 27 Rowley Archebal	1	1		1	
Mar 28 Roach Robert	3			3	
Apr 4 Rogers John	1	1		2	
Apr 4 Rose Jesse	2	1		3	

Mo.	day	chargeable w/tax	white males 16+	/blacks 16+	12+	H	other
Apr	27	Richards William	3	10	1	5	
Apr	29	Rogers Robert				1	
May	5	Read Margrett				1	
May	5	·Read John		1			
Mar	14	Sudden John	1	13	3	8	
Mar	16	Swillivant Lettuce				3	
Mar	17	Swillivant Darby Sen.ʳ tax free				2	
Mar	17	Swillivant Benj.ᵃ	1			4	
Mar	17	Swillivant Daniel	2			3	
Mar	18	Stone Joseph	2			2	
Mar	18	Stone William	2			3	
Mar	19	Strother George	1	9	2	6	
Mar	19	Slaven Jesse		1		3	
Mar	19	Swillivant Darby Jun.ʳ	1			2	
Mar	20	Swillivant Frances	2	1		4	
Mar	20	Swillivant Darby Y?	1			1	
Mar	21	Sudtherd William	2			1	
Mar	27	Seydmore Joshua	2			2	
Mar	27	Snellings William	1			4	
[folio 31]							
Mar	27	Snelling Enoch	1			2	
Mar	30	Snelling John	1			2	
Mar	30	Snipe Nathaˡ	1	1	·	2	
Mar	30	Smith John	3	2		6	
Mar	30	Stripling William	1			2	
Mar	30	Sherrett William	1			1	
Mar	30	Smith Henry	2	5	1	8	
Apr	11	Schooler Thomas	1			3	
Apr	11	Spence William tax free				3	
Apr	11	Sharp Linsfield	2	8	2	5	
Apr	11	Sharp Thomas	3	5		3	
Apr	11	Smith Samuel	1	5		3	
Apr	11	Sutor John	1				

Mo. day chargeable w/tax	white males 16+	/blacks 16+	12+	H	other
Apr 11 Stringfellow James	2	1	1	4	
Apr 13 Stephens Richards	2	1		4	
Apr 29 Skinker Thomas	1	6	2	5	
Apr 29 Scott Sarah	1			3	
May 2 Speckt Andrew	1				
May 2 Smith John	1				
May 2 Stone William	1				
May 2 Smith John Ju^r	1				
May 2 Selden Samuel	2	35	8	15	4 coach&char whls
May 5 Stripling Elizabeth		1			
May 5 Stringfellow Henry	1				
May 5 Stipes John	1	1			
May 5 Stringfellow George	1			1	
Mar 16 Templeman Jane				2	
Mar 30 Thompson John	1			1	
Mar 30 Taylor Robert	1				
Mar 30 Treslow Benj^a	1			1	
Apr 8 Threlkell Jesse	1			1	
Apr 11 Timmons John	1			3	
Apr 11 Tate William	1			1	
Apr 11 Troop Thomas	1			1	
Apr 13 Turner James	2			3	
Apr 13 Turner Absolum	3			3	
[folio 32]					
Apr 27 Threlkell George	1			4	
Apr 28 Turner Benj^a	1			1	
Apr 29 Taylor Samuel	1			1	
Apr 29 Turner Griffin	3			5	
May 2 Triplett Daniel	3	5	2	1	
May 5 Tyler Alice	2	7	1	5	
May 5 Taylor William	1	9		3	
May 5 Travis Peggy		1			
May 5 Tisly John	1			3	

Mo. day chargeable w/tax	white males 16+	/blacks 16+	12+	H	other
May 5 Terrier John	3	1		4	
May 5 Vowles Richards	2	1		1	2 chair whls
May 5 Vowles Henry	1	7		2	2 chr whls,ord lic.
Mar 14 White George	1	2		4	
Mar 14 Wright Robert	1	3	1	3	
Mar 14 Walker William	3	4	1	3	
Mar 16 Wisharts Est^e		4		4	
Mar 16 Waugh McCagby	3			3	
Mar 18 White George	1			1	
Mar 19 Washington Geo. Genl	1	8		3	
Mar 27 Waiten James tax free				1	
Mar 28 Weaks George	1	1		2	
Mar 30 Wallace John	2	6		8	
Mar 30 Wallace James		4		2	
Mar 30 West John	2	2		1	
Mar 30 Waugh George	1	18	1	8	1 stud horse
Apr 4 Wallace Thomas		2			
Apr 11 West John	1			4	
Apr 11 White Ann		1		1	
Apr 11 West Thomas	1			1	
Apr 11 White George	1	1		3	
Apr 27 Winlock William	2	4		3	
Apr 28 Woodard Mary	1	1		1	
Apr 28 Webb Aaron tax free				4	
Apr 28 Webb Moses	1			1	
Apr 28 Wright Samuel	1			2	
[folio 33]					
Apr 30 Wallace William	1	2	2	3	
Apr 30 Wellford Robert		1		2	
Apr 30 Weathers James	4	8	2	8	
Apr 30 Weaks Benjamin	1			3	
Apr 4 Young William	1			3	

Mo. day chargeable w/tax	white males 16+	/blacks 16+ 12+	H	other

Mo.	day	chargeable w/tax	white males 16+	/blacks 16+	12+	H	other
Jun	6	William Bassell	1		2		
Jun	7	Green Jesse	1		2		
		[Totals]	491	159			
			890	1122			

Excepted [sic] for William Alexander Comm.[r]

Stafford Sct. 21 June 1789

I certify the aforegoing List as agreeing with those returned to ....

W[m] Garrard CSC

[folio 34]

The Amt. Taxables Due Year 1789 in Stafford Cty.

890 Negros ab[v] 16 years @ 6/8 ea

£ 296.10.4

159 Negros from 12 to 16 @ do.	53.0.0
1122 Horses @ @ 16d Do.	74.16.0
4 chariot wheels @ 4 dollars	4.16.0
24 phaet & stage Wag[n] Do.@ 16/whl	19.4.0
18 Chair Do. @ 8/ each	7.4.0
4 stud horses @ £ 3.12	3.12.0
1 O. licence @	3.6.8
(sic)	£ 462.12.0
Ditto on land & lots - reducing one third	£ 375.9.6
	£ 838.1.6

End of 1789 personal property tax list

Stafford County
Virginia

Personal Property
Tax List

1789

[Arranged by date of tax enumeration]

Source: Virginia State Library, Archives Division. County Records. Stafford County Tax lists.

Form of return of taxable property to be made by the commissioners

List No. 1.

A List of the Taxable property within the district of Wm Mountjoy, commissioner in the county of Stafford for the year 1789
[Categories]:

Date of receiving lists from individuals;
Persons names chargeable with the tax;
[col. 1] - White males above 16 years;
[col. 2] - Blacks above 16 years;
[col. 3] - Blacks above 12 & under 16;
[col. 4] - Horses mares colts & mules;
[other]-Coach & chariot wheels;
   Phaeton & stage wagons;
   Chair wheels;
   Ordinaries;
   Stud horses;
   Rates of covering pr season;
   Doctors *[dropped after the first page].*

List No. 2.

A List of Taxable Property continued Viz.
[Categories]:

Months;
Days;
Proprietor's Names;
[col. 1] - White tythes;
[col. 2] - Neg.o tythes;
[col. 3] - Young Negros 12 to 16;
[col. 4] - Horses;
[other] - Coach & Char Wheels; Pha & stage wheels; Chairs;
   Studs; Rates pr season; O*[rdinary]*. licences;
   B*[illiard]* Tables; Doctors;

A List of the taxable property within the district of
Wm Mountjoy, commissioner in the county of Stafford for the year 1789

[Arranged by date of tax enumeration]

Mo.	day	chargeable w/tax	white males 16+	/blacks 16+	12+	H	other
Mar	10	William Anderson	1	1		1	
Mar	10	George Barns	1				
Mar	10	John Beagle	1			3	
Mar	10	George Burroughs	1	2	1	4	
Mar	10	William Carl	1			1	
Mar	10	Elizabeth Chissom	1			2	
Mar	10	George Coats	1			2	
Mar	10	Bradly Dent	2			2	
Mar	10	Archibild Douglis L.free	1			5	
Mar	10	Dennis Doyall	1	1		3	
Mar	10	Dennis Doyall Junr	1			2	
Mar	10	Patterson Doyall	1			2	
Mar	10	Joseph Dunaway	1				
Mar	10	Thomas Dunaway	1			1	
Mar	10	John Fritter	1			2	
Mar	10	Thomas Hay L.free	2			3	
Mar	10	Able Holloway	1	1		2	
Mar	10	John Hore	1	1	1	1	
Mar	10	John Jones	2			4	
Mar	10	William Jones	2			3	1 stud horse
Mar	10	Charles Latham	1				
Mar	10	John Latham	1			2	
Mar	10	Thomas Loury	1				
Mar	10	John Miller	1			1	
Mar	10	William Monroe	1	2	1	2	
Mar	10	Joel Readish	2	4	2	8	
Mar	10	Charles Stern	1	1	1	1	

[arranged by date of tax enumeration]

Mo. day	chargeable w/tax	white males 16+	/blacks 16+	12+	H	other
Mar 10	Joel Striblin	1			1	
Mar 10	Thomas Striblin	1			1	
Mar 10	Charles Thornton	1			1	
Mar 10	Richard Walker	1	1	1	3	
Mar 10	Mark Walters L.free		1	1	3	1 stud horse @ 10/
Mar 10	George West	1	1		5	
Mar 10	William Young	1			1	
Mar 11	William Edrington	2	2	1	6	
Mar 11	Willis Edwards	1			1	
Mar 11	Ezekiel Payn	1			1	
Mar 11	Francis Payn	1				
Mar 11	James Payn	1			2	
Mar 11	John Payn	1			1	
Mar 11	William Payn	1			1	
Mar 14	James Barnot	1	2		1	
Mar 14	William Barnot	1			1	
Mar 14	Jerremiah Day	1				
Mar 14	Elisha Green	1			1	
Mar 14	William Hallowday	1			2	
Mar 14	George Mauzy	1		1		
Mar 14	Peter Mauzy (Fairfax)		2	1	3	
Mar 14	Peter Mauzy	1	1		4	
Mar 14	William Mauzy	1	2		2	
Mar 14	George Normon	1	3		6	
Mar 14	John Richards	1			1	
Mar 14	James Robinson	1			1	
Mar 14	William Robinson	1			2	
Mar 14	John Shelket	2			4	
Mar 14	Edward Snoxall	1			3	
Mar 14	John Snoxall	1			1	
Mar 14	Sarsfield Snoxall	1			3	
Mar 14	Henry Sudduth	1			3	
Mar 14	Moses Sudduth	1			1	
Mar 14	Thomas Sudduth	1			1	
Mar 20	Cuthbert Byrum	1			1	
Mar 21	Elijah Abbet	1			2	
Mar 21	Robert Ashby	2			4	

[arranged by date of tax enumeration]

Mo.	day	chargeable w/tax	white males 16+	/blacks 16+	12+	H	other
Mar	21	John Atchison	1			2	
Mar	21	Nath.n Atchison	1	2		3	
Mar	21	William Barbee	1			3	
Mar	21	Joseph Barber	1			3	
Mar	21	Joel Beagle	1			2	
Mar	21	Edward Bethel	1			3	
Mar	21	Byrum Bowlin	1			1	
Mar	21	William Bradly	1			3	
Mar	21	James Bridges	1			3	
Mar	21	John Bridwell /son to T.B	1				
Mar	21	George Byrum	2			1	
Mar	21	Shadrick Davis	1				
Mar	21	John Faning	1	1		2	
Mar	21	Josiah Faning	1		2	2	
Mar	21	Samuel Faunt	1			3	
Mar	21	William French	2	5	1	8	
Mar	21	Phillip Gardner	1	3		4	
Mar	21	John Garrison	1			2	
Mar	21	John Goldsmith	1	4		2	
Mar	21	Benjamin Grigory	1			3	
Mar	21	John Grigsby	1			1	
Mar	21	Peter Hansbrough	1	1		3	
Mar	21	Cuthbert Harding	1	1		2	
Mar	21	John Harding	1			3	
Mar	21	Henry Kendall	1	1	1	3	
Mar	21	Josua Kendall	1			3	
Mar	21	John Latham (son/Snodon)	1			3	
Mar	21	Lewis Mason	1	1		2	
Mar	21	James McBride	2			2	
Mar	21	John McCullough	1			2	
Mar	21	Henry McEntire	1	1	1	2	
Mar	21	William Patton	1				
Mar	21	Charles Porter	1	2		2	
Mar	21	John Primm	1	1		3	
Mar	21	Margaret Primm		1		4	
Mar	21	Hepborn Ralls	1			2	
Mar	21	Kenez Ralls	1		1	1	

Stafford Co., Va. personal property tax list - 1789

[arranged by date of tax enumeration]

Mo.	day	chargeable w/tax	white males 16+	/blacks 16+	12+	H	other
Mar	21	Rawleigh Ralls	1	2	1	3	
Mar	21	John Read	1			1	
Mar	21	Jonathan Read	1			3	
Mar	21	John Rogers	1		1	3	
Mar	21	Joseph Rogers	1				
Mar	21	Abigale Shelton				3	
Mar	21	George Shelton	1			2	
Mar	21	Wilson Shelton	1			3	
Mar	21	Rhoadnum Sims	1			3	
Mar	21	William Stark	1	1		3	
Mar	21	Edward Templeman	1			4	
Mar	21	Thomas Tharp	1			1	
Mar	22	Frances Hereford	1				
Mar	22	James Hore	1	1	1	3	
Mar	23	Jedediah Carter	1			3	
Mar	23	John Carter	1			1	
Mar	23	Henry Clifton	2	4	1	6	
Mar	23	Jessey Cooper	1			1	
Mar	28	Halifax Ashby	1			1	
Mar	28	William B. Stone	2	5	1	7	
Mar	28	John Banister	2			2	
Mar	28	Elijah Bell	1			2	
Mar	28	George Bell Jun.r	1			2	
Mar	28	George Bell Sen.r	1			2	
Mar	28	Jonathan Bell	1			2	
Mar	28	John Bridges	1			2	
Mar	28	Bazel Burroughs	1			2	
Mar	28	Harris Carter	2			1	
Mar	28	James Carter	1	1		2	
Mar	28	William Devene	1				
Mar	28	John Dillon				1	
Mar	28	William Dunaway	1			1	
Mar	28	William Franklin	1	1		2	
Mar	28	William Fritter	1			2	
Mar	28	George Garrison	3			2	
Mar	28	Benjamin Gie	1			1	
Mar	28	John Gie	1			4	

[arranged by date of tax enumeration]

Mo.	day	chargeable w/tax	white males 16+	/blacks 16+	12+	H	other
Mar	28	Samuel Groves	3	1		4	
Mar	28	William Groves	1		1	2	
Mar	28	George Harding	1	1		2	
Mar	28	Elias Hore	1			1	
Mar	28	Mary Hore		7		3	
Mar	28	William Hore	1		1	1	
Mar	28	Allen Mountjoy	3			3	
Mar	28	Phillip Nash	1			2	
Mar	28	Charles Nixon	1			1	
Mar	28	Elizabeth Peyton	2	10	3	6	
Mar	28	Wharton Philbert	1				
Mar	28	Richard Poats	1	1		4	
Mar	28	Colvert Porter Jun.ʳ	1			1	
Mar	28	Colvert Porter	2	3	1	5	
Mar	28	Richard Ratliff	1			4	
Mar	28	William Richards	1	1		3	
Mar	28	Baily Riley	1			2	
Mar	28	James Riley	1			1	
Mar	28	Jessey Riley	1	1		2	
Mar	28	William Shacklet	1	1		4	
Mar	28	Joseph Slaughter	1				
Mar	28	John Smith	2			1	
Mar	28	William Stark	1	1	1	3	
Mar	28	Hawkin Stone	1	5	2	6	
Mar	28	Richard Stone	1	3	1	4	
Mar	28	Charles Stuart	1	6	1	6	
Mar	28	John Walters (Peaceneck)	1	1		1	
Mar	28	John Walters Jun.ʳ	2	1		4	
Mar	28	William Watson	1				
Mar	28	Henry Woodgerd	1			2	
Mar	30	Ja.ˢ Arrowsmith	1			3	
Mar	30	William Bant	1	1	1	6	
Mar	30	Thomas Barber	1			1	
Mar	30	Charles Bell	1			1	
Mar	30	Fielding Bell	1	2		3	
Mar	30	Mary Bell	1	1		3	
Mar	30	Dederick Benear (exempt)				2	

[arranged by date of tax enumeration]

Mo.	day	chargeable w/tax	white males 16+	/blacks 16+	H 12+		other
Mar	30	Clem. Billingslee	1	1		2	
Mar	30	James Billingslee	2	2		2	
Mar	30	John Bradly	1			1	
Mar	30	Philomon Bramel	3			2	
Mar	30	George Bridwell	1			2	
Mar	30	George Bridwell Jun.ʳ	1			3	
Mar	30	Sam. Bridwell	1			2	
Mar	30	Simon Bridwell	1			2	
Mar	30	William Brown	1			2	
Mar	30	John Browne	1		1	1	
Mar	30	Joseph Buchanan L.free				1	
Mar	30	John Butler	2	2		5	
Mar	30	William Byrum	1				
Mar	30	Brian Chadwell	2	3	1	4	
Mar	30	Perry Chinn	1			1	
Mar	30	John Clemmons	1			2	
Mar	30	James Cumberford L.free				1	
Mar	30	Mashack Davis	1			1	
Mar	30	John Delgair	1				
Mar	30	Moses Dick	1			1	
Mar	30	Christopher Dorson	1			1	
Mar	30	John Dorson	2			3	
Mar	30	William Dorson	2			2	
Mar	30	Rawleigh Wᵐ Downman	1	10	3	4	
Mar	30	Backer Edwards	1			3	
Mar	30	Jessey Edwards	2	1		3	
Mar	30	Isaac Eustace	2	10	1	7	2 chair wheels
Mar	30	James Faunt	3			5	
Mar	30	Reuben Franklen	1		1	2	
Mar	30	John Franklin Jun.ʳ	1			1	
Mar	30	John Franklin Sen.ʳ L.free	1			3	
Mar	30	Moses Fritter	2			2	
Mar	30	Moses Fritter Jun.ʳ	1			1	
Mar	30	William Gant	1	1		2	
Mar	30	Hannah Gough		1		3	
Mar	30	James Gough	1		1	2	
Mar	30	Richard Griffis	1			2	

[arranged by date of tax enumeration]

Mo.	day	chargeable w/tax	white males 16+	/blacks 16+	12+	H	other
Mar	30	Elisha Grigsby	1		1	1	
Mar	30	Ledia Hansbrough		1	1	2	
Mar	30	Thomas Harding	1		1	3	
Mar	30	William Innis	1				
Mar	30	John Johnston	1			1	
Mar	30	John Jones Jun.ʳ	2			1	
Mar	30	Anthony Kendall	2	?		2	
Mar	30	Charles Kendall	1	2		2	
Mar	30	Daniel Kendall	1			4	
Mar	30	Josua Kendall	1	4		4	
Mar	30	James Kirk	1			2	
Mar	30	Sarah Kirk	1			2	
Mar	30	Merryman Kitchen	1	1		3	
Mar	30	Ann Knight	1	3		1	
Mar	30	Christopher Knight	1			5	
Mar	30	John Lawlis	2			3	
Mar	30	Francis Linum	1				
Mar	30	John Lunsford	1			3	
Mar	30	Charles Martin	1			1	
Mar	30	Daniel Mason	3	1	1	6	
Mar	30	Fielding Mason	1			2	
Mar	30	Richard Mason	1	1		4	
Mar	30	Benjamin Million	3			2	
Mar	30	Robert Million	3	1		5	
Mar	30	James More	1			1	
Mar	30	Richard Morton	1	1		1	
Mar	30	John Nicholson	1			1	
Mar	30	Jesse Payn	1			1	
Mar	30	Kelly Payn	1			1	
Mar	30	John Poats	1			2	
Mar	30	Moses Poats	1	2		5	
Mar	30	James Primm	1	2		3	
Mar	30	Butler Ramey	1			2	
Mar	30	Aaron Read	1			3	
Mar	30	Thomas Right	3	2		6	
Mar	30	William Rising	1				
Mar	30	Benjamin Rogers	1			2	

[arranged by date of tax enumeration]

Mo.	day	chargeable w/tax	white males 16+	/blacks 16+	12+	H	other
Mar	30	William Ross	2	1		5	
Mar	30	John Scott Harding	2			4	
Mar	30	William Shelton	2			6	
Mar	30	James Sims	1			3	
Mar	30	Richard Sims	2			3	
Mar	30	Richard Taylor	1			2	
Mar	30	George Thorn	1			1	
Mar	30	Thomas Tolson	1			2	
Mar	30	John Tuttle	1			1	
Mar	30	Peter Walters	1			3	
Mar	30	Allen Way	1			1	
Mar	30	William West	2			3	
Mar	30	Jessey Woodgerd	1			1	
Mar	31	Samuel Hudson	1	2		3	
Mar	31	George Randol	2			2	
Apr	13	George Abbet	1			1	
Apr	13	Ja.s Abbet	1			1	
Apr	13	Mary Ann Payn				1	
Apr	13	Daniel Antrum	3			7	
Apr	13	Amus Atchison	2			4	
Apr	13	Nath.n Banister	1			4	
Apr	13	Enough Benson	2	3	2	5	
Apr	13	Joseph Botts	2	6	1	5	
Apr	13	William Botts	2	3		4	
Apr	13	William Branson	1				
Apr	13	Daniel C. Brent	4	36	11	25	
Apr	13	Eleanor Brent		2	1	9	4 coach&char. whls.
Apr	13	Henry Bridwell	1			1	
Apr	13	Jacob Bridwell L.free				3	
Apr	13	John Bridwell	2			2	
Apr	13	Moses Bridwell	3	4	1	3	
Apr	13	Benjamin Brock	1			1	
Apr	13	Josua Carney	3	1	2	8	
Apr	13	Joseph Combs	2	4	1	3	
Apr	13	Seth Combs	1	9		7	
Apr	13	Joseph Cooper L.free				2	
Apr	13	William Cummins	2			3	

[arranged by date of tax enumeration]

Mo.	day	chargeable w/tax	white males 16+	/blacks 16+	12+	H	other
Apr	13	Charles Davis	2			1	
Apr	13	Lewis Disher	1				
Apr	13	Anthony Ficklin	2	5		6	
Apr	13	Joseph Franklin Sen.ʳ L.free				4	
Apr	13	Richard Fristoe L.free		1		1	
Apr	13	William Garrard	1	9		3	
Apr	13	Moses Grigsby Sen.ʳ	2			1	
Apr	13	William Harding	3	1	1	7	
Apr	13	Asie Holloway	2			3	
Apr	13	Isaac Holloway	1			1	
Apr	13	John Holloway	2			3	
Apr	13	Alexander Jameson	2	1		2	
Apr	13	Gabril Jones	2	4	2	2	
Apr	13	Jerremiah Knight	2	1		4	
Apr	13	John Knight	1			1	
Apr	13	Chandrid Lewis	1			1	
Apr	13	Moses Lunsford	1			3	
Apr	13	James Nailer	1			5	
Apr	13	Edward Normon	1	5	3	7	
Apr	13	Robert Painter	2			4	
Apr	13	Benjamin Pritchet	1	4		8	1 stud horse
Apr	13	William Right	2			2	
Apr	13	Presly Sims	1			2	
Apr	13	Nathaniel Smith	1	1		3	
Apr	13	Jerremiah Stark	2	2		5	
Apr	13	John Stark Sen.ʳ	1			1	
Apr	13	Francis Steen	1	5		4	
Apr	13	John Stern	1	3		2	
Apr	13	John Stork		3		2	
Apr	13	Alexander Taylor	2			2	
Apr	13	William Taylor	2	8	1	5	2 chair wheels
Apr	13	Benjamin Tolson	1			2	
Apr	13	Elizabeth Tolson		3	1	5	
Apr	13	Charles Walters	1		1	3	
Apr	13	John Walters	1	2	1	4	
Apr	13	George Wells	2	3		4	
Apr	13	William West	1	1		4	

Stafford Co., Va. personal property tax list - 1789

[arranged by date of tax enumeration]

Mo.	day	chargeable w/tax	white males 16+	/blacks 16+	12+	H	other
Apr	13	Nathaniel Williams	1	5			
Apr	13	Benjamin Willits	1			1	
Apr	23	Bathsheba Waller				2	
Apr	23	Mary Waller		2	1	5	
Apr	24	Robert Buchan		5	1	8	
Apr	24	Williamson Chandler	2	2	1	2	
Apr	24	Hannah Dickenson	1	6	3	9	
Apr	24	Elizabeth Hollowday				1	
Apr	24	Thomas Mallery	1			1	
Apr	24	Gabrel Sullaven	2			3	
Apr	24	George Withers	1	2		2	
Apr	25	Peter Cash	1			1	
Apr	25	Catharine Conaway		3		4	
Apr	25	William Edwards Jun.r	1	2		1	
Apr	25	William Edwards Sen.r	1	1		3	
Apr	25	Ann Gaddis	1	5		5	
Apr	25	William Gie	2			7	
Apr	25	William Tolson	1	1		3	
Apr	26	John Browne	2	13	3	8	
Apr	26	John Markham	1	6	1	2	
Apr	26	William Mountjoy	1	5	1	6	
Apr	26	John Murray	1	7		4	
Apr	30	James Kendall	1		1	1	
Apr	30	John Kendall	3	2	3	5	
Apr	30	Peter Knight Sen.r	3			4	
Apr	30	Uriah Knight	1			2	
May	11	Mary Ann Bronaugh	1	12	1	6	2 chair whls.
May	11	Charles Carter	1	23	4	13	
May	11	John Cash	2	29	6	14	
May	11	Phillip Foxworthy	1			2	
May	11	Vintsin Foxworthy	1			2	
May	11	Richard Johnston Sen.r	1	1		4	2 chair wheels
May	11	David Jones	2			2	
May	11	Peter Knight Jun.r	1		1	2	
May	11	Alexander McEntire	1	3		3	
May	11	William Mullin	3	5		6	
May	11	Vallentine Peyton	1	9	2	5	4 phaeton wheels

[arranged by date of tax enumeration]

Mo.	day	chargeable w/tax	white males 16+	/blacks 16+	12+	H	other
May	11	Joseph Readish	2	4		3	
May	11	Thomas Sedden	2	13	4	9	
May	11	John Stark	2	1		4	
May	11	Baily Washington Jun.ʳ	1	10	2	5	
May	11	Baily Washington Sen.ʳ	1	12	1	7	4 coach wheels
May	11	William Williams	1			1	
May	13	John Fitzgerald	1				
May	16	Edward Barber	1			2	
May	16	George Brent	3	39	5	12	
May	16	John Brent		4?	1	1	
May	16	Thomas Bridwell	2			1	
May	16	William Bridwell	3	3		4	
May	16	Cuthbert Combs	2	6		7	
May	16	James Ford	1	3	1	6	
May	16	Thomas Fristoe	1	1		2	
May	16	Joseph Gie	1				
May	16	Robert Green	3			3	
May	16	Henry Hiden	1			2	
May	16	George Holloway	1				
May	16	Mary Holloway				1	
May	16	Steaphen Johnston	1			3	
May	16	Wordon Kendall	1			2	
May	16	James Lee	1			2	
May	16	John Mason	1	4		5	
May	16	Mary McDaniel				1	
May	16	Thomas Mountjoy	1	10		7	
May	16	James Peak	1			1	
May	16	Richard Sims Sen.ʳ L.free				2	
May	16	Joanna Tolson	1			1	
May	16	Ann Vaun				1	
May	16	Margaret Williams	1	3		3	
May	23	William Adie	1	9		7	
May	23	John Agin	1			1	
May	23	John Francis Mercer	2	37	4	14	
May	29	Snodon Latham	1			2	
Jun	1	Benjamin Withers				4	
Jun	1	John Withers	2	12	2	11	

[arranged by date of tax enumeration]

Mo.	day	chargeable w/tax	white males 16+	/blacks 16+	12+	H	other
Jun	3	John Mountjoy	1		1	3	
Jun	4	Elijah Threlkeld	1	11	1	12	
Jun	8	Daniel Bell	1				
Jun	8	Aaron Botts	1	4	1	7	
Jun	8	Travers Daniel Sen.r	2	21	3	17	2 chair wheels
Jun	8	Jane Eavs [name struck through]					
Jun	8	Causom Horton	2			2	
Jun	8	Aron Kendall	1	1		1	
Jun	8	Jessey Kendall	1			3	
Jun	8	William Phillips	2	7	1	5	
Jun	8	Lynzey Pollard	1				
Jun	8	Jane Silvey	1			2	
Jun	8	Jessey Stone	3			3	
Jun	12	William Waller	3	3	3	6	
Jun	13	John Esque	1			1	
Jun	13	Benjamin Green	1			1	
Jun	13	John R. Peyton	2	11	3	10	
Jun	17	Thomas Barbee L.free				2	
Jun	17	Uriah Bradshaw	2			4	
Jun	17	Robert Brent	1		1	8	
Jun	17	T. Browne	1	18	3	11	
Jun	17	William Bruce	1		1	2	
Jun	18	Mary Ann Ralls		3		2	
Jun	18	Thomas Rakestraw	1				
Jun	18	Richard Reid	1		1	4	
Jun	19	Susanah Wormsly		1		2	
Jun	26	Elizabeth Dunaway				1	
Jun	26	William Harrod	2			3	
Jun	26	Thomas Heth L.free		1			
Jun	26	Margaret Matthews		6	1	4	2 chair wheels
Jun	26	Ann Moncure		11	2	5	
Jun	26	Ursly Morton		1	2	2	
Jun	27	Isaac Eavs	1			1	
Jun	27	Haden Edwards	1	5	1	4	2 chair wheels
Jun	27	William Fristoe	3			4	
Jun	27	Elijah Thompson	1			3	
Jun	27	Samuel Thompson	1	1		6	

[arranged by date of tax enumeration]

Mo.	day	chargeable w/tax	white males 16+	/blacks 16+	12+	H	other
Jun	27	George Williams	1	7	1	3	
Jun	28	Benjamin Ficklin	1	2		5	
Jun	28	Francis Foushee	3	3		3	
Jun	28	John Green	2			3	
Jun	28	Walter Greyham	1	8	2	7	ordinary license
Jun	29	Wm Harding	1				[of] Chapawamsick
Jun	29	John Hardy	1	6	2	8	
Jun	29	John Hedgman	1	17	4	6	
Jun	30	Gavin Lawson	2	19	5	13	4 phaeton wheels
Jul	8	Jessey Bails	1			1	
Jul	8	James Battoe L.free				2	
Jul	8	William Battow	1			3	
Jul	8	Benjamin Bowlin	1			1	
Jul	8	Benjamin Bridwell	1			1	
Jul	10	Joseph Amblee	1			1	
Jul	10	Thos Amblee	2			5	
Jul	10	Isaac Branson	1			1	
Jul	10	William Bridwell	1			1	
Jul	10	Joseph Brown	2	4	1	6	
Jul	10	Nimrod Byrum	1				
Jul	10	Peter Byrum	1			1	
Jul	10	Sarah Byrum	1				
Jul	16	Thomas Beach	1			1	
Jul	16	Spencer Bowlin	1			1	
Jul	17	John Bruing	1			1	
Aug	22	John Dunbar	1	1	1	2	
Aug	22	Isaac Gaskins	1			3	
Aug	22	Asie Holloway Junr	1			2	
Aug	22	Michal Houson	1			1	
Aug	22	Reuben Rogers	1			1	
Aug	22	William Rout	1	2		3	
Aug	22	John Warren	1			2	
Aug	22	Augustin Weadon	1			2	
Aug	24	Wm Bobs	1				
Aug	24	John Chiverault	1				
Aug	24	Ja.^s Cloe Senr L.free				4	
Aug	24	Travers Daniel Junr	1	12	3	11	

[arranged by date of tax enumeration]

Mo.	day	chargeable w/tax	white males 16+	/blacks 16+	12+	H	other
Aug	24	John Dilley	1			3	
Aug	24	William Eaton	3			2	
Aug	24	Solomon Gollohorn	1			1	
Aug	24	John Gun	1			2	
Aug	24	Hannah Stark	1		1	2	
Aug	25	John Bails	1			2	
Aug	25	Ja.^{S} Cloe Junr	1			1	
Aug	25	Asie Cummins	3			4	
Aug	25	William Gollohorn	1			5	
Aug	25	[no given name] Green	1			1	
Aug	25	Moses Grigsby Junr	1				
Aug	25	William Randol	3			4	
Aug	25	Ann Rogers				2	
Aug	25	George Walters	1			3	
Aug	27	Aaron Garrison	1			1	
Aug	27	William George	1				
Aug	27	John Grey	1			2	
Aug	27	John Holloway	2			4	
Aug	27	Epraim Knight	1			2	
Aug	27	Charles Mifflin L.free				2	
Aug	27	James Murphy	1			1	
Aug	27	James Ocain	1	1		4	
Aug	27	Hezekiah Olover [sic]	1			3	
Aug	27	Elizabeth Overall		5		6	
Aug	27	Josia Stone	1	5		4	2 chair wheels
Aug	27	Samuel Striblin	1			1	
Aug	28	Robert B. Morton	1	8	1	3	2 chair wheels
Aug	28	John Faunt	1			1	
Aug	28	Walter Greyham	1	3		7	ordinary license
Aug	28	James Horton	1			3	
Aug	28	John Horton	2	6	1	6	
Aug	28	Edward Mountjoy	2			6	
Aug	28	John Mountjoy	1	6	1	9	1 stud horse
Aug	28	James Oglesby	1			2	
Aug	28	Edward Pearson	2			3	
Aug	28	William Poats	1		1	4	
Aug	28	Thomas Tennant	1			3	

[arranged by date of tax enumeration]

Mo.	day	chargeable w/tax	white males 16+	/blacks 16+	12+	H	other
Aug	28	William Tunzgate	1			3	
Aug	28	Tho.ˢ G. Tyler	1	2	3	5	1 stud horse @ 15/
Aug	28	James Walker	1			1	
Aug	28	Thomas Wells	1			1	
Aug	29	Mary Nelson		1		1	
Aug	29	Samuel Parker	1			1	
Aug	29	Thomas Powell	1				
Aug	29	John Rankings	1				
Sep	8	John Abbet Sen.ʳ	1			2	
Sep	8	Benjamin Adie	2	5	2	6	
n.d.		John Brooker	1			1	
n.d.		George Bussell	1			2	

[The following two names are struck through on the list:]

~~Charles Mifflin L free~~				2
~~James Murphy~~	1			6

* * * * *

* * *

*

[End of date-arranged 1789 returns for William Mountjoy]

A List of Property continued Viz.

[Arranged by date of tax enumeration]

Mo.	day	Proprietor's name	white males 16+	/blacks 16+	12+	H	other
Mar	11	Alexander William	1	15	2	9	4 phaet & stg whls
Mar	11	Ditto Tho.ˢ Casson		4	1	6	
Mar	11	Pilcher Moses	2	2		3	
Mar	13	Bruce William	3	2	1	4	
Mar	13	Garner John	1			2	
Mar	13	McFarlin Alexander Revᵈ				1	
Mar	13	Nooe Zepheniah	1	5	2	3	2 chair whls
Mar	14	Barnett William	3	3		5	
Mar	14	Black Margrett	2			5	
Mar	14	Day Elizabeth		1		1	
Mar	14	Day John	2	1			
Mar	14	Guttery Thomas	1			1	
Mar	14	Hord James	1	7	1	6	
Mar	14	Hord Jesse	1	6		6	
Mar	14	Pettet Benjamin	3	1		3	
Mar	14	Sudden John	1	13	3	8	
Mar	14	Walker William	3	4	1	3	
Mar	14	White George	1	2		4	
Mar	14	Wright Robert	1	3	1	3	
Mar	16	Carter Henry	1			1	
Mar	16	Chinon Joseph	1		1	5	
Mar	16	Cox George	1			3	
Mar	16	Curtice Aaron	2			1	
Mar	16	Garner William	1			1	
Mar	16	Jones George	1				
Mar	16	Lang James	1	1		1	
Mar	16	McDonol Hew	1			1	
Mar	16	Miner Elizabeth		1		1	
Mar	16	Payn Thomas	1	1		1	
Mar	16	Rawlins John	1			3	
Mar	16	Swillivant Lettuce				3	
Mar	16	Templeman Jane				2	
Mar	16	Waugh McCagby	3			3	

[arranged by date of tax enumeration]

Mo. day	chargeable w/tax	white males 16+	/blacks 16+	12+	H	other
Mar 16	Wisharts Este		4		4	
Mar 17	Cox Vincent Jun.ʳ	1		1	3	
Mar 17	Edmonds William	1	2	1	1	
Mar 17	Fines Patrick	2	1		3	
Mar 17	Fox Natha.ˡ	2	8	3	8	2 chair wheels
Mar 17	Fugett Daniel	1			1	
Mar 17	Fugett Frances	1			1	
Mar 17	Fugitt Benjᵃ	1		2	3	
Mar 17	Pilcher Mildred	2	2		2	
Mar 17	Swillivant Benj.ᵃ	1			4	
Mar 17	Swillivant Daniel	2			3	
Mar 17	Swillivant Darby Sen.ʳ tax free				2	
Mar 18	Ball William	3	2	1	6	[line badly faded]
Mar 18	Brooks Thomas	1			1	
Mar 18	Chelkett William	1			3	
Mar 18	Curtice George	2			3	
Mar 18	Donathan Gerrard	1	1	1	3	
Mar 18	Lang Robert	1			2	
Mar 18	Limbrick William	1			2	
Mar 18	Newton Thomas	2	2	1	4	
Mar 18	Pates Aaron	2			2	
Mar 18	Robertson Thomas					
Mar 18	Row John	1			1	
Mar 18	Stone Joseph	2			2	
Mar 18	Stone William	2			3	
Mar 18	White George	1			1	
Mar 19	Bryant John	1		2	3	
Mar 19	Carter George	1			1	
Mar 19	Downman B Joseph	1	8	3	6	
Mar 19	Henson Elijah	2			3	
Mar 19	Hill Jesse	2	3		5	
Mar 19	Hooe Harris Est.	2	7	3	5	
Mar 19	Limbrick Frances	2			3	
Mar 19	Limbrick George	1				
Mar 19	Newton Margrett		2		6	

[arranged by date of tax enumeration]

Mo.	day	chargeable w/tax	white males 16+	/blacks 16+	12+	H	other
Mar	19	Perry Thomas Est.e	1	12	2	12	
Mar	19	Slaven Jesse		1		3	
Mar	19	Strother George	1	9	2	6	
Mar	19	Swillivant Darby Jun.r	1			2	
Mar	19	Washington Geo. Genl	1	8		3	
Mar	20	Berry Sarah	1	1		3	
Mar	20	Butler William	1	1		3	
Mar	20	Cox Charnox	1		1	3	
Mar	20	Cox Presly	1			1	
Mar	20	Edwards Andrew	1	6	1	8	
Mar	20	Fletcher Rachel	1	1		4	
Mar	20	Gollehorn Solomon	1			2	
Mar	20	Payn John	2	1		3	
Mar	20	Pilcher Daniel	1			1	
Mar	20	Pilcher Richard	3			3	
Mar	20	Puzey Stephen	3			1	
Mar	20	Swillivant Darby Y?	1			1	
Mar	20	Swillivant Frances	2	1		4	
Mar	21	Colney Elisha	1			1	
Mar	21	Fitzhugh Henry	2	10	2	5	
Mar	21	Jett George	1				
Mar	21	Jett Presly	1			1	
Mar	21	Lathrum George	3	1		5	
Mar	21	Lowry James Jun.r	2	1		2	
Mar	21	Lowry James Sen.r	1			3	
Mar	21	Sudtherd William	2			1	
Mar	23	Allison Henry	1			1	
Mar	23	Barrett Barth.o	1		1	3	
Mar	23	Berry Richard	1			1	
Mar	23	Brown James	1			2	
Mar	23	Brown William	1			2	
Mar	23	Cox Vincent Sen.r	2			2	
Mar	23	Curtice John	2			4	
Mar	23	Curtice Richard	1			1	
Mar	23	Curtice Theodocius	1				

[arranged by date of tax enumeration]

Mo.	day	chargeable w/tax	white males 16+	/blacks 16+	12+	H	other
Mar	23	Curtice William	1			2	
Mar	23	Gollehorn Thomas	1			2	
Mar	23	Kenny John	2	1		3	
Mar	23	Ketchen William	1				
Mar	23	Leach Andrew	1			1	
Mar	23	Leach Benj.a	4			2	
Mar	23	McGuire Rachel	1			3	
Mar	23	Payton Ann	2			3	
Mar	23	Payton James	2			2	
Mar	23	Robertson John	1	1	1	1	
Mar	24	McFarlen Obed	1			5	1 stud horse
Mar	24	Monday Aaron	1			2	
Mar	26	Bowen Burkett	1	3	2	5	1 stud @ 10/
Mar	27	Groves Thomas	1			2	
Mar	27	Jacobs William	2	3	1	3	
Mar	27	Porch Thomas	1	9	3	8	
Mar	27	Rowley Archebal	1	1		1	
Mar	27	Seydmore Joshua	2			2	
Mar	27	Snelling Enoch	1			2	
Mar	27	Snellings William	1			4	
Mar	27	Waiten James tax free				1	
Mar	28	Anderson John	2			4	
Mar	28	Briggs David	2	12	5	8	
Mar	28	Jones Henry	2	2		3	
Mar	28	Lathrum John	2	1	1	3	
Mar	28	Logy Alexander	1	1		4	
Mar	28	Patterson Perry	1				
Mar	28	Patterson Thomas	1			1	
Mar	28	Roach Robert	3			3	
Mar	28	Weaks George	1	1		2	
Mar	30	Allentharp Jacob	2			4	
Mar	30	Beasly Phillip	1			2	
Mar	30	Berry Anth.o	1			3	
Mar	30	Berry Thomas	2	1	1	2	
Mar	30	Brimmer Isaac	1				

[arranged by date of tax enumeration]

Mo. day chargeable w/tax	white males 16+	/blacks 16+	12+	H	other
Mar	30	Brimmer John	1			1	
Mar	30	Brown Walter	1			3	
Mar	30	Burton James	1			4	
Mar	30	Burton Natha.^l	1			3˙	
Mar	30	Cahal James	1			1	
Mar	30	Conner John	1			3	
Mar	30	Faunt George	1	3	1	4	
Mar	30	Faunt John	1			4	
Mar	30	Horton William	1			3	
Mar	30	Jett William	3			4	
Mar	30	Kerk Jeremiah	1	3	1	3	
Mar	30	Ketchen James	1			4	
Mar	30	Leach James	1	2	1	3	
Mar	30	Limbrick John	1			1	
Mar	30	Martin Charles	2	1		3	
Mar	30	Martin Thomas	1			1	
Mar	30	Newton John	1	5	2	6	
Mar	30	Parmer Rawley	2	1	1	2	
Mar	30	Porch Esum	1	1	2	3	
Mar	30	Sherrett William	1			1	
Mar	30	Smith Henry	2	5	1	8	
Mar	30	Smith John	3	2		6	
Mar	30	Snelling John	1			2	
Mar	30	Snipe Natha^l	1	1		2	
Mar	30	Stripling William	1			2	
Mar	30	Taylor Robert	1				
Mar	30	Thompson John	1			1	
Mar	30	Treslow Benj^a	1			1	
Mar	30	Wallace James		4		2	
Mar	30	Wallace John	2	6		8	
Mar	30	Waugh George	1	18	1	8	1 stud horse
Mar	30	West John	2	2		1	
Apr	4	Buchanan Andrew	2	8	1	7	4 phaet & 2 chr whls
Apr	4	Donavan Joseph	1	2	1	2	
Apr	4	England John	3	1		2	

[arranged by date of tax enumeration]

Mo.	day	chargeable w/tax	white males 16+	/blacks 16+	12+	H	other
Apr	4	Hunter Adam forge	3	47	2	14	
Apr	4	Lavender John Ju.r	1				
Apr	4	Lavender Joseph	1				
Apr	4	Lavender Robrt	1			4	
Apr	4	Newton William	2	9	1	6	
Apr	4	Rogers John	1	1		2	
Apr	4	Rose Jesse	2	1		3	
Apr	4	Wallace Thomas		2			
Apr	4	Young William	1			3	
Apr	8	Alexander Phillip	1	8	3	4	
Apr	8	Bowen Thomas		1		3	
Apr	8	Burton Gerrard	1			3	
Apr	8	Burton William	1			1	
Apr	8	Kenyon James Est.		6	2	8	
Apr	8	Threlkell Jesse	1			1	
Apr	10	Ballard Thomas	1	3		2	
Apr	10	Fitzhugh William	1	54	8	20	4 ph.whls,2chr whls
Apr	10	Jackson William	1			2	
Apr	10	Marquiss Antho	1			2	
Apr	10	Martin Daniel	1			1	
Apr	10	Massey Thomas	1	3		6	
Apr	11	Allison Thomas	1	3		3	
Apr	11	Barbee John	1			1	
Apr	11	Benson James	2	3	1	5	
Apr	11	Benson Zachariah	1				
Apr	11	Bolling Charles	1			1	
Apr	11	Bolling James	3			1	
Apr	11	Bolling Thomas	2			1	
Apr	11	Burton Samuel	2	1		1	
Apr	11	Fitzhugh Thomas	2	25	1	14	4 phaeton whls
Apr	11	Foster Seth	1			3	
Apr	11	Hall John	1			2	
Apr	11	Hefferlin Martin	1			1	
Apr	11	Hord Killis	4	5		5	
Apr	11	Hord Peter	1	2		3	

[arranged by date of tax enumeration]

Mo.	day	chargeable w/tax	white males 16+	/blacks 16+	12+	H	other
Apr	11	Hord Rhoden	2	4		6	
Apr	11	Hudson David	1	1		3	
Apr	11	Jackson Robert	1			4	
Apr	11	Jackson Rosanah	1			3	
Apr	11	Lathrum Anth.o	2			3	
Apr	11	Lathrum George	1			2	
Apr	11	Martin Samuel	2			3	
Apr	11	Mattox Lazarus	2	1		5	
Apr	11	Munrow Daniel	2	2		6	
Apr	11	Munrow William tax free				1	
Apr	11	Musselman Henry	1				
Apr	11	Patterson George	1				
Apr	11	Payne Daniel	2	1	1	1	
Apr	11	Payton John	2			3	
Apr	11	Schooler Thomas	1			3	
Apr	11	Sharp Linsfield	2	8	2	5	
Apr	11	Sharp Thomas	3	5		3	
Apr	11	Smith Samuel	1	5		3	
Apr	11	Spence William tax free				3	
Apr	11	Stringfellow James	2	1	1	4	
Apr	11	Sutor John	1				
Apr	11	Tate William	1			1	
Apr	11	Timmons John	1			3	
Apr	11	Troop Thomas	1			1	
Apr	11	West John	1			4	
Apr	11	West Thomas	1			1	
Apr	11	White Ann		1		1	
Apr	11	White George	1	1		3	
Apr	13	Arrowsmith Thomas	2	1		4	
Apr	13	Carter Joseph	1	2	1	3	
Apr	13	Crop James Jn.r	1	4		6	
Apr	13	Crop James Sen.r	1	3	1	3	
Apr	13	Crop John	1	9	1	6	
Apr	13	Dowdle James	1	5		3	
Apr	13	Humphrys William	3	1	1	6	

[arranged by date of tax enumeration]

Mo.	day	chargeable w/tax	white males 16+	/blacks 16+	12+	H	other
Apr	13	Kerk Jesse	1	1		1	
Apr	13	Laitman Daniel	1	1		4	
Apr	13	Lewis Conyard	1			1	
Apr	13	Linn Simon	1			1	
Apr	13	More Edward	1	6	2	5	
Apr	13	Mortimore Charles		4		2	
Apr	13	Mulbury John	2			2	
Apr	13	Musselman Christian	2			2	
Apr	13	Pollard John Est.^{e}	2	7	2	5	
Apr	13	Stephens Richards	2	1		4	
Apr	13·	Turner Absolum	3			3	
Apr	13	Turner James	2			3	
Apr	19	Patterson Hezekiah	1			1	
Apr	19	Pow Elizabeth				1	
Apr	23	Conyers John	4	3	0	3	
Apr	25	Allison David	2	2	1	1	
Apr	25	Brauder William	2	3	1	3	
Apr	25	Colquohound Walter	1	3		1	
Apr	25	Ditto Hanstead	1	7	2	5	
Apr	25	Faunt Joseph	1	3	1	3	2 chair whls
Apr	25	Fugett Frances Junr	1			2	
Apr	25	Gordon Bazell	2	1		1	
Apr	25	Hunter Adam @ home	3	16	6	9	4 phaeton whls
Apr	25	Lewis Ann		1			
Apr	25	Lucus Leonard	1			1	
Apr	25	McFarlin Walter	1				
Apr	27	Ball John	1			1	
Apr	27	Fennal Jonathan	2	5	1	5	
Apr	27	Harwood Allice	1	1		3	
Apr	27	Henson Sarah				3	
Apr	27	Hewitt Susannah		7	1	3	
Apr	27	Hewitt William	1	13	3	8	
Apr	27	Hore Edward	2	3		6	
Apr	27	Jett Frances	1	2	2	4	
Apr	27	Richards William	3	10	1	5	

Stafford Co., Va. personal property tax list - 1789

[arranged by date of tax enumeration]

Mo.	day	chargeable w/tax	white males 16+	/blacks 16+	12+	H	other
Apr	27	Threlkell George	1			4	
Apr	27	Winlock William	2	4		3	
Apr	28	Banks Francis		8	2	5	
Apr	28	Bolling William	1			1	
Apr	28	Fickling Fielding	1				
Apr	28	Hord Thomas	2	2		5	
Apr	28	Lathrum John	1			1	
Apr	28	Lavender Robert Jun[r]	1			1	
Apr	28	Mannoa (sic) John	1			3	
Apr	28	Manson Auther	4	14	2	14	
Apr	28	Martin Lewis	1			1	
Apr	28	Massey Elizabeth				1	
Apr	28	Massey Taliaferrow	1				
Apr	28	Meal Samuel	1			1	
Apr	28	Turner Benj[a]	1			1	
Apr	28	Webb Aaron tax free				4	
Apr	28	Webb Moses	1			1	
Apr	28	Woodard Mary	1	1		1	
Apr	28	Wright Samuel	1			2	
Apr	29	Barber William	1			1	
Apr	29	Hall Benjamin	1			2	
Apr	29	Hill Leonard	1	5		4	
Apr	29	Horton Charles	1				
Apr	29	Humphrys Daniel	1			1	
Apr	29	James George	2	6		5	
Apr	29	Jones Charles	2	2	1	5	
Apr	29	Jones Evins	3	1		4	
Apr	29	Jones George	1			3	
Apr	29	Jones James	1			4	
Apr	29	Lee James	1			2	
Apr	29	Rogers Robert				1	
Apr	29	Scott Sarah	1			3	
Apr	29	Skinker Thomas	1	6	2	5	
Apr	29	Taylor Samuel	1			1	
Apr	29	Turner Griffin	3			5	

[arranged by date of tax enumeration]

Mo.	day	chargeable w/tax	white males 16+	/blacks 16+	12+	H	other
Apr	30	Devenport William	1	2		1	
Apr	30	Patten Rachel	1	3		2	
Apr	30	Wallace William	1	2	2	3	
Apr	30	Weaks Benjamin	1			3	
Apr	30	Weathers James	4	8	2	8	
Apr	30	Wellford Robert		1		2	
May	1	Buckner Richard	1	4		2	
May	1	Carter Charles		6	1	2	
May	1	Carter Robert Wor	1	17		6	
May	1	Conyers Benjamin	1				
May	1	Cotney John	1	4		4	
May	1	Pilcher John tax free				4	
May	2	Ballard William	1			1	
May	2	Barrett Jacob	1				
May	2	Bates Joseph Tax free				2	
May	2	Bell John	2	4		4	
May	2	Bowers Michal	2	3	2	4	
May	2	Critchett James	1				
May	2	Dunbar Robert	3	4		8	
May	2	Fenton John	1				
May	2	Hany William	2	5		4	
May	2	Lyon James	1				
May	2	Manson Alexander	2	2	1	2	
May	2	McCloud James	1				
May	2	Norwood Joseph	2		1		
May	2	Payn John Jun.ʳ	1				
May	2	Payton Thomas	1	2		2	
May	2	Pilcher Mason	2	6	1	5	
May	2	Puzey Olden	1				
May	2	Selden Samuel	2	35	8	15	4 coach & chrt whls
May	2	Smith John	1				
May	2	Smith John Juʳ	1				
May	2	Speckt Andrew	1				
May	2	Stone William	1				
May	2	Triplett Daniel	3	5	2	1	

[arranged by date of tax enumeration]

Mo. day chargeable w/tax			white males 16+	/blacks 16+	12+	H	other
May	5	Collins Thomas	1	4		5	
May	5	Graves Daniel	1				
May	5	Graves George	1				
May	5	Graves George	1	1	1		
May	5	Graves Polly				3	
May	5	Graves William	3	1		6	
May	5	Hill Henry	1				
May	5	James John	3	14	5	16	
May	5	Lathrum John Sen.ʳ	1	2		4	
May	5	Lee Thomas	2	32	7	20	
May	5	Lotspeak William	2	1		˙2	
May	5	Lunsford Joanah		1		4	
May	5	McCloud John	1				
May	5	McKetterick Anthony	2	10	1	10	2 chair whls
May	5	McMillon William	1				
May	5	Read John		1			
May	5	Read Margrett				1	
May	5	Stipes John	1	1			
May	5	Stringfellow George	1			1	
May	5	Stringfellow Henry	1				
May	5	Stripling Elizabeth		1			
May	5	Taylor William	1	9		3	
May	5	Terrier John	3	1		4	
May	5	Tisly John	1			3	
May	5	Travis Peggy		1			
May	5	Tyler Alice	2	7	1	5	
May	5	Vowles Henry	1	7		2	2 chr whls & ordinary lic.

[arranged by date of tax enumeration]

Mo.	day	chargeable w/tax	white males 16+	/blacks 16+	12+	H	other
May	5	Vowles Richards	2	1		1	2 chair whls
May	9	Ball Burgess		23	1	12	
Jun	6	William Bassell	1			2	
Jun	7	Green Jesse	1			2	

* * * * *

* * *

*

[End of date-arranged 1789 personal property tax list]

Stafford County
Virginia

Personal Property
Tax List

1790

Source: Virginia State Library, Archives Division. County Records. Stafford County Tax lists.

Form of return of taxable property to be made by the commissioners

List No. 1.

A List of the Taxable property within the district of Wm Mountjoy, commissioner in the county of Stafford for the year 1790
[Categories]:

Date of receiving lists from individuals;

Persons names chargeable with the tax;

[col. 1] -	White males above 16 years;
[col. 2] -	Blacks above 16 years;
[col. 3] -	Blacks above 12 & under 16 years;
[col. 4] -	Horses mares colts & mules;
[other] -	Coach & Chariott wheels;

Phaeton & stage wagon wheels;

Chair wheels;

Ordinary licence;

no. of stud horses;

Rates of covering pr season.

List No. 2.

A List of Taxable Property taken in the Year 1790 by William Alexander Commissioner of Stafford County
[Categories]:

Months;

Days;

Proprietor's Names;

[col. 1] -	White tythes;
[col. 2] -	Negro^s 16 upwards;
[col. 3] -	D^o from 12 to 16;
[col. 4] -	Horses;
[other] -	Coach & Char^{lio}t Wheels;

Phaet. & stage wls;

Chairs D.^o;

O*[rdinary]* licences;

B*[illiard]*Tables;

Studs;

Rates pr season;

Doctors;

[folio 1]

A List of the Taxable property within the district of Wᵐ Mountjoy, commissioner in the county of Stafford for the year 1790

Mo.	day	chargeable w/tax	white males 16+	/blacks 16+	12+	H	other
Mar	20	George Abbott	1			1	
Apr	3	Thomas Ambler	2			5	
Apr	5	John Agin	1			1	
Apr	5	Amus Atchison	2			5	
Apr	5	Nathⁿ Atchison	3	2		4	
Apr	5	Halafax Ashby	1			1	
Apr	5	John Atchison	2			1	
Apr	12	Elijah Abbot	1			2	
Apr	12	James Arrosmith	1			3	
Apr	12	Daniel Antrum	3			6	
Apr	12	John Abbot Senʳ (L.free)				3	
May	1	Benjamin Aedy	1	9		5	
Aug	10	Joseph Ambler	1			1	
Aug	28·	Robert Ashby	3			2	
Aug	28	William Aedy	2	9	1	6	
Aug	28	William Anderson	1	1		1	
Mar	20	John Bridges	1			1	
Mar	20	Joseph Brown	2	4	2	5	
Mar	20	James Billingsley	2	3		4	
Mar	20	George Byrum	2			2	
Mar	20	William Bradly	2			3	
Mar	20	John Brown	1			1	
Mar	20	Ge.º Bell Jun.ʳ	1			3	
Mar	27	Ge.º Burroughs	1	3	1	3	
Mar	27	Benj.ᵃ Burroughs	1		2	2	
Mar	27	John Burroughs	1			1	
[folio 2]							
Mar	27	John Banister	1			2	
Apr	3	Philamon Bramit	3			2	

Mo.	day	chargeable w/tax	white males 16+	blacks 16+	12+	H	other
Apr	3	Charles Bradly	1				
Apr	5	John Beagle	3			3	
Apr	5	William Bruce	1			2	
Apr	5	Thomas Beagle	1				
Apr	5	William Byrum	1			1	
Apr	5	John Brooker	1				
Apr	5	Nath.n Banester	2			3	
Apr	5	Jonathan Bell	1			2	
Apr	5	Ge.o Bell Sen.r	1	2		3	
Apr	5	Senate Byrum	1				
Apr	5	Ge.o Bredwell Jun.r	1			4	
Apr	5	Cuthbert Byrum	1			1	
Apr	12	Joseph Botts	2	6		5	
Apr	12	Thomas Barbe (L.free)				2	
Apr	12	William Brown	1			3	
Apr	12	Bazel Burroughs	1			3	
Apr	12	Jacob Bridwell (L.free)				3	
Apr	12	Enough Benson	2	3	1	6	
Apr	12	Uriah Bradshaw	1			4	
Apr	12	William Botts	2	3		3	
Apr	12	William Baul	1	2	1	6	
Apr	12	Mary Ann Burroughs	1	10	1	6	
Apr	12	Fielding Bell	1	1		3	
[folio 3]							
Apr	12	John Browne	1	13	4	7	2 chair wheels
Apr	28	Elijah Bell	1			2	
May	8	William Barnot	1			1	
May	10	Dedreck Benear (L.free)				2	
May	15	James Bridges	2			2	
May	15	Edward Barber	1			2	
Jun	14	George Brent	2	12	1	5	
Jun	14	John Bridwell	2			2	
Jun	14	Ann Brent	1	19	1	9	
Jun	20	John Bruing	2			2	

478   Stafford Co., Va. personal property tax list -1790

Mo.	day	chargeable w/tax	white males 16+	/blacks 16+	H 12+	other
Jul	12	Daniel C. Brent	3	41	8	20
		"				4 coach whls & 2 chr whls.
Jul	17	William Barbee	1			3
Jul	28	Thomas Beach	1			1
Aug	9	Mary Bell		3		2
Aug	9	James Brown	1			1
Aug	14	Jessey Bails	1			1
Aug	14	Ann Botts		5	1	4
Aug	14	William Battoe	1			3
Aug	14	James Battoe (L.free)				2
Aug	14	William Bridwell	1			1
Aug	14	Simon Bridwell	1			1
Aug	14	John Bradly	1			
Aug	19	Spencer Bowlin	1			1
Aug	20	Isaac Branson	1			1
Aug	20	Edward Bethell	1			3
Aug	23	Joseph Barber	1	1		3
Aug	23	Clem Billingsley	1	1		2
Aug	23	Robert Buihan	1	5	1	8
Sep	12	Ge.o Bridwell Sen.r	1			1
Sep	12	George Burns	1			
[folio 4]						
Sep	12	James Barnot	1	1		
Sep	12	Henry Bridwell	1			1
Sep	12	Sam. Bridwell	1			2
Sep	12	William Bridwell	3	3		5
Oct	2	Joel Beagle	2			2
Oct	2	John Bridwell	1			
Oct	2	Moses Bridwell	3	5	1	3
Oct	8	Benj.a Bowlin	1			2
Oct	8	Peter Byrum	1			1
Oct	8	Nimrod Byrum	1			
Oct	8	William Bobo	1			
Oct	8	Rawleigh T. Browne	1	18	3	11
Oct	11	Thomas Bridwell	1			3

Mo.	day	chargeable w/tax	white males 16+	/blacks 16+	12+	H	other
Oct	11	George Bussel	1			2	
Oct	11	Robert Brent	1				
Oct	11	Daniel Brent Jun.ʳ	1				
Oct	11	William Branson	1				
Oct	11	Benjamin Brock	1			3	
Mar	20	James Carter	1		1	2	
Mar	27	Perry Chinn	1			2	
Mar	27	Renn Carter	1	1		1	
Apr	3	Asia Cummins	4			6	
Apr	3	Cuthbert Combs	2	6	1	7	
Apr	5	William Cummins	2			4	
Apr	12	Harris Carter	2			2	
Apr	12	Brian Chadwell	1	2	1	4	
Apr	12	James Cain	1			2	
Apr	12	James Camberford (L.free)				1	
[folio 5]							
Apr	12	John Carney	2	1	2	6	
Apr	12	Jessey Carney	1			1	
Apr	12	William Cole	1			1	
Apr	12	Jedediah Carter	1			3	
Apr	12	Joseph Cooper (L.free)				2	
Apr	28	Jessey Cooper	1			1	
May	10	John Cook	2	28	6	15	
May	10	Catherine Conaway		3	2	3	
May	24	John Carter	1			1	
May	24	Henry Clifton	2	5	2	4	
May	24	George Coats	1	1	1	1	
May	24	Joseph Combs	1	4	1	4	
Jun	14	Charles Carter	1	27	4	15	
Jul	12	Seth Combs	1	9		7	
Aug	9	Williamson Chandler	1	1	1	2	
Aug	19	Elizabeth Chissom	1			3	
Aug	19	John Chiverall	1			1	
Sep	12	Ja.ˢ Cloe Jun.ʳ	1			1	
Sep	12	Elijah Conner	1				

Mo.	day	chargeable w/tax	white males 16+	/blacks 16+	12+	H	other
Oct	2	Peter Cash	1			1	
Oct	2	Ja.S Cloe Sen.r (L.free)	1			1	
Mar	17	Hannah Dickenson	1	5	3	13	
Mar	20	John Dillon				1	
Mar	20	Archabald Douglis	1			6	
Mar	20	John Dorson	1			3	
Mar	20	Bradly Dent	2			2	
Apr	5	Jerremiah Day	1				
Apr	5	Mashack Davis	1			1	
[folio 6]							
Apr	12	Moses Dick	1			1	
Apr	12	John Dalgair	1		1		
Apr	12	Charles Davis	2			1	
Apr	28	Elizabeth Dunaway				1	
Apr	28	Thomas Dunaway	1			2	
May	15	Dennis Doyall Sen.r	1	1		3	
May	15	Dennis Doyall Jun.r	1			1	
Jun	25	Patterson Doyall	1				
Aug	8	John Dunbar	2	1		2	
Aug	13	William Dorson	2			3	
Aug	14	Shadreck Davis	1			3	
Aug	14	Joseph Dunaway	1			2	
Sep	2	Lewis Dishue *[sic]*	1				
Sep	2	William Devene	1				
Sep	2	Christopher Dorson	1			1	
Oct	2	William Dunaway	1			1	
Oct	8	Travers Daniel Jun.r	1	12	2	12	2 chair wheels
Oct	11	John Dilley	2			2	
Oct	11	Travers Daniel Sen.r	1	24	1	1	
Oct	15	Rawleigh W. Downman	1	10	3	6	
Oct	15	Daw & Burn	2	3		1	1 ordinary licence
Mar	27	William Edrington	2	2	4	5	
Mar	27	John Edrington	1			1	
Apr	3	Willis Edwards	1			1	
Apr	5	William Eaton	4			3	

Mo.	day	chargeable w/tax	white males 16+	/blacks 16+	12+	H	other
Apr	5	William Edwards	1	5	1	4	
May	1	Jessey Edwards	2	1	4?		
[folio 7]							
May	10	Isaac Eustace	2	10	3	8	4 phaeton wheels
May	10	Isaac Eavs	1				
Jun	18	John Eshew	1				
Aug	14	Haden Edwards	1	5		4	
Aug	14	Baker Edwards	1			3	
Aug	14	Travers Edwards	1			1	
Mar	20	John H. Foushee	1			1	
Mar	20	William Franklin	1			2	
Mar	27	John Faunt	1			1	
Apr	5	Vintsin Foxworthy	1			1	
Apr	5	Phillip Foxworthy	1			1	
Apr	5	John Fritter	1			2	
Apr	5	William Fritter	1			3	
Apr	5	Reuben Franklin	1		1	2	
Apr	5	Joseph Franklin Jun.r	1			1	
Apr	5	John Franklin L.free				2	
Apr	12	Sam. Faunt	2			4	
Apr	12	Joseph Franklin L.free	1			4	
Apr	12	Anthony Ficklin	2	7	1	6	
Apr	12	Rich.d Fristoe L.free				2	
Apr	12	James Ford	1	3	1	5	
Apr	12	Benj.a Ficklin	1	1		4	
Apr	12	Moses Fritter Jun.r	1			1	
Apr	12	Francis Foushee	2	3		3	
Aug	19	Moses Fritter Sen.r	1			1	
Aug	19	Enough Fritter	1			1	
Aug	19	James Faunt	2			4	
[folio 8]							
Aug	12	John Fitzgerald	1				
Oct	2	Thomas Fristoe	1	1		2	
Oct	2	William Fristoe	3			5	
Oct	2	William Faning	1		1	2	

Mo.	day	chargeable w/tax	white males 16+	/blacks 16+	12+	H	other
Oct	11	William French	2	6	2	8	
Mar	20	John Garrison	2			2	
Mar	20	William Gant	1	1		2	
Mar	20	John Green	1			2	
Mar	27	Phillip Gardner	1	4		4	
Apr	3	Robert Green	2			3	
Apr	3	Elizabeth Garrison				1	
Apr	3	Elijah Green	1				
Apr	5	John Gie	1			3	
Apr	5	Hannah Gough	1	1		3	
Apr	12	William Groves	1			2	
Apr	12	Moses Grigsby Sen.ʳ	1			1	
Apr	12	Elisha Grigsby	1		1	2	
Apr	12	James Gough	1		2	1	
Apr	12	Isaac Gaskins	1	1		3	
Apr	12	George Garrison	3			2	
May	15	George Green	1	1		2	
May	24	Benjamin Gie	1			1	
May	24	William Gie	4			5	
Jun	14	Mary Garrard	2	10		3	
Jun	20	Sollomon Gollohorn	1			2	
Aug	9	William Gollohorn	1			4	
Aug	13	Aaron Garrison	1				
[folio 9]							
Aug	14	John Grigsby	1			1	
Aug	20	John Grey	1			2	
Aug	20	Sam. Groves	1	1		3	
Aug	31	Ann Gaddis	1	5		4	
Aug	31	Moses Grigs Jun.ʳ	1				
Aug	31	William George	1				
Oct	2	Benjamin Grigory	1			3	
Oct	2	John Gun	1			2	
Mar	20	William Hore [Hoie?]	1		1	1	
Mar	20	Peter Hansbrough	1	1	2	3	
Mar	20	Lidia Hansbrough		1	1	2	

Mo.	day	chargeable w/tax	white males 16+	/blacks 16+	12+	H	other
Mar	27	William Harding	5	2	1	7	
Mar	27	John Harding	1	1		4	
Apr	3	George Holloway	2			1	
Apr	5	Thomas Harding	1		1	3	
Apr	12	Henry Hiden	1			2	
Apr	12	Isaac Holloway	1			1	
Apr	12	John Holloway Sen.ʳ	4			4	
Apr	12	Asia Holloway	2			4	
Apr	12	Thomas Hay L.free	2			4	
Apr	12	William Holloday	1	1		3	
Apr	12	Causom Horton	2			2	
Apr	12	George Harding	1		1	2	
Apr	12	Sam. Hudson	1	2		3	
Apr	12	John Hore	1	2		1	
Apr	12	John S. Harding	2			3	
Apr	12	Thomas Heth L.free		1			
[folio 10]							
May	15	Cuthbert Harding	1			2	
Aug	14	John Hardy	1	8	2	8	
Aug	16	John Hedgman	1	16	5	5	
Aug	20	John Horton	2	7		8	
Aug	20	Henry Horton	1			1	
Aug	20	Elijah Horton	1			4	
Aug	20	James Horton	1			3	
Aug	21	William Harrod	2			3	
Aug	21	William Hereford	1	1		1	2 chair wheels
Aug	21	Thomas Hereford	1	7		4	
Aug	21	Isaac Holloway	1			2	
Aug	21	Mary Hore		7		3	
Aug	21	Elias Hore	1	1		1	
Aug	21	James Hore	1	2	1	4	
Oct	11	John Holloway Jun.ʳ	2			6	
Mar	20	William Jones	3			3	1 stud horse
Apr	5	Charles Jones	1				
Apr	12	Gabril Jones	2	4		5	

Mo.	day	chargeable w/tax	white males 16+	/blacks 16+	12+	H	other
Apr	12	John Jones	1			1	
Apr	12	John Jones	2			6	
Apr	12	David Jones	1	1		2	
Apr	12	Alexander Jameson	2			1	
Apr	15	John Jameson	1				
Aug	14	Elizabeth Jones				1	
Aug	14	John Johnston	1			1	
Aug	14	George Johnston	1			1	
Aug	14	Steaphen Johnston	1			2	
Aug	14	William Jones	1				
[folio 11]							
Mar	27	Christopher Knight	1			4	
Apr	3	John Knight Sen.r	1			1	
Apr	3	Charles Kendall	1	2	2	2	
Apr	5	Josua Kendall Sen.r	1	4	1	4	
Apr	5	Henry Kendall	1	1	1	4	
Apr	12	Merryman Ketchen	2	1	1	2	
Apr	12	Anthony Kendall	1			3	
Apr	12	Uriah Knight	1			2	
Apr	12	Peter Knight Sen.r	3	1		5	
Apr	12	Peter Knight Jun.r	1	1	1	2	
Apr	12	Daniel Kendall	1	1		2	
May	10	Jessy Kendall	1			4	
May	10	John Kendall	3	3	2	7	
May	10	Jerremiah Knight	2	1		5	
Aug	19	Sarah Kirk	1			1	
Aug	20	James Kendall	1			1	
Aug	20	Aaron Kendall	1		1	1	
Aug	20	Ephraem Knight	1			2	
Aug	21	Josua Kendall Jun.r	1			2	
Aug	21	Thomas Kenney	1	1		1	
Mar	28	Gaven Lawson	2	17	4	15	4 phaeton wheels
Apr	5	John Latham Sen.r	1			3	
Apr	12	Snodon Latham	2			2	
Apr	12	Francis Linum	1				

Mo.	day	chargeable w/tax	white males 16+	/blacks 16+	12+	H	other
Apr	12	John Lawlis	1			3	
May	10	John Lunsford	1	1		3	
May	15	Charles Latham	1			1	
[folio 12]							
Jun	15	Dennis Linum	1				
Aug	14	Moses Lunsford	1			2	
Aug	14	Anthony Long	1			2	
Mar	20	Richard Morton	1	1		1	
Mar	27	Henry McEntire	1	1	1	2	
Apr	3	Allen Mountjoy	4			4	
Apr	3	Ewel Mason	1			1	
Apr	5	Richard Mason	1	1		5	
Apr	5	Lewis Mason	1		1	4	
Apr	12	James More	1			1	
Apr	12	Edward Mountjoy	2			6	
Apr	12	Peter Mauzy Jun.ʳ	1	1		4	
Apr	12	John Murray	1	7		4	
Apr	12	William Mullin	3	5	1	7	
Apr	12	Robert Melion	2	1		5	
Apr	12	Alexand McEntire	1	3		3	
Apr	12	Daniel Mason	3	2	2	5	
Apr	28	Ann Moncure	1	10	2	6	
May	8	William Mauzy	1	2		4	
May	8	John F. Mercer	1	47	6	18	
May	10	Charles Martin	1			1	
May	23	Thomas Mountjoy	1	8	2	6	2 chair wheels
Jun	2	Thomas Mallery	1			1	
Jun	2	Mary McDaniel				1	
Jun	2	Charles Mifflin L.free				2	
Jul	12	William Mountjoy	1	5	1	5	
Aug	9	Ursly Morton		3	1	2	
Aug	9	James McBride	1			1	
[folio 13]							
Aug	10	John Markham	1	5	2	3	
Aug	13	William Melion	1			2	

Stafford Co., Va. personal property tax list -1790

Mo.	day	chargeable w/tax	white males 16+	/blacks 16+	12+	H	other
Aug	13	Benjamin Melion	3			2	
Aug	24	William Monroe	1	2		2	
Aug	24	John Mountjoy	1		1	2	
Oct	8	Peter Mauzy Sen.r		2	1	3	
Oct	8	John Mountjoy	1	6	1	9	
Oct	10	John Mason	1	4		5	
Oct	10	John Minton	1		1	1	
Oct	10	Robert B. Morton	1	11		4	
Apr	12	Mary Nelson		1		1	
Apr	12	Edward Normon	1	3	3	7	
Apr	12	George Normon	1	3		6	
May	22	Charles Nixon	1			1	
Aug	9	John Nicholson	1			1	
May	18	James Oglesby	1			1	
Aug	20	Hezekiah Ollover	1	1		3	
Oct	10	Elizabeth Overall		6		4	
Mar	20	James Primm	1	1		3	
Mar	20	Thomas Powell	1			1	
Mar	20	William Phillips	1	7	1	6	
Mar	27	Thomas Porter	1	3	1	5	
Apr	3	Moses Poats	1			4	
Apr	5	Wharton Philbert	1			1	
Apr	12	Robert Painter	2			4	
Apr	12	Charles Porter	2	2		3	
[folio 14]							
Apr	12	William Poats	2		1	4	
May	8	William Payn	1			3	
May	8	Kelley Payn	1			1	
May	8	Ezekiel Payn	1			2	
May	8	Jessey Payn	1			1	
May	8	James Payn	1			2	
May	8	Mary Ann Payn				1	
May	10	Benjamin Pritchett	2	3		9	
May	15	Margaret Primm				3	
May	15	John Primm	1	1	1?	3	

Mo.	day	chargeable w/tax	white males 16+	/blacks 16+	12+	H	other
May	15	Elizabeth Peyton	3	9	1	8	
May	24	Richard Poats	1		1	4	
Jun	8	Colvert Porter	1			1	
Aug	9	Peter Pilcher	1			2	
Aug	13	William Pattin	1				
Aug	13	Edward Pearson	1			2	
Aug	14	James Peak	1				
Aug	18	Sam. Parker	1			2	
Aug	18	John R. Peyton	1	13	1	9	
Aug	18	John Payn	1				
Aug	18	Linzey Pollard	1				
Oct	8	Francis Payn	1				
Oct	8	John Poats	1	1	1	3	
Oct	8	Vallentine Peyton	2	10	1	5	
Mar	20	Jessey Riley	1			2	
Mar	20	James Riley	1			1	
Mar	20	Richard Ratliff	1		2	4	
[folio 15]							
Mar	20	Butler Reimy	1			2	
Apr	12	William Rout	1	1	1	4	
Apr	12	Joel Readish	2	4	2	7	
Apr	12	William Randol	3	1		4	
Apr	12	James Robeson	1			1	
Apr	12	Richard Reid	1		1	3	
Apr	12	Aaron Reid	1			3	
Apr	12	John Randol	1				
Apr	12	Mary Ann Ralls		4		2	
Apr	12	John Richards	1			1	
Apr	29	William Richards	1	1		2	
May	10	John Rogers	2	1		3	
May	10	Benjamin Rogers	1			2	
May	10	Ann Rogers				2	
May	10	George Randol	2			1	
Apr	24	Thomas Right	3	2	2	6	
Jun	14	Baily Riley	2			4	

Mo.	day	chargeable w/tax	white males 16+	/blacks 16+	12+	H	other
Jun	14	William Robeson	3			2	
Jun	14	Rawling Ralls	1	1	2	2	
Jun	14	Charles Ralls	2	3	1	4	
Aug	5	John R. Rawlins	1			2	
Aug	9	Kenez Ralls	2	1		1	
Aug	19	John Rankings	1	1		1	
Aug	19	Thomas Rakestraw	1				
Oct	8	William Ross	1	3		5	
Oct	8	Joseph Readish	2	3	1	3	
Oct	8	Reuben Rogers	1			1	
Oct	10	Jonathan Reid	1			3	
Oct	10	Joseph Rogers	1				

[folio 16]

Mo.	day	chargeable w/tax	white males 16+	/blacks 16+	12+	H	other
Oct	10	Hepbron Ralls	1			2	
Oct	15	William Right	1			3	
Mar	17	Thomas Sedden	1	13	4	9	
Mar	20	Jane Silvey	1			2	
Mar	20	William Shacklett	3	1		3	
Mar	27	Richard Sims Junr	2			5	
Mar	27	George Shelton	1			2	
Mar	27	Francis Stern	1	4	3	4	
Mar	27	Abigale Shelton	1			3	
Mar	27	Jerremaih Stark	2	2		5	
Mar	27	Wilson Shelton	1			3	
Apr	3	Richard Stone	1	3	4	4	
Apr	3	Rhoadnum Sims	2			3	
Apr	3	James Sims	1			2	
Apr	5	Sarsfield Snoxall	1			2	
Apr	5	William Stark	1	1	1	3	
Apr	5	Richard Sims L.free	1			3	
Apr	12	Nath.^{n} Smith	1	1		2	
Apr	12	Gabrel Sullaven	2			4	
Apr	12	John Smith	2			1	
Apr	12	John Stark	1			1	
Apr	12	Hannah Stark	1	1		2	

Mo.	day	chargeable w/tax	white males 16+	/blacks 16+	12+	H	other
Apr	12	Charles Stern	1	1	1	2	
Apr	12	Charles Stuart	1	6	1	6	
Apr	12	John Stark Sen.ʳ	2	1		3	
Apr	12	Henry Sudduth	1			2	
Apr	12	Hawkin Stone	1	5	2	6	
Apr	12	John Shelket	1	1		4	
[folio 17]							
Apr	12	William B. Stone	2	5	3	7	
Apr	12	Thomas Sudduth	1			1	
May	8	John Snoxall	1			2	
May	8	Moses Sudduth	1			1	
May	10	William Shelton	2			4	
May	10	John Stern	1	2		3	
May	10	Joseph Slaughter	1				
May	15	William Stark	1	1	1	3	
Aug	9	Edward Snoxall	1			3	
Aug	14	Josias Stone	1	5		4	2 chair wheels
Aug	14	John Stark		4		2	
Aug	20	Ezekiel Skinner	1			1	
Oct	8	Presly Sims	1			1	
Oct	15	Jessey Stone	3			3	
Mar	17	Richard Taylor	1			2	
Apr	12	William Tolson	1	1		3	
Apr	12	Sam. Thompson	1	2		6	
Apr	12	Alexander Taylor	3			2	
Apr	12	Benjamin Tolson	1	1	2	4	
Apr	12	John Tuttle	1			1	
May	10	John Tharp L.free				1	
May	10	Charles Thornton	1			1	
May	10	Thomas Tennant	1		1	3	
Aug	13	Joanna Tolson	1	1		1	
Aug	13	Elizabeth Tolson		1		6	
Aug	20	Edward Templeman	2			3	
Aug	21	Elijah Thompson	1	1		4	
[folio 18]							

Mo.	day	chargeable w/tax	white males 16+	/blacks 16+	H 12+		other
Aug	28	Allen Thomas	1			2	
Aug	28	Jessey Taylor	1				
Aug	28	Tho.ˢ G. Tyler	2	3	2	5	
Aug	28	Elijah Threlkeld	2	13	3	11	
Oct	8	Thomas Tolsen [sic]	1			1	
Oct	11	Hannah Taylor		4	2	5	2 chair wheels
Aug	19	Frances Underwood	1			1	
Aug	8	Ann Vaughan				3	
Mar	20	Jessey Woodgerd	1			1	
Mar	20	Benjamin Withers	1			3	
Apr	3	William Williams	1			2	
Apr	3	Allen Way	1			1?	
Apr	5	John Walters	1			1	
Apr	5	Peter Walters	1			3	
Apr	12	William Williams	1			1	
Apr	12	John Walters Sen.ʳ	2	3		4	
Apr	12	Charles Walters	1			2	
Apr	12	Mark Walters L.free		1		4	
Apr	12	Baily Walters	1			1	
Apr	12	William West	1			3	
Apr	12	John West	1				
Apr	12	Thomas Wells	1			1	
Apr	12	George Wells	3	3		4	
May	8	John Whitfield	1				
[folio 19]							
May	10	George Withers	1	3		2	
May	24	Margaret Williams	1	3	1	5	
May	24	Nath.ⁿ Williams	1	7	3	3	
May	26	Barsheba Waller				2	
May	26	Mary Waller		2	2	5	
Jun	14	George Williams	1	6	1	2	
Jun	14	Richard Walker	1	1		4	
Jun	14	John Withers	1	12	4	9	
Jul	2	William Waller	3	4	3	7	
Aug	9	Baily Washington Jun.ʳ	2	22	4	10	4 phaeton wheels

Mo.	day	chargeable w/tax	white males 16+	/blacks 16+	12+	H	other
Aug	13	Henry Woodgerd	1			2	
Aug	13	William West	1			6	
Aug	13	William Watson	3			1	
Aug	20	James Walker	1			1	
Aug	20	Susanah Wormsly		1		3	
Aug	21	John Walters	1			3	
Oct	10	Augustin Weadon	1		1	3	
Oct	15	George Walters	1			4	
Oct	15	John Warren	1			2	
Aug	9	William Young	1			1	
		Totals	161	868	201	1459	

[End of Mountjoy's returns]

[folio 20]

A List of Taxable Property taken in the Year 1790 by*[William]* Alexander commissioner of Stafford County

Mo.	day	chargeable w/tax	white males 16+	/blacks 16+	12+	H	other
Mar	10	William Alexander	1	21	6	20	4 phaeton wheels
Mar	10	Ditto Casson's Est.[a]					
Mar	20	Allison Henry	1				
Apr	5	Alexander Philip's Est.[a]	1	10	2	5	
Apr	12	Alexander W[m] Scho*[Blurred]*				4	
Apr	12	Arrowsmith Thomas	3	1		5	
Apr	12	Anderson John	1			3	
May	4	Allison Thomas	1	4	2	4	
May	22	Allison David	2	2	1	1	
Jun	14	Anderson John				3	
Jun	19	Adams John	1			1	
Mar	20	Ball William	2	3		4	
Mar	20	Burton Gerrard	1			2	
Mar	20	Black Margrett	1			6	
Mar	20	Berry Rich.[d]	1			1	
[ink stain]		Bruce William	3	2		4	
?	?	Butler William	1	1	1	4	
Mar	29	Brissus Isaac	1				
Mar	29	Burnett William	3	3		6	
Apr	5	Bensen John			1	1	
Apr	7	Brooks Margrett		1		1	
Apr	9	Bryant John	2	2	1	3	
Apr	9	Bates Joseph	1			2	
Apr	9	Benson Zachariah	1				
Apr	9	Berry William		1		2	
Apr	11	Brown James	1			3	
Apr	11	Brown William	2			4	
Apr	11	Bolling James	3			3	
Apr	12	Bolling Charles	1			1	
Apr	12	Berry Anthony	1			4	
Apr	12	Berry Thomas	2	1	2	3	
Apr	12	Buckner Richard	1	4		2	

Mo.	day	chargeable w/tax	white males 16+	/blacks 16+	12+	H	other
[folio 21]							
Apr	16	Buchanan Andrew	1	9	1	7	2 chair wheels
Apr	16	Ditto Hooe's Est.[a]		7	1	3	
May	1	Bridges David	1	1	1	6	
May	1	Robert Branhams	1	2		1	
May	1	Benson James	2	4	1	8	
May	1	Bridges William	1				
May	1	Burton Samuel	2	1		1	
May	1	Ballard Thomas	2	3	1	3	
May	1	Bowen Burkitt	1	3	2	5	
May	1	Bowens Michal	2	2		5	
May	22	Briggs David	1	11	2	9	
May	22	Bell John	3	3	1	5	
May	22	Beasly Phillip	1			1	
May	25	Burton William	1			1	
Jun	14	Brown Walter	2			3	
Jun	25	Ball Burgess	2	26	4	12	
		"					4coach whls & 4 phaeton whls
Jul	14	Brimmer John	1			1	
Jul	14	Bussell Benjamin	1	1'		4	
Jul	14	Bolling Thomas	2			7	
Jul	15	Banks Fran.[s]		8		5	2 chair whls
Jul	15	Brimmer Isaac	1				
Jul	15	Burton Nath.[l]	1	1		4	
Jul	15	Barbe *[sic]* John	1			1	
Jul	15	Barber William	1			1	
Jul	15	Burton Samuel	1	1		1	
Jul	15	Bolling William	1			1	
Mar	20	Curtice Richard	1			1	
Mar	20	Curtice John	2			4	
Mar	20	Cox John	1			2	
Mar	24	Carter Henry	2			2	
Mar	29	Curtice George	2			3	
Mar	29	Chinn Joseph	1			2	
Mar	29	Clemmons John	1	1		3	
Mar	31	Chilton William	2			2	
Apr	7	Curtice Aaron	2				
[folio 22]							
Apr	7	Cox George	1			5?	

Mo.	day	chargeable w/tax	white males 16+	/blacks 16+	12+	H	other
Apr	7	Cox Presley	1			1	
Apr	9	Cox Vincent Sen.ʳ	2			3	
Apr	9	Cox Vincent Jun.ʳ	1	1		2	
Apr	9	Cashal James	1			1	
Apr	9	Conyers John	4	3	1	4	
Apr	9	Conyers Benj.ᵃ	1				
Apr	12	Carter Joseph	1	2	1	4	
Apr	12	Conner John	1			2	
Apr	12	Crop James Jun.ʳ	1	5	2	6	
Apr	12	Crop James Sen.ʳ	1	4	1	4	
Apr	12	Callender Phillip	1			4	
Apr	19	Curtice William	1			3	
Apr	19	Curtice Thad.ˢ	1			1	
May	1	Colney Elijah	1		1	2	
May	8	Citchen William	1				
May	22	Collins Tho.ˢ	1	5	1	4	
Jun	19	Colquhoun Walter	1	3		1	
Jul	14	Colney Elijah	1			1	
Jul	15	Crop John	1	7	1	9	
Jul	16	Colney George	1	3		4	
Jul	16	Corbin Henry	1			2	
Jul	16	Carter Robert	1	17		5	
Apr	12	Devenport William	1	1	1	1	
May	1	Dowdle James	2	6		5	
May	22	Dunbar Robert	3	2	1	10	
May	22	Day John	2	1			
May	22	Day Elizabeth		1		1	
Jun	21	Downman B Joseph	1	10	4	8	
Jul	14	Danovan James	1	3	2	4	
Jul	15	David John	1				
Mar	20	Edwards James	1				
Apr	12	England John	2			5	
[folio 23]							
Mar	31	Fines Patrick	1	?		2	
Mar	31	Fugett Benjamin	1			2	
Mar	31	Fugett Francis Jun.ʳ				2	
Mar	31	Fugett Daniel	1			2	
Apr	9	Fennal Jonathan	2	7		5	
Apr	12	[surname faded] John	2			3	

Mo.	day	chargeable w/tax	white males 16+	/blacks 16+	12+	H	other
Apr	12	Fields Samuel	1				
Apr	12	Fitzhugh Thomas	2	28	1	12	4 phaeton wheels
Apr	21	Fitzhugh John	4	15	1	9	
Apr	21	Fitzhugh Henry	2	7	2	7	1 stud horse @ 1.
May	1	Faunt George	1	3	1	4	
May	25	Fitzhugh William	1	55	8	22	
		"	4phaeton whls,2chr whls & 1 stud @1.4				
Jul	13	Fox Natha.¹	1	5	3	12	2 chair wheels
Jul	15	Fickling Fielding	1				
Jul	16	Follis Thomas	1			1	
Jul	16	Faunt Joseph	1	2	1	3	2 chair wheels
Jul	16	Fugett Francis	1			2	
Mar	20	Gollehorne Soloman	1			3	
Mar	20	Gollihorn Thomas	1			2	
Mar	29	Garner John	1			2	
Mar	29	Garner William	2			2	
Apr	12	Graves William	3	1		5	
Apr	12	Gullery Thomas	1			1	
Apr	20	Graves Catharine	1			2	
May	22	Gordon Samuel	2	1		1	
Jul	14	Graves Daniel	1				
Jul	14	Graves Polly				3	
Jul	14	Graves George	1				
Jul	16	Gum Epram free neg.	1				
Jul	16	Green Jesse	1			1	
[folio 24]							
Mar	20	Henson Elijah	2			2	
Apr	12	Hord Kellis	4	6	1	5	
Apr	12	Hill Jesse	2	3		4	
Apr	12	Hord Peter	2	2		4	
Apr	12	Humphrys William	3	2		6	
Apr	16	Hooe Robt	2	3		4	
Apr	20	Hinson Sarah	1			3	
May	1	Hord James	1	7	1	7	
May	1	Hudson David	1			1	
May	1	Humphrys Daniel	1			1	
May	1	Hall Benjamin	1			1	
May	22	Hany William	2	2		4	
May	22	Hill Henry	1				

Mo.	day	chargeable w/tax	white males 16+	/blacks 16+	12+	H	other
Jun	19	Horton William	1			4	
Jul	14	Hudson Elizabeth		1			
Jul	15	Hore Edward	2	2		6	
Jul	15	Hall John	1			1	
Jul	15	Hill Jelly & sisters				2	
Jul	16	Hickerson Joseph	1			2	
Jul	16	Horton Charles	1				
Jul	16	Hord Thomas	1	1		5	
Jul	16	Hord Rhodan	2	3		6	
Jul	16	Heffertin Martin	1			1	
Jul	16	Hill Leonard	1	6		3	
Jul	16	Harwood Allice	1	1		3	
Jul	17	Hewett William	1	14	1	11	
Jul	17	Adam Hunter forge	2	44	3	12	2 chair wheels
Jul	17	Ditto @ home	3	24	6	14	4 phaeton wheels
Jul	17	Hewett Susanna		7	1	5	
[folio 25]							
Mar	20	Jett Presly	1			2	
Mar	29	Jones George	1				
Mar	31	Jones John	1	1		1	
Apr	3	Jones Henry	3		1	3	
Apr	12	Jett William	3			3	
Apr	12	Jackson Robert	2			3	
Apr	12	Jackson Rosana				3	
Apr	12	Jackson William	1			2	
Apr	20	James John	3	14	3	17	
Apr	20	Jacobs William	2	3	1	2	
Apr	20	Jacobs Robert	1			1	
Apr	20	Jett George	1			1	
May	1	Jones George	1			3	
May	1	Jones Evin	2	1		3	
May	1	Jones Charles	1	2	1	4	
May	8	Jett Francis	2	2	2	5	
Jul	16	James George	1	6	1	4	
Mar	20	Kenney John	1			3	
Apr	9	Kitchen Charles	2			5	
Apr	12	Kenny Andrew	2			1	
May	8	Kitchen William	1				
Jul	14	Kenny John Jun.r	1			1	

Mo.	day	chargeable w/tax	white males 16+	/blacks 16+	12+	H	other
Mar	20	Leach Benjamin	1			3	
Mar	20	Lang James	2			1	
Mar	20	Lang Robert	1	1	1	4	
Mar	20	Leach Andrew	2			2	
Mar	20	Limbrick George	1			1	
Mar	20	Limbrick Francis	2			3	
Mar	31	Limbrick William	1			2	
Apr	12	Leach James	1	1	1	3	
Apr	12	Latham John	1	2		5	
Apr	12	Lowry James Jun.ʳ	1			2	
[folio 26]							
Apr	12	Lowry James Tax free				2	
Apr	12	Latham John	1	2		3	
Apr	20	Lee L. Thomas	2	30	9	20	
May	1	Lathum Anthony	2			3	
May	22	Lewis Conrod	1			1	
May	22	Lotspeck William	2			1	
May	22	Lyon James	1			1	
May	22	Lucas John	1				
Jun	14	Legy Alexander	1	1	1	4	
Jun	14	Lathum George	2	1		4	
Jul	12	Lavender Robert	1			1	
Jul	14	Lavender Robert Jun.ʳ	2			3	
Jul	14	Lathum John	1			1	
Jul	16	Lunsford Toahan [?]		1		4	
Jul	16	Lewis Ann				2	
Jul	16	Limbrick John	1			1	
Mar	20	McGuire Rachel	2			3	
Mar	20	Moss John	1				
Mar	29	Miner Elizabeth		1	1	1	
Mar	31	Monday Aaron	1			2	
Apr	12	Massey Thomas	2	4		6	
Apr	12	Martin Thomas	1			1	
Apr	12	Munrow William Tax free			1		
Apr	12	Martin Samuel	2			3	
Apr	12	Moreland Thomas	1		1	2	
Apr	12	McFarlin Obed	1			3	
Apr	12	Musselman Christian	3			3	
Apr	12	Martin Charles	2			4	

Mo.	day	chargeable w/tax	white males 16+	/blacks 16+ 12+		H	other
Apr	12	Munrow Daniel	1	1		2	
Apr	12	Martin Charles	1			1	
Apr	12	McCulluck John	1			2	
May	1	Meals Samuel	1			1	
May	1	Martin Lewis	1			1	
May	5	Mortimer Charls		4		2	
[folio 27]							
May	22	McCloud James	2	1			
May	22	McCloud John	1				
May	22	McMillion William	1				
Jun	19	Mauson Alexander	2	2	1	2	
Jun	25	McKetterick Anthony	1	9	1	9	
Jul	14	Marquess Anthony	1			1	
Jul	15	Mulberry John	1			1	
Jul	15	More Edward	2	7	2	5	
Jul	15	Martin Daniel	1			1	
Jul	15	Monnon John	1			3	
Jul	15	Massey Taliafero	1			1	
Jul	15	Munrow William	1				
Jul	15	Mauson Auther	3	15	2	14	
Jul	16	Monteath Jas.	1	1	1	2	
Mar	29	Nooe Zepheniah	1	3	2	6	2 chair wheels
Apr	9	Nash Philip	1			1	
Apr	12	Newton John	2	6	1	5	
Apr	16	Newton Margrett		2		4	
Apr	16	Newton Isaac	1	7		5	
Apr	16	Newton Thomas	1	4		6	
Jul	14	Norwood Joseph	1		1		
Jul	14	Normon William	1				
[folio 28]							
Mar	20	Payton Charles	1			2	
Mar	20	Payton Ann	2	1	1	2	
Mar	20	Payne John	2			3	
Mar	20	Pilcher Daniel	1			1	
Mar	29	Payne Thomas	1	1		2	
Mar	31	Pilcher Moses	3	2		3	
Mar	31	Pilcher Mildred		1	1	1	
Mar	31	Pusee James	1			1	
Mar	31	Pates Aaron	1			1	

Mo.	day	chargeable w/tax	white males 16+	/blacks 16+	12+	H	other
Mar	31	Payton James	1			1	
Mar	31	Pates Lewis	1				
Apr	7	Pates Allice	1			3	
Apr	9	Pilcher Richard	3			4	
Apr	9	Pusee Stephen	3			1	
Apr	12	Pettett Benjamin	2	1		3	
Apr	12	Patterson George	1			1	
May	1	Patterson Perry W^m	1				
May	1	Patterson Thomas	2			1	
May	1	Pattin John	1			1	
May	8	Thos Porch	1	11	2	8	
May	22	Payn Daniel	2	2		1	
May	26	Pilcher John Tax free				4	
May	14	Payner John Junr	1				
May	14	Paxton John	1			3	
May	28	Posey Thos Col.^o	1	13		28	
Jul	15	Payton Thomas	1	2		2	
Jul	15	Payne John	1				
Jul	15	Porch Esom	1	3		3	
Jul	16	Patterson Hezekiah	1			1	
Jul	16	Parmes Raughley	2	1	1	2	
Jul	16	Pon Elizabeth				1	
Jul	16	Pattin Rachell	1	1		2	
Jul	16	Pilcher Barsheba		6	1	5	
[folio 29]							
Mar	20	Rowley Archibal	2			1	
Mar	20	Robertson Thomas	2			2	
May	12	Ransdal John	1				
May	12	Rowley Archibal	1	1		1	
Jun	19	Richards William	4	10	4	7	
Jul	14	Rose Jesse	1	1		2	
Jul	14	Rose William	1			2	
Jul	14	Robertson George	1				
Jul	15	Read John		1			
Jul	15	Rogers Nancy				1	
Jul	15	Rogers Robert				2	
Jul	15	Rawley Michal	1				
Jul	15	Rogers John forge	1	3		3	
Jul	15	Rogers John	1			1	

Stafford Co., Va. personal property tax list -1790

Mo.	day	chargeable w/tax	white males 16+	blacks 16+	12+	H	other
Jul	15	Row John	1			1	
Mar	20	Souillivant Darby young	1			1	
Mar	20	Snellings Enoch	1			2	
Mar	20	Snellings William	1			3	
Mar	20	Souillivant Daniel	1	1		2	
Mar	20	Souillivant Benj.^a	1			4	
Mar	20	Souillivant Darby Tax free			1		
Mar	20	Souillivant Darby Jn.^r	1			2	
Mar	29	Souillivant Lettice				3	
Mar	31	Stone William	1	1		3	
Mar	31	Stone Joseph	2			2	
Apr	9	Souillivant Fran^s	1	1		4	
Apr	12	Smith John	2	2		5	
Apr	12	Sharp Linsfield	2	7	2	5	
Apr	12	Spence William Tax free	1			3	
Apr	12	Smith Henry	3	4		3	
Apr	12	Suton John	2			2	
Apr	12	Stripling Joel	1			1	
Apr	12	Stripling Thomas	1			1	

[folio 30]

Mo.	day	chargeable w/tax	white males 16+	blacks 16+	12+	H	other
Apr	12	Suddon John	2	13	1	8	
Apr	16	Strother George	3	10	1	9	
Apr	16	Snellings John	1			1	
Apr	20	Selden Samuel	3	38	6	15	4 phaeton wheels
Apr	20	Seydmore Joshua	1		1	1	
Apr	20	Sudthard William	2			1	
May	1	Stringfellow Townshand	1			1	
May	1	Sharp Thomas J^r	3	4	1	3	
May	22	Sudthard William	1				
May	22	Sanders James	1			1	
Jun	14	Smith Joseph	1	5	2	4	
May	28	Scott Sarah	1		1	1	
Jul	14	Schooler Thomas	2			3	
Jul	14	Snipe Nathl	1			3	
Jul	15	Smith John Junr	1				
Jul	15	Stephens Richard	2	2		3	
Jul	15	Smith John free Negro	1				
Jul	15	Samuel Smith	3	4		3	
Jul	15	Sutor William	1				

Mo.	day	chargeable w/tax	white males 16+	/blacks 16+	12+	H	other
Jul	16	Simpson John	1				
Jul	16	Skinker Thomas	1	6	3	5	
Jul	16	Stringfellow George	1				
Mar	29	Templeman Moses	1				
Apr	7	Templeman Jane				3	
Apr	9	Terrur John	3	1		3	
Apr	9	Turner Wm Griffin	3			5	
Apr	9	Turner Absolum	3			5	
Apr	20	Tyler Allice	2	8	1	6	
Apr	20	Tesly John	1			3	
May	1	Temmons John	1			3	
May	1	Truslow Benjamin	1			1	
May	26	Triplett Daniel	3	6	2	2	4 phaeton wheels
May	26	Taylor Robert	1				
[folio 31]							
May	25	Threlkeld Jesse	1			1	
Jun	9	Travis Margrett		1			
Jul	14	Threkell [sic] George	1			3	
Jul	15	Turner James	2			2	
Jul	15	Turner Benjamin	1			1	
Jul	16	Taylor Samuel	1			2	
Jul	16	Troop Thomas	2			1	
Jul	16	Tate William	1			1	
Jul	20	Taylor William		4			
May	22	Vowles Zachariah	2	1		1	
Jun	19	Vowles Henry	1	8	1	1	2 chair wheels
Mar	20	Walker Thomas	2	4	1	3	
Mar	24	Waugh McCagby	2			4	
Mar	29	Wisharts Esta		5		5	
Apr	12	West John Junr	2	1		2	
Apr	12	White George	1	1		3	
Apr	12	Weaks George	2			2	
Apr	12	William Walker	3	3	1	3	
Apr	12	Waugh Lee George	2	17	1	9	
May	1	Wright Samuel	1			1	
May	1	White George	1			1	
May	22	Wallace B. William	2	3	2	6	
May	22	Weather James	4	10	2	9	
May	22	Wallace Thomas		2		2	

Stafford Co., Va. personal property tax list -1790

Mo.	day	chargeable w/tax	white males 16+	/blacks 16+	12+	H	other
May	22	Welch Langton	1				
Jun	19	West Thos. & comp[a]	2	2	1	1	
[folio 32]							
Jul	12	Wallace James		4		2	
Jul	12	Wallace John	2	4	1	8	
Jul	12	Weaks Benjamin	1				
Jul	12	Woodard Mary	1	1		1	
Jul	12	Webb Aaron	1			4	
Jul	12	Webb Moses	1			1	
Jul	16	Wright Samuel	1			1	
Jul	16	Write [?] Ann		1		1	
Jul	16	West John	2			4	
Jul	16	Winlock William	1	3		3	
Jul	16	Wellford Robert		1		3	
Apr	12	Young William	2	1		3	
		Totals	502	852	149	1125	

Examined agreeable to same
Val Peyton

(continued on page 503)

Mo.	day	chargeable w/tax	white /blacks males 16+ 16+ 12+		H	other

[folio 33]

Whites above 16 years   502
Negro tithes Do.   852 @ 5/each£ 213.   d.
Do. from 12 to 16 years   149 @ Do.   37.   5
Horses Mares &c.   1125 @ 1/   56.   5
Coach Wheels   4 @ 18/   3.   12
Pha & stage waggon Ditto   28 @ 12/   16.   16
Chairs Ditto   18 @ 26/   5.   8
Or. Licences   1 @ 50/   2.   10
Stud Horses   4 @ £ 4/8   4.   8
£ 337.0.0
Rhody Hord properly not aded   1.0.0
£ 338.1.0

70369$^1/_2$ Acres Amo^{t}g to £ 33885.8.10
Tax @ 1$^1/_2$ pct. 5 Ditto of ...[?] of Lotts 835
£ 551.19.9 $^1/_2$
Deduct one half   £ 275.19.10 $^3/_4$

Total Amot of Tax for Year 1790   £ 614.0.10 $^3/_4$

Excepted[sic]
Wm Alexander Comm^r

[End of Alexander's returns]

[End of 1790 personal property tax list]

[this page blank]

Stafford County
Virginia

Personal Property
Tax List

1790

[Arranged by date of tax enumeration]

Source: Virginia State Library, Archives Division. County Records. Stafford County Tax lists.

Form of return of taxable property to be made by the commissioners

List No. 1.
A List of the Taxable property within the district of Wm Mountjoy, commissioner in the county of Stafford for the year 1790
[Categories]:
> Date of receiving lists from individuals;
> Persons names chargeable with the tax;
> *[col. 1]* - White males above 16 years;
> *[col. 2]* - Blacks above 16 years;
> *[col. 3]* - Blacks above 12 & under 16 years;
> *[col. 4]* - Horses mares colts & mules;
> *[other]-*Coach & Chariott wheels;
>> Phaeton & stage wagon wheels;
>> Chair wheels;
>> Ordinary licence;
>> no. of stud horses;
>> Rates of covering pr season.

List No. 2.
A List of Taxable Property taken in the Year 1790 by William Alexander Commissioner of Stafford County
[Categories]:
> Months;
> Days;
> Proprietor's Names;
> *[col. 1]* - White tythes;
> *[col. 2]* - Negro^s 16 upwards;
> *[col. 3]* - D^o from 12 to 16;
> *[col. 4]* - Horses;
> *[other]* - Coach & Char^tt Wheels;
>> Phaet. & stage wls;
>> Chairs D.^o;
>> O*[rdinary]*. licences;
>> B*[illiard]*Tables;
>> Studs;
>> Rates pr season;
>> Doctors;

A List of the Taxable property within the district of Wm Mountjoy, commissioner in the county of Stafford for the year 1790

[Arranged by date of tax enumeration]

Mo.	day	chargeable w/tax	white males 16+	/blacks 16+	12+	H	other
Mar	17	Hannah Dickenson	1	5	3	13	
Mar	17	Thomas Sedden	1	13	4	9	
Mar	17	Richard Taylor	1			2	
Mar	20	George Abbott	1			1	
Mar	20	Ge.o Bell Jun.r	1			3	
Mar	20	James Billingsley	2	3		4	
Mar	20	William Bradly	2			3	
Mar	20	John Bridges	1			1	
Mar	20	John Brown	1			1	
Mar	20	Joseph Brown	2	4	2	5	
Mar	20	George Byrum	2			2	
Mar	20	James Carter	1		1	2	
Mar	20	Bradly Dent	2			2	
Mar	20	John Dillon				1	
Mar	20	John Dorson	1			3	
Mar	20	Archabald Douglis	1			6	
Mar	20	William Franklin	1			2	
Mar	20	William Gant	1	1		2	
Mar	20	John Garrison	2			2	
Mar	20	John Green	1			2	
Mar	20	John H. Foushee	1			1	
Mar	20	Lidia Hansbrough		1	1	2	
Mar	20	Peter Hansbrough	1	1	2	3	
Mar	20	William Hore [Hoie?]	1		1	1	
Mar	20	William Jones	3			3	1 stud horse
Mar	20	Richard Morton	1	1		1	
Mar	20	William Phillips	1	7	1	6	
Mar	20	Thomas Powell	1			1	
Mar	20	James Primm	1	1		3	

507

[arranged by date of tax enumeration]

Mo.	day	chargeable w/tax	white males 16+	/blacks 16+	12+	H	other
Mar	20	Richard Ratliff	1		2	4	
Mar	20	Butler Reimy	1			2	
Mar	20	James Riley	1			1	
Mar	20	Jessey Riley	1			2	
Mar	20	William Shacklett	3	1		3	
Mar	20	Jane Silvey	1			2	
Mar	20	Benjamin Withers	1			3	
Mar	20	Jessey Woodgerd	1			1	
Mar	27	John Banister	1			2	
Mar	27	Benj.ª Burroughs	1		2	2	
Mar	27	Ge.º Burroughs	1	3	1	3	
Mar	27	John Burroughs	1			1	
Mar	27	Renn Carter	1	1		1	
Mar	27	Perry Chinn	1			2	
Mar	27	John Edrington	1			1	
Mar	27	William Edrington	2	2	4	5	
Mar	27	John Faunt	1			1	
Mar	27	Phillip Gardner	1	4		4	
Mar	27	John Harding	1	1		4	
Mar	27	William Harding	5	2	1	7	
Mar	27	Christopher Knight	1			4	
Mar	27	Henry McEntire	1	1	1	2	
Mar	27	Thomas Porter	1	3	1	5	
Mar	27	Abigale Shelton	1			3	
Mar	27	George Shelton	1			2	
Mar	27	Wilson Shelton	1			3	
Mar	27	Richard Sims Jun.ʳ	2			5	
Mar	27	Jerremaih Stark	2	2		5	
Mar	27	Francis Stern	1	4	3	4	
Mar	28	Gaven Lawson	2	17	4	15	4 phaeton wheels
Apr	3	Thomas Ambler	2			5	
Apr	3	Charles Bradly	1				
Apr	3	Philamon Bramit	3			2	

[arranged by date of tax enumeration]

Mo.	day	chargeable w/tax	white males 16+	/blacks 16+	12+	H	other
Apr	3	Cuthbert Combs	2	6	1	7	
Apr	3	Asia Cummins	4			6	
Apr	3	Willis Edwards	1			1	
Apr	3	Elizabeth Garrison				1	
Apr	3	Elijah Green	1				
Apr	3	Robert Green	2			3	
Apr	3	George Holloway	2			1	
Apr	3	Charles Kendall	1	2	2	2	
Apr	3	John Knight Sen.r	1			1	
Apr	3	Ewel Mason	1			1	
Apr	3	Allen Mountjoy	4			4	
Apr	3	Moses Poats	1			4	
Apr	3	James Sims	1			2	
Apr	3	Rhoadnum Sims	2			3	
Apr	3	Richard Stone	1	3	4	4	
Apr	3	Allen Way	1			1?	
Apr	3	William Williams	1			2	
Apr	5	John Agin	1			1	
Apr	5	Halafax Ashby	1			1	
Apr	5	Amus Atchison	2			5	
Apr	5	John Atchison	2			1	
Apr	5	Nathn Atchison	3	2		4	
Apr	5	Nath.n Banester	2			3	
Apr	5	John Beagle	3			3	
Apr	5	Thomas Beagle	1				
Apr	5	Ge.o Bell Sen.r	1	2		3	
Apr	5	Jonathan Bell	1			2	
Apr	5	Ge.o Bredwell Jun.r	1			4	
Apr	5	John Brooker	1				
Apr	5	William Bruce	1			2	
Apr	5	Cuthbert Byrum	1			1	
Apr	5	Senate Byrum	1				
Apr	5	William Byrum	1			1	

[arranged by date of tax enumeration]

Mo.	day	chargeable w/tax	white males 16+	/blacks 16+	12+	H	other
Apr	5	William Cummins	2			4	
Apr	5	Mashack Davis	1			1	
Apr	5	Jerremiah Day	1				
Apr	5	William Eaton	4			3	
Apr	5	William Edwards	1	5	1	4	
Apr	5	Phillip Foxworthy	1			1	
Apr	5	Vintsin Foxworthy	1			1	
Apr	5	John Franklin L.free				2	
Apr	5	Joseph Franklin Jun.r	1			1	
Apr	5	Reuben Franklin	1		1	2	
Apr	5	John Fritter	1			2	
Apr	5	William Fritter	1			3	
Apr	5	John Gie	1			3	
Apr	5	Hannah Gough	1	1		3	
Apr	5	Thomas Harding	1		1	3	
Apr	5	Charles Jones	1				
Apr	5	Henry Kendall	1	1	1	4	
Apr	5	Josua Kendall Sen.r	1	4	1	4	
Apr	5	John Latham Sen.r	1			3	
Apr	5	Lewis Mason	1		1	4	
Apr	5	Richard Mason	1	1		5	
Apr	5	Wharton Philbert	1			1	
Apr	5	Richard Sims L.free	1			3	
Apr	5	Sarsfield Snoxall	1			2	
Apr	5	William Stark	1	1	1	3	
Apr	5	John Walters	1			1	
Apr	5	Peter Walters	1			3	
Apr	12	Elijah Abbot	1			2	
Apr	12	John Abbot Senr (L.free)				3	
Apr	12	Mary Ann Burroughs	1	10	1	6	
Apr	12	Mary Ann Ralls		4		2	
Apr	12	Daniel Antrum	3			6	
Apr	12	James Arrosmith	1			3	

[arranged by date of tax enumeration]

Mo.	day	chargeable w/tax	white males 16+	/blacks 16+	12+	H	other
Apr	12	William B. Stone	2	5	3	7	
Apr	12	Thomas Barbe (L.free)				2	
Apr	12	William Baul	1	2	1	6	
Apr	12	Fielding Bell	1	1		3	
Apr	12	Enough Benson	2	3	1	6	
Apr	12	Joseph Botts	2	6		5	
Apr	12	William Botts	2	3		3	
Apr	12	Uriah Bradshaw	1			4	
Apr	12	Jacob Bridwell (L.free)				3	
Apr	12	William Brown	1			3	
Apr	12	John Browne	1	13	4	7	2 chair wheels
Apr	12	Bazel Burroughs	1			3	
Apr	12	James Cain	1			2	
Apr	12	James Camberford (L.free)				1	
Apr	12	Jessey Carney	1			1	
Apr	12	John Carney	2	1	2	6	
Apr	12	Harris Carter	2			2	
Apr	12	Jedediah Carter	1			3	
Apr	12	Brian Chadwell	1	2	1	4	
Apr	12	William Cole	1			1	
Apr	12	Joseph Cooper (L.free)				2	
Apr	12	John Dalgair	1		1		
Apr	12	Charles Davis	2			1	
Apr	12	Moses Dick	1			1	
Apr	12	Sam. Faunt	2			4	
Apr	12	Anthony Ficklin	2	7	1	6	
Apr	12	Benj.a Ficklin	1	1		4	
Apr	12	James Ford	1	3	1	5	
Apr	12	Francis Foushee	2	3		3	
Apr	12	Joseph Franklin L.free	1			4	
Apr	12	Rich.d Fristoe L.free				2	
Apr	12	Moses Fritter Jun.r	1			1	
Apr	12	George Garrison	3			2	

Stafford Co., Va. personal property tax list - 1790

[arranged by date of tax enumeration]

Mo.	day	chargeable w/tax	white males 16+	/blacks 16+	12+	H	other
Apr	12	Isaac Gaskins	1	1		3	
Apr	12	James Gough	1		2	1	
Apr	12	Elisha Grigsby	1		1	2	
Apr	12	Moses Grigsby Sen.ʳ	1			1	
Apr	12	William Groves	1			2	
Apr	12	George Harding	1		1	2	
Apr	12	Thomas Hay L.free	2			4	
Apr	12	Thomas Heth L.free		1			
Apr	12	Henry Hiden	1			2	
Apr	12	William Holloday	1	1		3	
Apr	12	Asia Holloway	2			4	
Apr	12	Isaac Holloway	1			1	
Apr	12	John Holloway Sen.ʳ	4			4	
Apr	12	John Hore	1	2		1	
Apr	12	Causom Horton	2			2	
Apr	12	Sam. Hudson	1	2		3	
Apr	12	Alexander Jameson	2			1	
Apr	12	David Jones	1	1		2	
Apr	12	Gabril Jones	2	4		5	
Apr	12	John Jones	1			1	
Apr	12	John Jones	2			6	
Apr	12	Anthony Kendall	1			3	
Apr	12	Daniel Kendall	1	1		2	
Apr	12	Merryman Ketchen	2	1	1	2	
Apr	12	Peter Knight Jun.ʳ	1	1	1	2	
Apr	12	Peter Knight Sen.ʳ	3	1		5	
Apr	12	Uriah Knight	1			2	
Apr	12	Snodon Latham	2			2	
Apr	12	John Lawlis	1			3	
Apr	12	Francis Linum	1				
Apr	12	Daniel Mason	3	2	2	5	
Apr	12	Peter Mauzy Jun.ʳ	1	1		4	
Apr	12	Alexand McEntire	1	3		3	

[arranged by date of tax enumeration]

Mo.	day	chargeable w/tax	white males 16+	/blacks 16+	12+	H	other
Apr	12	Robert Melion	2	1		5	
Apr	12	James More	1			1	
Apr	12	Edward Mountjoy	2			6	
Apr	12	William Mullin	3	5	1	7	
Apr	12	John Murray	1	7		4	
Apr	12	Mary Nelson		1		1	
Apr	12	Edward Normon	1	3	3	7	
Apr	12	George Normon	1	3		6	
Apr	12	Robert Painter	2			4	
Apr	12	William Poats	2		1	4	
Apr	12	Charles Porter	2	2		3	
Apr	12	John Randol	1				
Apr	12	William Randol	3	1		4	
Apr	12	Joel Readish	2	4	2	7	
Apr	12	Aaron Reid	1			3	
Apr	12	Richard Reid	1		1	3	
Apr	12	John Richards	1			1	
Apr	12	James Robeson	1			1	
Apr	12	William Rout	1	1	1	4	
Apr	12	John S. Harding	2			3	
Apr	12	John Shelket	1	1		4	
Apr	12	John Smith	2			1	
Apr	12	Nath.^{n} Smith	1	1		2	
Apr	12	Hannah Stark	1	1		2	
Apr	12	John Stark Senr	2	1		3	
Apr	12	John Stark	1			1	
Apr	12	Charles Stern	1	1	1	2	
Apr	12	Hawkin Stone	1	5	2	6	
Apr	12	Charles Stuart	1	6	1	6	
Apr	12	Henry Sudduth	1			2	
Apr	12	Thomas Sudduth	1			1	
Apr	12	Gabrel Sullaven	2			4	
Apr	12	Alexander Taylor	3			2	

[arranged by date of tax enumeration]

Mo.	day	chargeable w/tax	white males 16+	/blacks 16+	H 12+		other
Apr	12	Sam. Thompson	1	2		6	
Apr	12	Benjamin Tolson	1	1	2	4	
Apr	12	William Tolson	1	1		3	
Apr	12	John Tuttle	1			1	
Apr	12	Baily Walters	1			1	
Apr	12	Charles Walters	1			2	
Apr	12	John Walters Sen.r	2	3		4	
Apr	12	Mark Walters L.free		1		4	
Apr	12	George Wells	3	3		4	
Apr	12	Thomas Wells	1			1	
Apr	12	John West	1				
Apr	12	William West	1			3	
Apr	12	William Williams	1			1	
Apr	15	John Jameson	1				
Apr	24	Thomas Right	3	2	2	6	
Apr	28	Elijah Bell	1			2	
Apr	28	Jessey Cooper	1			1	
Apr	28	Elizabeth Dunaway				1	
Apr	28	Thomas Dunaway	1			2	
Apr	28	Ann Moncure	1	10	2	6	
Apr	29	William Richards	1	1		2	
May	1	Benjamin Aedy	1	9		5	
May	1	Jessey Edwards	2	1	4?		
May	8	Mary Ann Payn				1	
May	8	William Barnot	1			1	
May	8	John F. Mercer	1	47	6	18	
May	8	William Mauzy	1	2		4	
May	8	Ezekiel Payn	1			2	
May	8	James Payn	1			2	
May	8	Jessey Payn	1			1	
May	8	Kelley Payn	1			1	
May	8	William Payn	1			3	
May	8	John Snoxall	1			2	

[arranged by date of tax enumeration]

Mo.	day	chargeable w/tax	white males 16+	/blacks 16+	12+	H	other
May	8	Moses Sudduth	1			1	
May	8	John Whitfield	1				
May	10	Dedreck Benear (L.free)				2	
May	10	Catherine Conaway		3	2	3	
May	10	John Cook	2	28	6	15	
May	10	Isaac Eavs	1				
May	10	Isaac Eustace	2	10	3	8	4 phaeton wheels
May	10	Jessy Kendall	1			4	
May	10	John Kendall	3	3	2	7	
May	10	Jerremiah Knight	2	1		5	
May	10	John Lunsford	1	1		3	
May	10	Charles Martin	1			1	
May	10	Benjamin Pritchett	2	3		9	
May	10	George Randol	2			1	
May	10	Ann Rogers				2	
May	10	Benjamin Rogers	1			2	
May	10	John Rogers	2	1		3	
May	10	William Shelton	2			4	
May	10	Joseph Slaughter	1				
May	10	John Stern	1	2		3	
May	10	Thomas Tennant	1		1	3	
May	10	John Tharp L.free				1	
May	10	Charles Thornton	1			1	
May	10	George Withers	1	3		2	
May	15	Edward Barber	1			2	
May	15	James Bridges	2			2	
May	15	Dennis Doyall Jun.ʳ	1			1	
May	15	Dennis Doyall Sen.ʳ	1	1		3	
May	15	George Green	1	1		2	
May	15	Cuthbert Harding	1			2	
May	15	Charles Latham	1			1	
May	15	Elizabeth Peyton	3	9	1	8	
May	15	John Primm	1	1	1?	3	

[arranged by date of tax enumeration]

Mo.	day	chargeable w/tax	white males 16+	/blacks 16+	12+	H	other
May	15	Margaret Primm				3	
May	15	William Stark	1	1	1	3	
May	18	James Oglesby	1			1	
May	22	Charles Nixon	1			1	
May	23	Thomas Mountjoy	1	8	2	6	2 chair wheels
May	24	John Carter	1			1	
May	24	Henry Clifton	2	5	2	4	
May	24	George Coats	1	1	1	1	
May	24	Joseph Combs	1	4	1	4	
May	24	Benjamin Gie	1			1	
May	24	William Gie	4			5	
May	24	Richard Poats	1		1	4	
May	24	Margaret Williams	1	3	1	5	
May	24	Nath.^{n} Williams	1	7	3	3	
May	26	Barsheba Waller				2	
May	26	Mary Waller		2	2	5	
Jun	2	Thomas Mallery	1			1	
Jun	2	Mary McDaniel				1	
Jun	2	Charles Mifflin L.free				2	
Jun	8	Colvert Porter	1			1	
Jun	14	Ann Brent	1	19	1	9	
Jun	14	George Brent	2	12	1	5	
Jun	14	John Bridwell	2			2	
Jun	14	Charles Carter	1	27	4	15	
Jun	14	Mary Garrard	2	10		3	
Jun	14	Charles Ralls	2	3	1	4	
Jun	14	Rawling Ralls	1	1	2	2	
Jun	14	Baily Riley	2			4	
Jun	14	William Robeson	3			2	
Jun	14	Richard Walker	1	1		4	
Jun	14	George Williams	1	6	1	2	
Jun	14	John Withers	1	12	4	9	
Jun	15	Dennis Linum	1				

[arranged by date of tax enumeration]

Mo.	day	chargeable w/tax	white males 16+	/blacks 16+	12+	H	other
Jun	18	John Eshew	1				
Jun	20	John Bruing	2			2	
Jun	20	Sollomon Gollohorn	1			2	
Jun	25	Patterson Doyall	1				
Jul	2	William Waller	3	4	3	7	
Jul	12	Daniel C. Brent	3	41	8	20	
		"					4 coach whls & 2 chr whls.
Jul	12	Seth Combs	1	9		7	
Jul	12	William Mountjoy	1	5	1	5	
Jul	17	William Barbee	1			3	
Jul	28	Thomas Beach	1			1	
Aug	5	John R. Rawlins	1			2	
Aug	8	John Dunbar	2	1		2	
Aug	8	Ann Vaughan				3	
Aug	9	Mary Bell		3		2	
Aug	9	James Brown	1			1	
Aug	9	Williamson Chandler	1	1	1	2	
Aug	9	William Gollohorn	1			4	
Aug	9	James McBride	1			1	
Aug	9	Ursly Morton		3	1	2	
Aug	9	John Nicholson	1			1	
Aug	9	Peter Pilcher	1			2	
Aug	9	Kenez Ralls	2	1		1	
Aug	9	Edward Snoxall	1			3	
Aug	9	Baily Washington Jun.r	2	22	4	10	4 phaeton wheels
Aug	9	William Young	1			1	
Aug	10	Joseph Ambler	1			1	
Aug	10	John Markham	1	5	2	3	
Aug	12	John Fitzgerald	1				
Aug	13	William Dorson	2			3	
Aug	13	Aaron Garrison	1				
Aug	13	Benjamin Melion	3			2	
Aug	13	William Melion	1			2	

Stafford Co., Va. personal property tax list - 1790

[arranged by date of tax enumeration]

Mo.	day	chargeable w/tax	white males 16+	/blacks 16+	12+	H	other
Aug	13	William Pattin	1				
Aug	13	Edward Pearson	1			2	
Aug	13	Elizabeth Tolson		1		6	
Aug	13	Joanna Tolson	1	1		1	
Aug	13	William Watson	3			1	
Aug	13	William West	1			6	
Aug	13	Henry Woodgerd	1			2	
Aug	14	Jessey Bails	1			1	
Aug	14	James Battoe (L.free)				2	
Aug	14	William Battoe	1			3	
Aug	14	Ann Botts		5	1	4	
Aug	14	John Bradly	1				
Aug	14	Simon Bridwell	1			1	
Aug	14	William Bridwell	1			1	
Aug	14	Shadreck Davis	1			3	
Aug	14	Joseph Dunaway	1			2	
Aug	14	Baker Edwards	1			3	
Aug	14	Haden Edwards	1	5		4	
Aug	14	Travers Edwards	1			1	
Aug	14	John Grigsby	1			1	
Aug	14	John Hardy	1	8	2	8	
Aug	14	George Johnston	1			1	
Aug	14	John Johnston	1			1	
Aug	14	Steaphen Johnston	1			2	
Aug	14	Elizabeth Jones				1	
Aug	14	William Jones	1				
Aug	14	Anthony Long	1			2	
Aug	14	Moses Lunsford	1			2	
Aug	14	James Peak	1				
Aug	14	John Stark		4		2	
Aug	14	Josias Stone	1	5		4	2 chair wheels
Aug	16	John Hedgman	1	16	5	5	
Aug	18	Sam. Parker	1			2	

[arranged by date of tax enumeration]

Mo.	day	chargeable w/tax	white males 16+	/blacks 16+	12+	H	other
Aug	18	John Payn	1				
Aug	18	Linzey Pollard	1				
Aug	18	John R. Peyton	1	13	1	9	
Aug	19	Spencer Bowlin	1			1	
Aug	19	Elizabeth Chissom	1			3	
Aug	19	John Chiverall	1			1	
Aug	19	James Faunt	2			4	
Aug	19	Enough Fritter	1			1	
Aug	19	Moses Fritter Sen.ʳ	1			1	
Aug	19	Sarah Kirk	1			1	
Aug	19	Thomas Rakestraw	1				
Aug	19	John Rankings	1	1		1	
Aug	19	Frances Underwood	1			1	
Aug	20	Edward Bethell	1			3	
Aug	20	Isaac Branson	1			1	
Aug	20	John Grey	1			2	
Aug	20	Sam. Groves	1	1		3	
Aug	20	Elijah Horton	1			4	
Aug	20	Henry Horton	1			1	
Aug	20	James Horton	1			3	
Aug	20	John Horton	2	7		8	
Aug	20	Aaron Kendall	1		1	1	
Aug	20	James Kendall	1			1	
Aug	20	Ephraem Knight	1			2	
Aug	20	Hezekiah Ollover	1	1		3	
Aug	20	Ezekiel Skinner	1			1	
Aug	20	Edward Templeman	2			3	
Aug	20	James Walker	1			1	
Aug	20	Susanah Wormsly		1		3	
Aug	21	William Harrod	2			3	
Aug	21	Thomas Hereford	1	7		4	
Aug	21	William Hereford	1	1		1	2 chair wheels
Aug	21	Isaac Holloway	1			2	

[arranged by date of tax enumeration]

Mo.	day	chargeable w/tax	white males 16+	/blacks 16+	12+	H	other
Aug	21	Elias Hore	1	1		1	
Aug	21	James Hore	1	2	1	4	
Aug	21	Mary Hore		7		3	
Aug	21	Josua Kendall Jun.ʳ	1			2	
Aug	21	Thomas Kenney	1	1		1	
Aug	21	Elijah Thompson	1	1		4	
Aug	21	John Walters	1			3	
Aug	23	Joseph Barber	1	1		3	
Aug	23	Clem Billingsley	1	1		2	
Aug	23	Robert Buihan	1	5	1	8	
Aug	24	William Monroe	1	2		2	
Aug	24	John Mountjoy	1		1	2	
Aug	28	William Aedy	2	9	1	6	
Aug	28	William Anderson	1	1		1	
Aug	28	Robert Ashby	3			2	
Aug	28	Tho.ˢ G. Tyler	2	3	2	5	
Aug	28	Jessey Taylor	1				
Aug	28	Allen Thomas	1			2	
Aug	28	Elijah Threlkeld	2	13	3	11	
Aug	31	Ann Gaddis	1	5		4	
Aug	31	William George	1				
Aug	31	Moses Grigs Jun.ʳ	1				
Sep	2	William Devene	1				
Sep	2	Lewis Dishue [sic]	1				
Sep	2	Christopher Dorson	1			1	
Sep	12	James Barnot	1	1			
Sep	12	Ge.ᴼ Bridwell Sen.ʳ	1			1	
Sep	12	Henry Bridwell	1			1	
Sep	12	Sam. Bridwell	1			2	
Sep	12	William Bridwell	3	3		5	
Sep	12	George Burns	1				
Sep	12	Ja.ˢ Cloe Jun.ʳ	1			1	
Sep	12	Elijah Conner	1				

[arranged by date of tax enumeration]

Mo.	day	chargeable w/tax	white males 16+	blacks 16+	12+	H	other
Oct	2	Joel Beagle	2			2	
Oct	2	John Bridwell	1				
Oct	2	Moses Bridwell	3	5	1	3	
Oct	2	Peter Cash	1			1	
Oct	2	Ja.s Cloe Sen.r (L.free)	1			1	
Oct	2	William Dunaway	1			1	
Oct	2	William Faning	1		1	2	
Oct	2	Thomas Fristoe	1	1		2	
Oct	2	William Fristoe	3			5	
Oct	2	Benjamin Grigory	1			3	
Oct	2	John Gun	1			2	
Oct	8	William Bobo	1				
Oct	8	Benj.a Bowlin	1			2	
Oct	8	Nimrod Byrum	1				
Oct	8	Peter Byrum	1			1	
Oct	8	Travers Daniel Jun.r	1	12	2	12	2 chair wheels
Oct	8	Peter Mauzy Sen.r		2	1	3	
Oct	8	John Mountjoy	1	6	1	9	
Oct	8	Francis Payn	1				
Oct	8	Vallentine Peyton	2	10	1	5	
Oct	8	John Poats	1	1	1	3	
Oct	8	Joseph Readish	2	3	1	3	
Oct	8	Reuben Rogers	1			1	
Oct	8	William Ross	1	3		5	
Oct	8	Presly Sims	1			1	
Oct	8	Rawleigh T. Browne	1	18	3	11	
Oct	8	Thomas Tolsen [sic]	1			1	
Oct	10	Robert B. Morton	1	11		4	
Oct	10	John Mason	1	4		5	
Oct	10	John Minton	1		1	1	
Oct	10	Elizabeth Overall		6		4	
Oct	10	Hepbron Ralls	1			2	
Oct	10	Jonathan Reid	1			3	

[arranged by date of tax enumeration]

Mo.	day	chargeable w/tax	white males 16+	/blacks 16+ 12+		H	other
Oct	10	Joseph Rogers	1				
Oct	10	Augustin Weadon	1		1	3	
Oct	11	William Branson	1				
Oct	11	Daniel Brent Jun.ʳ	1				
Oct	11	Robert Brent	1				
Oct	11	Thomas Bridwell	1			3	
Oct	11	Benjamin Brock	1			3	
Oct	11	George Bussel	1			2	
Oct	11	Travers Daniel Sen.ʳ	1	24	1	1	
Oct	11	John Dilley	2			2	
Oct	11	William French	2	6	2	8	
Oct	11	John Holloway Jun.ʳ	2			6	
Oct	11	Hannah Taylor		4	2	5	2 chair wheels
Oct	15	Daw & Burn	2	3		1	1 ordinary licence
Oct	15	William Right	1			3	
Oct	15	Jessey Stone	3			3	
Oct	15	Rawleigh W. Downman	1	10	3	6	
Oct	15	George Walters	1			4	
Oct	15	John Warren	1			2	

* * * * *

* * *

*

[End of date-arranged returns for William Mountjoy]

A List of Taxable property taken in the Year 1790
by [William]] Alexander Commissioner of Stafford County
[Arranged by date of tax enumeration]

Mo.	day	chargeable w/tax	white males 16+	/blacks 16+	12+	H	other
Mar	10	William Alexander	1	21	6	20	4 phaeton wheels
Mar	10	Ditto Casson's Est.[a]					
Mar	20	Allison Henry	1				
Mar	20	Ball William	2	3		4	
Mar	20	Berry Rich.[d]	1			1	
Mar	20	Black Margrett	1			6	
Mar	20	Burton Gerrard	1			2	
Mar	20	Cox John	1			2	
Mar	20	Curtice John	2			4	
Mar	20	Curtice Richard	1			1	
Mar	20	Edwards James	1				
Mar	20	Gollehorne Soloman	1			3	
Mar	20	Gollihorn Thomas	1			2	
Mar	20	Henson Elijah	2			2	
Mar	20	Jett Presly	1			2	
Mar	20	Kenney John	1			3	
Mar	20	Lang James	2			1	
Mar	20	Lang Robert	1	1	1	4	
Mar	20	Leach Andrew	2			2	
Mar	20	Leach Benjamin	1			3	
Mar	20	Limbrick Francis	2			3	
Mar	20	Limbrick George	1			1	
Mar	20	McGuire Rachel	2			3	
Mar	20	Moss John	1				
Mar	20	Payne John	2			3	
Mar	20	Payton Ann	2	1	1	2	
Mar	20	Payton Charles	1			2	
Mar	20	Pilcher Daniel	1			1	
Mar	20	Robertson Thomas	2			2	
Mar	20	Rowley Archibal	2			1	
Mar	20	Snellings Enouch	1			2	
Mar	20	Snellings William	1			3	

[arranged by date of tax enumeration]

Mo.	day	chargeable w/tax	white males 16+	/blacks 16+	12+	H	other
Mar	20	Souillivant Benj.a	1			4	
Mar	20	Souillivant Daniel	1	1		2	
Mar	20	Souillivant Darby Tax free			1		
Mar	20	Souillivant Darby Jn.r	1			2	
Mar	20	Souillivant Darby young	1			1	
Mar	20	Walker Thomas	2	4	1	3	
Mar	24	Carter Henry	2			2	
Mar	24	Waugh McCagby	2			4	
Mar	29	Brissus Isaac	1				
Mar	29	Burnett William	3	3		6	
Mar	29	Chinn Joseph	1			2	
Mar	29	Clemmons John	1	1		3	
Mar	29	Curtice George	2			3	
Mar	29	Garner John	1			2	
Mar	29	Garner William	2			2	
Mar	29	Jones George	1				
Mar	29	Miner Elizabeth		1	1	1	
Mar	29	Nooe Zepheniah	1	3	2	6	2 chair wheels
Mar	29	Payne Thomas	1	1		2	
Mar	29	Souillivant Lettice				3	
Mar	29	Templeman Moses	1				
Mar	29	Wisharts Esta		5		5	
Mar	31	Chilton William	2			2	
Mar	31	Fines Patrick	1	?		2	
Mar	31	Fugett Benjamin	1			2	
Mar	31	Fugett Daniel	1			2	
Mar	31	Fugett Francis Jun.r				2	
Mar	31	Jones John	1	1		1	
Mar	31	Limbrick William	1			2	
Mar	31	Monday Aaron	1			2	
Mar	31	Pates Aaron	1			1	
Mar	31	Pates Lewis	1				
Mar	31	Payton James	1			1	
Mar	31	Pilcher Mildred		1	1	1	
Mar	31	Pilcher Moses	3	2		3	

[arranged by date of tax enumeration]

Mo.	day	chargeable w/tax	white males 16+	/blacks 16+	12+	H	other
Mar	31	Pusee James	1			1	
Mar	31	Stone Joseph	2			2	
Mar	31	Stone William	1	1		3	
Apr	3	Jones Henry	3		1	3	
Apr	5	Bensen John			1	1	
Apr	5	Alexander Philip's Est.[a]	1	10	2	5	
Apr	7	Brooks Margrett		1		1	
Apr	7	Cox George	1			5?	
Apr	7	Cox Presley	1			1	
Apr	7	Curtice Aaron	2				
Apr	7	Pates Allice	1			3	
Apr	7	Templeman Jane				3	
Apr	9	Bates Joseph	1			2	
Apr	9	Benson Zachariah	1				
Apr	9	Berry William		1		2	
Apr	9	Bryant John	2	2	1	3	
Apr	9	Cashal James	1			1	
Apr	9	Conyers Benj.[a]	1				
Apr	9	Conyers John	4	3	1	4	
Apr	9	Cox Vincent Jun.[r]	1	1		2	
Apr	9	Cox Vincent Sen.[r]	2			3	
Apr	9	Fennal Jonathan	2	7		5	
Apr	9	Kitchen Charles	2			5	
Apr	9	Nash Philip	1			1	
Apr	9	Pilcher Richard	3			4	
Apr	9	Pusee Stephen	3			1	
Apr	9	Souillivant Fran[s]	1	1		4	
Apr	9	Terrur John	3	1		3	
Apr	9	Turner Absolum	3			5	
Apr	9	Turner Wm Griffin	3			5	
Apr	11	Bolling James	3			3	
Apr	11	Brown James	1			3	
Apr	11	Brown William	2			4	
Apr	12	[surname faded] John	2			3	
Apr	12	Alexander W[m] Scho[Blurred]				4	

Stafford Co., Va. personal property tax list - 1790

[arranged by date of tax enumeration]

Mo.	day	chargeable w/tax	white males 16+	/blacks 16+	12+	H	other
Apr	12	Anderson John	1			3	
Apr	12	Arrowsmith Thomas	3	1		5	
Apr	12	Berry Anthony	1			4	
Apr	12	Berry Thomas	2	1	2	3	
Apr	12	Bolling Charles	1			1	
Apr	12	Buckner Richard	1	4		2	
Apr	12	Callender Phillip	1			4	
Apr	12	Carter Joseph	1	2	1	4	
Apr	12	Conner John	1			2	
Apr	12	Crop James Jun.ʳ	1	5	2	6	
Apr	12	Crop James Sen.ʳ	1	4	1	4	
Apr	12	Devenport William	1	1	1	1	
Apr	12	England John	2			5	
Apr	12	Fields Samuel	1				
Apr	12	Fitzhugh Thomas	2	28	1	12	4 phaeton wheels
Apr	12	Graves William	3	1		5	
Apr	12	Gullery Thomas	1			1	
Apr	12	Hill Jesse	2	3		4	
Apr	12	Hord Kellis	4	6	1	5	
Apr	12	Hord Peter	2	2		4	
Apr	12	Humphrys William	3	2		6	
Apr	12	Jackson Robert	2			3	
Apr	12	Jackson Rosana				3	
Apr	12	Jackson William	1			2	
Apr	12	Jett William	3			3	
Apr	12	Kenny Andrew	2			1	
Apr	12	Latham John	1	2		5	
Apr	12	Latham John	1	2		3	
Apr	12	Leach James	1	1	1	3	
Apr	12	Lowry James Tax free				2	
Apr	12	Lowry James Jun.ʳ	1			2	
Apr	12	Martin Charles	2			4	
Apr	12	Martin Charles	1			1	
Apr	12	Martin Samuel	2			3	
Apr	12	Martin Thomas	1			1	

[arranged by date of tax enumeration]

Mo.	day	chargeable w/tax	white males 16+	/blacks 16+	12+	H	other
Apr	12	Massey Thomas	2	4		6	
Apr	12	McCulluck John	1			2	
Apr	12	McFarlin Obed	1			3	
Apr	12	Moreland Thomas	1		1	2	
Apr	12	Munrow Daniel	1	1		2	
Apr	12	Munrow William Tax free			1		
Apr	12	Musselman Christian	3			3	
Apr	12	Newton John	2	6	1	5	
Apr	12	Patterson George	1			1	
Apr	12	Pettett Benjamin	2	1		3	
Apr	12	Sharp Linsfield	2	7	2	5	
Apr	12	Smith Henry	3	4		3	
Apr	12	Smith John	2	2		5	
Apr	12	Spence William Tax free	1			3	
Apr	12	Stripling Joel	1			1	
Apr	12	Stripling Thomas	1			1	
Apr	12	Suddon John	2	13	1	8	
Apr	12	Suton John	2			2	
Apr	12	Waugh Lee George	2	17	1	9	
Apr	12	Weaks George	2			2	
Apr	12	West John Jun[r]	2	1		2	
Apr	12	White George	1	1		3	
Apr	12	William Walker	3	3	1	3	
Apr	12	Young William	2	1		3	
Apr	16	Buchanan Andrew	1	9	1	7	2 chair wheels
Apr	16	Ditto Hooe's Est.[a]		7	1	3	
Apr	16	Hooe Robt	2	3		4	
Apr	16	Newton Isaac	1	7		5	
Apr	16	Newton Margrett		2		4	
Apr	16	Newton Thomas	1	4		6	
Apr	16	Snellings John	1			1	
Apr	16	Strother George	3	10	1	9	
Apr	19	Curtice Thad.[s]	1			1	
Apr	19	Curtice William	1			3	
Apr	20	Graves Catharine	1			2	

Stafford Co., Va. personal property tax list - 1790

[arranged by date of tax enumeration]

Mo.	day	chargeable w/tax	white males 16+	/blacks 16+	12+	H	other
Apr	20	Hinson Sarah	1			3	
Apr	20	Jacobs Robert	1			1	
Apr	20	Jacobs William	2	3	1	2	
Apr	20	James John	3	14	3	17	
Apr	20	Jett George	1			1	
Apr	20	Lee L. Thomas	2	30	9	20	
Apr	20	Selden Samuel	3	38	6	15	4 phaeton wheels
Apr	20	Seydmore Joshua	1		1	1	
Apr	20	Sudthard William	2			1	
Apr	20	Tesly John	1			3	
Apr	20	Tyler Allice	2	8	1	6	
Apr	21	Fitzhugh Henry	2	7	2	7	1 stud horse @ 1.
Apr	21	Fitzhugh John	4	15	1	9	
May	1	Ballard Thomas	2	3	1	3	
May	1	Benson James	2	4	1	8	
May	1	Bowen Burkitt	1	3	2	5	
May	1	Bowens Michal	2	2		5	
May	1	Bridges David	1	1	1	6	
May	1	Bridges William	1				
May	1	Burton Samuel	2	1		1	
May	1	Colney Elijah	1		1	2	
May	1	Dowdle James	2	6		5	
May	1	Faunt George	1	3	1	4	
May	1	Hall Benjamin	1			1	
May	1	Hord James	1	7	1	7	
May	1	Hudson David	1			1	
May	1	Humphrys Daniel	1			1	
May	1	Jones Charles	1	2	1	4	
May	1	Jones Evin	2	1		3	
May	1	Jones George	1			3	
May	1	Lathum Anthony	2			3	
May	1	Martin Lewis	1			1	
May	1	Meals Samuel	1			1	
May	1	Patterson Perry Wm	1				
May	1	Patterson Thomas	2			1	

[arranged by date of tax enumeration]

Mo.	day	chargeable w/tax	white males 16+	/blacks 16+ 12+		H	other
May	1	Pattin John	1			1	
May	1	Robert Branhams	1	2		1	
May	1	Sharp Thomas J^r	3	4	1	3	
May	1	Stringfellow Townshand	1			1	
May	1	Temmons John	1			3	
May	1	Truslow Benjamin	1			1	
May	1	White George	1			1	
May	1	Wright Samuel	1			1	
May	4	Allison Thomas	1	4	2	4	
May	5	Mortimer Charls	.	4		2	
May	8	Citchen William	1				
May	8	Jett Francis	2	2	2	5	
May	8	Kitchen William	1				
May	8	Thos Porch	1	11	2	8	
May	12	Ransdal John	1				
May	12	Rowley Archibal	1	1		1	
May	14	Paxton John	1			3	
May	14	Payner John Junr	1				
May	22	Allison David	2	2	1	1	
May	22	Beasly Phillip	1			1	
May	22	Bell John	3	3	1	5	
May	22	Briggs David	1	11	2	9	
May	22	Collins Thos	1	5	1	4	
May	22	Day Elizabeth		1		1	
May	22	Day John	2	1			
May	22	Dunbar Robert	3	2	1	10	
May	22	Gordon Samuel	2	1		1	
May	22	Hany William	2	2		4	
May	22	Hill Henry	1				
May	22	Lewis Conrod	1			1	
May	22	Lotspeck William	2			1	
May	22	Lucas John	1				
May	22	Lyon James	1			1	
May	22	McCloud James	2	1			
May	22	McCloud John	1				

Stafford Co., Va. personal property tax list - 1790

[arranged by date of tax enumeration]

Mo.	day	chargeable w/tax	white males 16+	/blacks 16+	12+	H	other
May	22	McMillion William	1				
May	22	Payn Daniel	2	2		1	
May	22	Sanders James	1			1	
May	22	Sudthard William	1				
May	22	Vowles Zachariah	2	1		1	
May	22	Wallace B. William	2	3	2	6	
May	22	Wallace Thomas		2		2	
May	22	Weather James	4	10	2	9	
May	22	Welch Langton	1				
May	25	Burton William	1			1	
May	25	Fitzhugh William	1	55	8	22	
May	25	*Fitzhugh William*	4 phaeton whls,2 chair wheels & 1 stud @ £1.4				
May	25	Threlkeld Jesse	1			1	
May	26	Pilcher John Tax free				4	
May	26	Taylor Robert	1				
May	26	Triplett Daniel	3	6	2	2	4 phaeton wheels
May	28	Posey Tho.s Col.o	1	13		28	
May	28	Scott Sarah	1		1	1	
Jun	9	Travis Margrett		1			
Jun	14	Anderson John				3	
Jun	14	Brown Walter	2			3	
Jun	14	Lathum George	2	1		4	
Jun	14	Legy Alexander	1	1	1	4	
Jun	14	Smith Joseph	1	5	2	4	
Jun	19	Adams John	1			1	
Jun	19	Colquhoun Walter	1	3		1	
Jun	19	Horton William	1			4	
Jun	19	Mauson Alexander	2	2	1	2	
Jun	19	Richards William	4	10	4	7	
Jun	19	Vowles Henry	1	8	1	1	2 chair wheels
Jun	19	West Thos. & compa	2	2	1	1	
Jun	21	Downman B Joseph	1	10	4	8	
Jun	25	Ball Burgess	2	26	4	12	
Jun	25	*Ball Burgess*	4 coach wheels & 4 phaeton wheels				
Jun	25	McKetterick Anthony	1	9	1	9	

[arranged by date of tax enumeration]

Mo.	day	chargeable w/tax	white males 16+	/blacks 16+	12+	H	other
Jul	12	Lavender Robert	1			1	
Jul	12	Wallace James		4		2	
Jul	12	Wallace John	2	4	1	8	
Jul	12	Weaks Benjamin	1				
Jul	12	Webb Aaron	1			4	
Jul	12	Webb Moses	1			1	
Jul	12	Woodard Mary	1	1		1	
Jul	13	Fox Natha.[l]	1	5	3	12	2 chair wheels
Jul	14	Bolling Thomas	2			7	
Jul	14	Brimmer John	1			1	
Jul	14	Bussell Benjamin	1	1'		4	
Jul	14	Colney Elijah	1			1	
Jul	14	Danovan James	1	3	2	4	
Jul	14	Graves Daniel	1				
Jul	14	Graves George	1				
Jul	14	Graves Polly				3	
Jul	14	Hudson Elizabeth		1			
Jul	14	Kenny John Jun.[r]	1			1	
Jul	14	Lathum John	1			1	
Jul	14	Lavender Robert Jun.[r]	2			3	
Jul	14	Marquess Anthony	1			1	
Jul	14	Normon William	1				
Jul	14	Norwood Joseph	1	1			
Jul	14	Robertson George	1				
Jul	14	Rose Jesse	1	1		2	
Jul	14	Rose William	1			2	
Jul	14	Schooler Thomas	2			3	
Jul	14	Snipe Nath[l]	1			3	
Jul	14	Threkell [sic] George	1			3	
Jul	15	Banks Fran.[s]		8		5	2 chair whls
Jul	15	Barbe [sic] John	1			1	
Jul	15	Barber William	1			1	
Jul	15	Bolling William	1			1	
Jul	15	Brimmer Isaac	1				
Jul	15	Burton Nath.[l]	1	1		4	

[arranged by date of tax enumeration]

Mo.	day	chargeable w/tax	white males 16+	/blacks 16+ 12+		H	other
Jul	15	Burton Samuel	1	1		1	
Jul	15	Crop John	1	7	1	9	
Jul	15	David John	1				
Jul	15	Fickling Fielding	1				
Jul	15	Hall John	1			1	
Jul	15	Hill Jelly & sisters				2	
Jul	15	Hore Edward	2	2		6	
Jul	15	Martin Daniel	1			1	
Jul	15	Massey Taliafero	1			1	
Jul	15	Mauson Auther	3	15	2	14	
Jul	15	Monnon John	1			3	
Jul	15	More Edward	2	7	2	5	
Jul	15	Mulberry John	1			1	
Jul	15	Munrow William	1				
Jul	15	Payne John	1				
Jul	15	Payton Thomas	1	2		2	
Jul	15	Porch Esom	1	3		3	
Jul	15	Rawley Michal	1				
Jul	15	Read John		1			
Jul	15	Rogers John forge	1	3		3	
Jul	15	Rogers John	1			1	
Jul	15	Rogers Nancy				1	
Jul	15	Rogers Robert				2	
Jul	15	Row John	1			1	
Jul	15	Samuel Smith	3	4		3	
Jul	15	Smith John Junr	1				
Jul	15	Smith John free Negro	1				
Jul	15	Stephens Richard	2	2		3	
Jul	15	Sutor William	1				
Jul	15	Turner Benjamin	1			1	
Jul	15	Turner James	2			2	
Jul	16	Carter Robert	1	17		5	
Jul	16	Colney George	1	3		4	
Jul	16	Corbin Henry	1			2	
Jul	16	Faunt Joseph	1	2	1	3	2 chair wheels

[arranged by date of tax enumeration]

Mo.	day	chargeable w/tax	white males 16+	/blacks 16+	12+	H	other
Jul	16	Follis Thomas	1			1	
Jul	16	Fugett Francis	1			2	
Jul	16	Green Jesse	1			1	
Jul	16	Gum Epram free neg.	1				
Jul	16	Harwood Allice	1	1		3	
Jul	16	Heffertin Martin	1			1	
Jul	16	Hickerson Joseph	1			2	
Jul	16	Hill Leonard	1	6		3	
Jul	16	Hord Rhodan	2	3		6	
Jul	16	Hord Thomas	1	1		5	
Jul	16	Horton Charles	1				
Jul	16	James George	1	6	1	4	
Jul	16	Lewis Ann				2	
Jul	16	Limbrick John	1			1	
Jul	16	Lunsford Toahan [?]		1		4	
Jul	16	Monteath Jas.	1	1	1	2	
Jul	16	Parmes Raughley	2	1	1	2	
Jul	16	Patterson Hezekiah	1			1	
Jul	16	Pattin Rachell	1	1		2	
Jul	16	Pilcher Barsheba		6	1	5	
Jul	16	Pon Elizabeth				1	
Jul	16	Simpson John	1				
Jul	16	Skinker Thomas	1	6	3	5	
Jul	16	Stringfellow George	1				
Jul	16	Tate William	1			1	
Jul	16	Taylor Samuel	1			2	
Jul	16	Troop Thomas	2			1	
Jul	16	Wellford Robert		1		·3	
Jul	16	West John	2			4	
Jul	16	Winlock William	1	3		3	
Jul	16	Wright Samuel	1			1	
Jul	16	Write [?] Ann		1		1	
Jul	17	Adam Hunter forge	2	44	3	12	2 chair wheels
Jul	17	Ditto @ home	3	24	6	14	4 phaeton wheels
Jul	17	Hewett Susanna		7	1	5	

Stafford Co., Va. personal property tax list - 1790

[arranged by date of tax enumeration]

Mo.	day	chargeable w/tax	white males 16+	/blacks 16+	12+	H	other
Jul	17	Hewett William	1	14	1	11	
Jul	20	Taylor William		4			
?	?	Bruce William	3	2		4	
?	?	Butler William	1	1	1	4	

* * * * *

* * *

*

[End of date-arranged 1790 personal property tax list]

Appendices

1. Legislative petition of the inhabitants of Stafford County, Oct. 15, 1776, seeking an alteration in the boundary line with King George County. [1]

To the Honourable the Speaker and Gentlemen of the House of Delegates
    The humble Petition of the Freeholders and inhabitants of the County of Stafford Sheweth
    That Petitions from the Inhabitants of the Counties of King George and Stafford were Presented the House of Burgesses under the old form of Government, praying a division of the said Counties, by a line from Potomack to Rappahannock River as a more conveniant boundary, and which were upon consideration thereof thought reasonable, and Commissioners appointed to settle the said line
    That upon the report of the said Commissioners to which your Petitioners beg leave to refer, a Bill was ordered to be brought in, and your Petitioners are informed would have passed into a law, had it not been for the the Governor's deserting his Government, and the Business of the Assembly thereby obstructed.
    That the said Assembly being now disolved, and a new form of Government established, your Petitioners, still desirous the alteration should take place, apprehend it necessary to revive their request to this Honourable House; And do therefore pray, that the Boundary, as set forth by the Commissioners in their said Report, to the late House of Assembly, may be now established by Law.
    And your Petitioners as in duty bound---

---

[1] Virginia State Library, Archives Division: Legislative Petitions, Stafford County, 1776-1789. 15 October 1776.

F. Thornton
John Washington
Henry Fitzhugh
William Hooe
Jo.n James
Willm. Fitzhugh
Alvin Mosby
Townshend Dade
Robert Stith
W. Gibbons Stuart
Lund Washington
Baldw. Dade
Thomas Fitzhugh
Joshua Browne
Enoch Benson
Anthony Ficklin
Robert Smith
David Archbill
Nasey West
Joseph West
Wm Griffin Turner
Simon Linn
Absalam Turner
Seth Foster
John Morrow
Wm Spence
Jeremiah Brown
Robt. Roach
Ric.d Brooks
Thos. Brooks

Benj.a Wittots [?]
Wm. Perfectt
John Callagan
Ben McCulley
James McCulley
Lewis Pritchett junr.
Mathew Grigg
John Skinner
Joseph Indicott
John Withers junr.
James Threlkeld
James Hiter
Thos. Whalebone
John Ballard
Steph Bright
Rhodm Hord
James Fant
John Bright
William Campbell
John Conner
John West
Joseph Fant
Jesse Kendall
John Crap
William Humphrey
Alexander Forbes
Gerard Banks
William Smith
Richard Davis
George White

John Smith

Samuel Martin

James Crap Senr.

John Hubbard

Ivin Jones

James Jones

Charles Jones

John Hardy

William Fristoe

Thomas Threlkeld

Lewis Lunsford

James Benson

Charles Benspn

Edward West

Robert White

Isaac Copage

Moses Copage

Daril [...]ron

Thomas Strother

Alexander Laskey

Thomas Skinker

John Thomas

James Allen

James Browne

Enoch Henslie

Philip Chapman

Thos. Ballard

Kellis Hord

James Paton

Samuel Smith

Anthony Berry

Andrew Wodrow

James Turner

Thomas James

James Stringfellow

Steven Smith

Peter Hord

Jesse Hord

Thomas Prim

Wm. Mullin

Jas. Jeffries

Charles Ficklen

George Villars

William Alexander

William Wood

Wm. Sturdy

Francis Day

Robert Jackson

Thomas Massey

Yel[n] Peyton

James Garrard

Appendix 2. *[A similarly-worded petition exists from the inhabitants of King George County].* [2]

John Thornton	William Peck
J. Skinker	Ger.d Wilkerson
John Fowards?	Sam.l Kendall Sen.r
Will Boon	Geo. Curtice
Geo. White	Law.s Ashton
Rich.d Davis	Dan.l Monroe
John Taliafero	Tho.s Jett
W.m Burgess	John Robertson
W. Bruce	Tho.s Smith
G. Marshall	W.m Bronaugh
Charles Deane Jr.	Anth.o Strother
John Etherington	John Lovett
Horatio Dade	Tho.s Hord
Francis Thornton	W. Grant
John Thornley Jr.	W.m Chadwell
Dan.l Briscoe	James D.....
John Wren	Jos. Rodgers
Joseph Robinson	Mich. Wallace
Thomas Peck	Andrew Wodroux?
Landon Carter	W.m Wallace
Thomas Berry	John Peck
John Dickie	Jed.y Pullen
John Crop	John Washington
William Wood	T. Turner
William Campbell	
Edward West	

---

[2] Virginia State Library, Archives Division: Legislative Petitions, Stafford County, 1776-1789. 15 October 1776.

3.   An act for altering and establishing the boundaries of the counties of Stafford and King George [1776]. [3]

WHEREAS the present situation of the counties of Stafford and King George is found to be very inconvenient to the inhabitants of those counties, in respect to their necessary attendance at their respective county courts and general musters, and they have petitioned that a more convenient boundary may be laid off between them:

Be it therefore enacted by the General Assembly of the commonwealth of Virginia, and it is hereby enacted by the authority of the same, That from and after the first day of January next the said counties of Stafford and King George shall be altered and bounded in the following manner, that is to say: Beginning at the mouth of Muddy creek, on the river Rappahannock, and running up the said creek, and the northwest branch thereof, to a small red oak, maple and persimon trees, at or near the head of the said branch, and between the plantations of Thomas and James Jones, thence north seventy one degrees east twenty five poles to a spring, said to be the head spring of Whipsewaughson creek, thence down the said creek to Potowmack creek, thence down Potowmack creek to Potowmack river, and thence down the said river, pursuing the old bounds of Stafford and King George, until it strikes Rappahannock river, thence up the said river to the beginning, and those parts of the said counties of Stafford and King George, shall be the lower county, and known by the name of King George; and for the upper county, beginning at the mouth of Potowmack creek, and running up the river Potowmack, and along the old bounds of Stafford

---

[3] From *Hening's Statutes at Large*, volume 9, pp. 244-245.

and King George, until it strikes the river Rappahanock, thence down the river Rappahannock to the mouth of Muddy Creek, the beginning of the dividing line, thence along the dividing line to the beginning, and those parts of the said counties of Stafford and King George within the said boundaries, to be known by the name of Stafford.

Provided, That nothing herein contained shall be construed to hinder the sheriffs or collectors of the said counties of Stafford and King George, as the same now stand, from collecting and making distress for any publick dues and officers fees which shall remain unpaid by the inhabitants of the said counties of Stafford and King George, at the time the siad alteration shall take place, but such sheriffs and collectors shall have the same power to collect and distrain for the said dues and fees, and shall be answerable for them in the same manner, as if this act had never been made; any law, custom, or usage, to the contrary thereof, in any wise notwithstanding.

And be it further enacted, by the authority aforesaid, That the courts of the said counties of Stafford and King George, respectively, shall have jurisdiction over all actions and suits, both in law and equity, which shall be depending before them at the time the said alteration shall take place, and may try and determine all such actions and suits, and issue process and award execution against the body or estate of the defendant or defendants in any such action or suit, in the same manner as if this act had never been made; any law, custom, or usage, to the contrary thereof, in any wise notwithstanding.

4. Petition to the House of Delegates to fix the court seat near
the center of the county. [4]

[In the lengthy petition it is noted that of the thirty justices
available to hear cases, only nine appeared at the previous August
Court, to wit: Baily Washington, Charles Carter, John James,
William Garrard, John Pollard, Harris Hooe, Robert Brent,
Thomas Montjoy, and James Garrard]
Signatories:

Traverse Daniel

John Fitzhugh

William Fitzhugh

James Hunter

Thomas Fitzhugh

William Hewitt

John Thornton

Daniel Payne

Daniel Triplett

Harris Hooe

Adam Hunter

John Pollard

James Kenyon

Gerard Banks

John Strode

Thomas Casson

Henry Armistead

William Newton

John Richards

Nathaniel Fox

James Crap

Thomas Skinker

Thomas Strother

Lincfield Sharp

Thomas Sharp

Kellis Hord

William Sulivan

Robert Laying?

George Curtis

John Curtis

William Curtis

William Ball

Lewis Payne

Thomas Bowen

Richard Night

George Doggett

John Bagnall

Robert Weston?

Daniel Miller

Henry Grigsby

---

[4] Virginia State Library, Archives Division: Legislative
Petitions, Stafford County, 1776-1789. 24 May 1779.

Aaron Pates
James Fagan
William Butler
William Limbrick
George Luncford
Anthony Strother
George Strother
John Newton
Thomas Whalebone
Barth.º Barrett
Charles Night
Patrick Fines
Francis Limbrick
Daniel Sulivan
Francis Jett
Abraham Newton
William Walker
Henry Glass
James Drake
George White
John Crapp
John Seddon
Andrew suter
Peter Hord
Lazarus Maddux
Thomas Hord
James Crap Jun.ʳ
Evan Jones
John Jones
James Jones
James Hord
William Mills West

John Palmer
Rawleigh Palmer
Rawleigh Palmer Jun.ʳ
Joseph Palmer
Thomas Twinham
Thomas McClannahan
Alexander Logey
John Doyle
Edward West
Edward West Jun.ʳ
John West Jun.ʳ
Hezekiah Proctor
Esly Schooler
William Campbell
James Benson
Thomas white
Spencer Haynie
Charles Benson
Moses Coppage
William Turner
Dan.ˡ Monrow
Tho.ˢ Turner Jun.ʳ
Nath.ˡ Hickeson
William Graves
William Mitchell
Benj.ᵃ Graves
Rich.ᵈ Davis
Martin Sulivan
W.ᵐ Sulivan
John Sulivan
John Mulberry
Jacob Mulberry

John Mulberry Jun.r

William Davis

Robert Jackson

John West

Stephen Smith

Samuel Smith

John Hubbard

Richard Coal

Thomas James

George James

William Jones

Charles Jones

Alex.r Simpson

...*[faded]* Simpson

Proctor Ballard

John Bright

John Hopwood

Peter Hopwood

George Stringfellow

Benj.a Pettit

William Hume

Thomas Vowles

William Wilson

Edward Moore

James Weeks

Henry Lee

John Harwood

George Fant

Joseph Reddish

Edw.d Bethell

Rob.t Harrison

And.w Boyle

John Albrite

Obed. McFarlin

Philip Calender

Matt.w Tibbit

James Stringfellow

Thomas Schooler

Zacharias Thompson

James Brown

William Humphries

William Jett

James Laverty

John Oliver

Thomas Ballard

William sharpe

Thomas Sharpe

Rob.t Sharpe

Edward Hoar

James Hiter

John Griffeth

Moses Threlkeld

James Threlkeld

Robert Elliston

John Minton

Benj.a Sharpe

Thomas Wallace

John Wallace

George Williamson

Reuben Burgess

Martin Heffertin

Robert Jackson Jun.r

George Jackson

William Monrow

Seth Foster
Anth.o Berry
Nath.l Burton
John Burton
James Burton
Richard Brookes
William Weeks
Henry [Brown?]
Jere.m Brown
John Rogers
Enoch Hensley
William Spence
Simon Lyn
Sam.l Martin
Ambrose Hord
Thomas Massey
Benj.a Massey
Philip Chapman
Joseph Fant
Samuel Mitchell
John Snelling
William Snelling
Tho.s Gallowhorn
William Simmon
William Suthard
William Allason
Moses Suthard
William Payne
Adam Newall
William McMillan
John Horner
John Day

Harmon Haner
Ja.s Williamson
John Boyes
Thomas Collins
John Brimmer
William Walker
William Winlock
John Mason
James Lyon
Ishamel Harmon
Ralph Smith
John Tonna
John Bradford
John Yeatman
William Wood
John Smith
Elijah Jones
John Row
Jesse Hord
David Hudson
John Ballard
Peter Hord
William Newton Jr.
Vincen Cox
William Horton
John Horton
William Lawson
Thomas Cortney
William Tyler
James Patton
Stephen Bright
James Turner

Isaac Coppage

Ignatius West

Rhodam Hord

George Weeks

John Conner

John Montroe

William West

John Mellit

James Brown

Jere.^m Pulliam

Joseph James

John Limbrick

Arnold Rogers

Nathl Snipe

Elisha Courtney

William Courtney

Christian Courtney

John Meal

John Baker

Solomon Walker

Moses Baker

Bartin Field

John Heckason

William Bishop

John Humphries

George Humphries

Jesse Humphries

Francis Nodan

Lynn Hite

Robt Snipe

John Matson

Saml Matson

John Kirkbride

Charles Martin

John Callinghan

John Underwood

John Bright

John Turner

William Hord

Elijah Jones

Thomas Schooler

George Jones

Seth Foster

Nathl Snipe Jr.

James Denovan

Richard Wine

Richd Wine Junr

Alex.^r Taylor

Benj.^a Suddoth

Benj.^a Suddoth Jr.

James Hord

Henry Jones

Thomas King

Mich.^l Thurman

Jos. Windcut

Blackle Martin

Jos. Rogers

Jos. Rogers Jr.

David Doile

John Mason

Smith Hansbrough

Peter Hansbrough

Alex. Mackentier

Danl Mason

John Baker
George Mason
William Mackentier
Thos Barby
Saml Bullock
Jos. Lewis
James Jeffries
Lewis Mason
John Gray
Jos. Reddish
George French
Benjamin Willitt
George Latherum
John Kendall
Chas Kendall
William Barby
Ephraim Knight
James Yelton
David Archbill
William Cummings
Asa Cummings
Peter Knight
Edmond Bowling
Daniel O'Cain
Henry Smith
William Smith
Joseph Smith
John Baker
Moses Baker
Francis Starn
John Serne
Dennis Doyle

James Kendall
Jeremiah Stark
John Sharp
Laurence Washington
George Kendall
Jerem.^{h} Kendall
Thos Edrington
John Fant
Saml Fant
John Horton
Enoch Horton
James Horton
Elijah Horton
Henry Horton
John Paterson
Mor.^{s} Hansbrough Jr.
Ja.^{s} Hansbrough Jr.
John Hagan
Leonard Hill
Jesse Hill
Anth.^{o} Ficklin
Enoch Benson
Benj.^{a} Ficklin
Jesse Kindle
James Vant
Griffin Turner
Jeremiah Reily?
Charles Ficklin
Richd Arrowsmith
Chas Thornton
Robert Smith
Richd Taylor

Absalom Turner

Adam Atcherson

David Archibald

Thomas Benson

John Heffernon

Robt Roach Sr.

Robt Roach Jr.

Thos Arrowsmith

------*[name too faded]*

William Roach

James Walker

William Bowlin

Ja.^s Arrowsmith

Ch.^s Lewis

Joshua Kendall Sr.

Henry Kendall

Joshua Kendall Jr.

William Parvitt

Dederick Bonear

John Nickelson

Peter Byrum Sr.

John Bradley

William Tungit

William Fritter

Moses Fritter Sr.

Moses Fritter Jr.

George Bussell

Thomas James

John Nelson

William Dunn

James Simpson

James Kindle Sr.

Bartley Kindall

John Kindall Jr.

Bennett Evins

Thos Turnum Jr.

Joseph West

John Grat

Gabriel Jones

Jesse Harlan

Israel Robinson

Frederick Klette

Francis Asman

John English

Edwd Singleton

John Ferney

Edward Wells

William Burgess Jr.

Micajah Hughes

William Kirk

John Stanley

William Allen

Saml R. Brooke

Edward Ferney

Philip Ferney

George Hood

Isaac Rose

-----*[faded]* Field

James Saunders

Jos. Lavinder

Jos.ⁱ Greenwood

James Thompson

Robt Lavinder

John Lavinder

William Haner
John Connyers
William Woodside
Benj^a Griffith
Robt Smith W.^{m}
John Shepherd
Archib.^{d} Rollon
Amos Thorp
Daniel Northup
John Reids
William Palmer
Harris Winlock
Abel Griffeth
John Pollitt
Henry Day
William Kayley
John Brown
John Banks
Henry Banks
Abner Vernon

5. Collector's Bond, Stafford County, Virginia, 8 April 1775 for Peter Hansbrough, David Briggs, and George Hamilton. [5]

Northern Neck of Virginia. Know all Men By these Presents that We Peter Hansbrough and David Briggs and George Hamilton do owe & stand justly indebted unto the Right Honourable Thomas Lord Fairfax Proprietor of the Northern Neck of Virginia the full & just Sum of One Thousand Pounds lawful Money of Great Britain to be paid unto him the said Thomas Lord Fairfax his Executors or Administrators to which Payment to be well and truly made we bind ourselves & each of us our & each of our Heirs Executors & Administrators jointly & severally by these Presents. In Witness whereof we have hereunto set our Hands & Seals. Dated this Eight Day of April One thousand seven hundred & seventy five.

The Condition of the above Obligation is such that Whereas Thomas Bryan Martin Esq.[r] of the Country of Frederick being fully authorized & impowered by the said Thomas Lord Fairfax to ask demand sue for decover & receive all & every the Rents Quitrents & all other Rights & Dues issuing growing & arising by by [sic] from & out of the said Northern Neck & whereas he the said Thomas Bryan Martin hath constituted deputed & appointed the above bound Peter Hansbrough to collect & receive all Debts Dues & Demands that are due & owing unto the said Thomas Lord Fairfax from all & every the Tenants & Landholders within the County of Stafford. If therefore the said Peter Hansbrough shall by himself or Deputies duly qualified with all possible

---

    [5] From Virginia State Library. Archives Division. Accessions No. 24062. Fairfax Family Northern Neck Proprietary Papers, 1688-1810. Folder C-19.

Dispatch ask demand & receive of all & every the Tenants & Landholders aforesaid their several Debts Dues Quitrents Fines & Forfeitures that *[folio 2]* that were due & owing to the said Lord Fairfax on the Feast Day of St. Michael the Archangel last past being in the Year of Our Lord God One thousand seven hundred & seventy four in good & lawful Money of Great Britain at the Rate off two Shillings for every hundred Acres of Land & so proportionally for a greater or lesser Quantity. And where such lawful Money of Great Britain or Bills of Exchange cannot be had then to receive the same in Current Money of Virginia at & after the Rate of twenty five per Centum Advance on such Current Money and where such Current Money cannot be had aforesaid then to receive good inspected Tobacco at & after the Rate of thirty two Pounds of Tobacco for every hundred Acres & so proportionally as aforesaid.   Furthermore if the said Peter Hansbrough shall well & truly pay or cause to be paid unto the said Lord Fairfax his Attorney or Attornies Agent or Agents what Money Bills of Exchange & Tobacco he & his Deputies shall receive on or before the Twenty ninth Day of September next ensuing & likewise return a true compleat & exact Rental then the above Obligation to be void or else to remain and be in full Force & Virtue

Signed sealed & delivered in presence of

George Lo??   David Briggs

John Bagle   George Hamilton

6. Stafford Court's recommendation for an addition of the number of justices and for William Garrard as Sheriff. 2 October 1781 [6]

Stafford Sct.   September Court 1781

The Court do recommend to his Excellency the Governour, the following Gentlemen, to wit, John Murray, Daniel Triplet, William Phillips, John Rouzy Peyton, William Alexander, & William Eustace, to be added to the Commission of the Peace, for this County.

Attest   Tho. ES Tyler CSC

List of Justices in the Present Commission

Baily Washington, Samuel Selden, Gowry Waugh, William Brent, John Brown, John James, Cha.[S] Carter, Arthur Morson, William Garrard, John Pollard, Daniel Payne, Gerrard Banks, Harris Hooe, William Fitzhugh, Thomas Mountjoy, John Moncure, Henry Washington, Raleigh T. Brown, William Hewitt, Thomas Fitzhugh, James Garrard & John Cooke Gts.

Col.[O] Charles Carter's Sheriffalty expiring at Next Court his Excellency is requested to send a Commission for that Office to William Garrard Gt. the next in Commissioner the Recommend.[n] of Sheriffs.

Tho. ES Tyler CSC
Stafford Sept. 25 81

End of Volume 2

---

[6] Virginia State Library, Archives Division. Civil Papers, 1779-1782. Stafford County, 1781.

A

Abbet
Elijah   289,   323,
    355, 388, 415, 448
George   189,   289,
    323, 415, 454
James   289,   323,
    355, 392, 415, 454
John 355, 392
John Sr. 415, 461
Abbett
George 355, 385
Abbot
Elijah 275, 476, 510
J. 273
James 218, 272
John 187, 218, 233
John Sr. 476, 510
Abbott
George 476, 507
John 253
Accakeek   Company
    103, 141
Accokick   Company
    66, 78, 92
Achison
John 289, 331
Adam
John 190
Adams
Daniel 24
Francis   103, 166,
    167
Gabriel   103, 157,
    159
George 24
John   5, 103, 148,
    164, 219, 245, 492,
    530
John Jr. 103, 174
John Sr. 24
Richard 24
William 24
Addams
John 103, 141
Addie
William 77
Addison
John 65, 72, 77

Adie
B. 279
Benjamin 179, 224,
    254, 289, 331, 355,
    394, 415, 461
Hugh 49, 51
William 65, 91, 179,
    224, 254, 279, 289,
    331, 355, 394, 415,
    457
William   Jr.   355,
    395
William   Sr.   355,
    394
Adis
William 212
Aedy
Aedy · 476, 520
Benjamin 476, 514
Agan
John 272, 274
Agin
John 289, 326, 355,
    394, 415, 457, 476,
    509
Aictheson
Nathan 186
Aitchason
Amos 253
John 251
Nathaniel 251
Aitcheson
Amos 186, 187
Albin
Thomas 103, 171
Albright
John 207
Albrite
John 544
Alesander
William 202
Aleson
William 289, 329
Alexander
Ann 49
Charles 65, 77, 91
John 49, 65, 77, 91,
    103, 142, 171, 172,
    306, 346
P. 278
P. T. 231
Phil T. 184

Philip (Estate) 492,
    525
Phillip 49, 306, 339,
    372, 407, 432, 467
Robert 5, 103, 157,
    173
Thomas 250
W. Schos? 492, 526
William   184,   207,
    232, 237, 251, 267,
    276, 306, 319, 339,
    346, 355, 372, 382,
    392, 401, 432, 444,
    462, 492, 503, 523,
    538, 552
Allanson
David 244
Allason
David 266
William 81, 91, 545
Allay
Nathan 254
Allen
.....ary 203
Andrew 61, 62
George 103, 156
James   77, 91, 99,
    538
John   5,   6, 49, 65,
    77, 91, 103, 174
John Jr. 103, 174
M. 282
Mary 194, 226, 245
William   5, 49, 65,
    85, 103, 141, 146,
    155, 156, 165, 171,
    236, 243, 548
Allensthorpe
Jacob 243
Allentharp
Jacob   306,   347,
    372, 401, 432, 465
Allentharpe
J. 282
Jacob 227
Allerton
Col. Isaak 103, 143
Isaac 5
Isaak 103, 143
Allexon
Thomas 61

Alley
  Nathaniel Benjamin
    213
Alliason
  David 372, 409
Allison
  David 306, 351,
    432, 469, 492, 529
  George 103, 143
  Henry 432, 464,
    492, 523
  Thomas 62, 372,
    408, 432, 467, 492,
    529
  William 269, 306,
    351
Ally
  Nathan Barton 179
Amblee
  Joseph 415, 459
  Thomas 415, 459
Ambler
  Decimus Filius 103,
    144
  Dissimus Phillius
    103, 145
  James 355, 393
  Joseph 476, 517
  Thomas 355, 393,
    476, 508
  William 355, 393
Ambrose
  John 49
Anderer
  Scott 20
Anderson
  David 5, 49, 65, 77,
    91, 103, 167
  John 306, 341, 432,
    465, 492, 526, 530
  William 23, 275,
    289, 328, 355, 394,
    415, 447, 476, 520
Andrew
  Andrew 319, 352
Andrews
  John 313, 345
Ann
  Mary Ann 477, 510
Antram
  Daniel 100, 270

Antrum
  Daniel 289, 331,
    355, 392, 415, 454,
    476, 510
  Levi 355, 392
  Levy 289, 331
Archbill
  David 537, 547
Archibald
  David 548
Archiball
  David 306, 348
Armistead
  Henry 542
Arrasmith
  .....mas 203
  Richard 193, 245
  T. 282
  Thomas 245
Arrington
  ----- 103, 149, 162
  Wansford 5, 103,
    104, 147, 152, 162,
    163, 165
Arrosmith
  James 271, 289,
    325, 476, 510
  Thomas 193, 306,
    346
Arrowsmith
  James 355, 385,
    415, 451, 548
  Richard 547
  Thomas 372, 406,
    432, 468, 492, 526,
    548
Artram
  Daniel 242
Asbury
  Thomas 104, 165
Ashby
  Halafax 476, 509
  Halifax 415, 450
  Henry 104, 152
  John 62, 65, 77, 91,
    104, 152
  Robert 28, 49, 65,
    77, 91, 104, 143,
    144, 151, 152, 163,
    289, 325, 415, 448,
    476, 520
  Robert Jr. 104, 152

Robert Sr. 104, 152
  S. 282
  Sarah 179, 217,
    226, 254, 289, 325,
    355, 392
  Stephen 104, 152
  Thomas 27, 70,
    104, 152
Ashford
  John 62
  Michael 104, 143,
    145, 155
  William 61
Ashley
  Robert 355, 386
Ashmore
  John 104, 172
Ashton
  Burdett 104, 162
  Capt. 104, 163
  Col. Henry 104,
    154, 169, 170
  Henry 104, 147,
    148, 159, 170
  Lawless? 539
  Peter 104, 161
Askins
  Edward 26
Asman
  Francis 548
Astbury
  Thomas 104, 156
Atcherson
  Adam 548
Atchison
  Amos 218, 235, 274
  Amus 289, 333,
    355, 391, 415, 454,
    476, 509
  J. 273
  John 217, 235, 355,
    388, 415, 448, 476,
    509
  Nathan 235, 274,
    289, 331, 355, 385,
    415, 448, 476, 509
  Nathaniel 217
Atwell
  Hugh 104, 170
Awbrey
  ----- 104, 169

Barnett
  William 432, 462
Barnot
  James   289, 326,
    357, 393, 415, 448,
    478, 520
  William   290, 326,
    356, 388, 415, 448,
    477, 514
Barns
  George   272, 290,
    327, 356, 388, 415,
    447
  Leonard 99
  Thomas 106, 170
Barnwell
  James 272
Barraway
  Patrick 21
Barret
  Bathholomew 230
Barrett
  Bartholomew   306,
    351, 372, 401, 432,
    464, 543
  Jacob 433, 471
Bartlett
  William 106, 170
Bartlit
  William 106, 159
Barton
  Bur 24
  James 24
  Thomas 5, 24, 25
  Thomas Jr. 25, 106,
    172
  Valentine   24, 106,
    147, 148
Bates
  Behethlem 253
  James 34
  John 307, 347
  Joseph   306, 339,
    372, 404, 433, 471,
    492, 525
  Robert 106, 156
  Thomas   191, 227,
    232, 246, 282, 372,
    402
Batt
  William 202

Battew
  William 106, 152
Batting
  Nicholas 106, 167
Batto
  William 255
Battoe
  James   179, 226,
    255, 292, 337, 357,
    398, 417, 459, 478,
    518
  John 255
  William   179, 226,
    291, 334, 355, 386,
    478, 518
Battooe
  ----- 106, 152
  J. 281
  James 65, 78, 92
  William 281
Battow
  William 417, 459
Battue
  Peter 33
Baul
  William   290, 327,
    356, 388, 477, 511
Baxter
  Abraham 49
  James 68
  Thomas 106, 162
Baylis
  ----- 106, 146
  John   49, 106, 146,
    147
Beach
  Alexander 5
  Thomas   61, 290,
    307, 334, 348, 356,
    386, 418, 459, 478,
    517
Beagle
  Joel   415, 449, 478,
    521
  John 260, 275, 290,
    326, 355, 385, 415,
    447, 477, 509
  John Sr. 355, 385
  Joseph   235, 253,
    289, 325, 355, 386
  Thomas   369, 398,
    477, 509

Bean
  William   106, 163,
    164
Bearh
  ----- 106, 146
Beasley
  Phillips 307, 341
Beasly
  Philip 373, 407
  Phillip   432, 465,
    493, 529
Beaver
  Francis   106, 149,
    168
Beavin
  Daniel 235
Bedgel
  John 190
Beech
  Thomas 62
Bell
  ----- 106, 151
  Alexander 106, 149
  Bell 218
  Charles   219, 356,
    388, 416, 451
  Christopher 106
  Daniel 417, 457
  Elijah   180, 213,
    255, 290, 328, 357,
    399, 416, 450, 477,
    514
  Fielding   356, 393,
    416, 451, 477, 511
  G. 282
  George   180, 215,
    290, 328, 329
  George Jr.   180,
    213, 224, 255, 416,
    450, 476, 507
  George Sr.   224,
    255, 357, 397, 416,
    450, 477, 509
  John   65, 78, 92,
    106, 149, 164, 207,
    215, 243, 268, 290,
    307, 329, 349, 373,
    409, 433, 471, 493,
    529
  John (Rev.)   106,
    149, 150, 151, 167
  John Jr. 106, 173

Jonathan 180, 213,
224, 255, 290, 330,
355, 386, 416, 450,
477, 509
Jonathan Sr. 213
Mary 188, 215, 260,
275, 290, 326, 357,
394, 416, 451, 478,
517
Thomas 215
William 215
Belton
Richard 245
Benear
Dederick 416, 451
Dedreck 477, 515
Dedrick 189
Derek 357, 396
Derk 291, 336
Bengey
John 306, 339
Beniers
Durke 267
Benitt
William 6
Benjamin
Gregory 257
Bennet
Mason 30
William 30, 106,
151
William Jr. 30
Bennett
John 106, 107, 152,
164
Bensen
John 492, 525
Benson
Charles 538, 543
Enoch 99, 190, 242,
265, 537, 547
Enough 290, 331,
356, 392, 417, 454,
477, 511
James 203, 227,
307, 342, 373, 407,
433, 467, 493, 528,
538, 543
Prue 356, 392
Robert 242
Thomas 548

Zachariah 265, 291,
336, 358, 400, 433,
467, 492, 525
Zachary 210
Berkeley
William 107, 168
Berkley
William 107, 159
Berlit
William 107, 159
Bern
John 317, 340
Bernard
----- 107, 161
Berry
.....than 203
A. 282
Anthony 191, 227,
245, 307, 346, 372,
402, 432, 465, 492,
526, 538, 545
Benjamin 199, 207,
230
Edward 29
Joseph 49
Richard 189, 307,
343, 372, 402, 432,
464, 492, 523
Sarah 201, 232,
250, 277, 306, 339,
372, 401, 432, 464
Thomas 13, 107,
201, 232, 276, 307,
344, 372, 402, 432,
465, 492, 526, 539
W. 277
William 188, 202,
259, 492, 525
Berryman
----- 107, 161
Benjamin 65
Elizabeth 49
Gilson 49, 65
James 50
John 6, 65, 77, 91
Bessick
Daniel 357, 393
Bethel
Edward 249, 265,
291, 334, 416, 449
William 107, 143

Bethell
----- 23
Edward 23, 356,
386, 478, 519, 544
William 23
Betty
Magdalin 290, 331
Bevans
Ann (widow) 107,
149
Morrice 24, 25
Beveridge
John 200
Bevins
Maurice 107, 162
Bigam
Christopher 21
Billingslee
Clement 290, 329,
357, 393, 416, 451
James 289, 325,
356, 388, 416, 451
James Sr. 289, 325
Billingsley
Clem 478, 520
James 476, 507
Billingsly
James 268
Bing
John 355, 385
Bingey
John 249, 277
Bingy
John 373, 406
Biram
Peter 50
Birdwell
Jacob 217
Bishell
Benjamin 207
Bishop
William 546
Biven
Maurice 6
Bivin
Maurice 107, 149,
165
Maurice (Mrs.) 107,
148
Bivins
Maurice 107, 164,
166

Black
  Margrett 307, 343, 372, 402, 432, 462, 492, 523
Blackburn
  ----- 107, 144, 152
  John 107, 174
  Richard 107, 144, 163
Blackley
  ----- 107, 167
  John 107, 164, 167
Blackman
  Daniel 28
  John 107, 145, 174
Blackwell
  ----- 107
Blake
  John 357, 400
Bland
  James 5, 107, 154, 162, 163, 166
  John 5, 107, 154
  Robert 107, 154
  Widow 6
  William 107, 108, 149, 154, 163, 165, 166
Blisford
  Charles 37
Blower
  John 108, 167
Blowers
  John 108, 150, 158
Bobo
  William 478, 521
Boboe
  William 357, 396
Bobs
  William 418, 459
Bolling
  .....mes 203
  Byram 270
  Charles 306, 341, 433, 467, 492, 526
  Edmund 243
  J. 282
  James 191, 246, 306, 341, 372, 405, 433, 467, 492, 525
  Samuel 194, 203, 227, 372, 405

Simon 307, 344
Spencer 210, 243
Thomas 191, 246, 306, 341, 372, 405, 433, 467, 493, 531
William 203, 207, 227, 246, 306, 307, 339, 344, 373, 406, 433, 470, 493, 531
William Sr. 307, 344
Bonear
  Dederick 548
Boon
  Will 539
Boring
  John 37
Bott
  Thomas 108, 152
Botts
  A. 280
  Aaron 179, 214, 224, 255, 356, 388, 417, 457
  Ann 478, 518
  Aron 290, 331
  Bernard 108, 170
  J. 280
  John 40, 91, 179, 214, 224, 255, 290, 331
  Joseph 179, 214, 224, 255, 291, 334, 356, 388, 417, 454, 477, 511
  Sabina 214, 224, 255
  Seth 40, 65, 78
  Thomas 6, 40, 49, 108, 150-152
  William 179, 214, 223, 254, 281, 290, 331, 356, 388, 417, 454, 477, 511
Bourn
  Daniel 5
Bowen
  B. 277
  Burkett 306, 344, 373, 406, 432, 465
  Burkitt 493, 528
  Mathew 61

Thomas 201, 232, 250, 278, 306, 339, 373, 407, 433, 467, 542
Bowens
  Michal 493, 528
Bower
  Michael 269
  Michal 307, 349
Bowers
  Michael 207, 236
  Michal 373, 409, 433, 471
Bowlin
  Benjamin 190, 290, 327, 356, 391, 417, 459, 478, 521
  Byrum 416, 449
  Spencer 356, 388, 418, 459, 478, 519
  William 548
Bowling
  Edmond 547
  Samuel 245
Boyce
  Christopher 108, 161
Boyer
  John 373, 409
Boyers
  Leonard 207
Boyes
  John 545
Boyle
  Andrew 544
Bradford
  ----- 6
  John 108, 158, 545
Bradley
  John 548
  William 356, 392
  William Sr. 356, 392
Bradly
  Charles 290, 330, 477, 508
  George 241, 271
  James 211
  John 219, 291, 336, 367, 387, 416, 451, 478, 518

John 180, 255, 290,
329, 356, 389, 416,
452
Joshua 5
Lawrence 292, 327,
358, 389
Sally 180
Thomas 49
William 50, 184,
202, 212, 225, 232,
277, 306, 339, 372,
401, 432, 464, 492,
534, 543
Buzan
----- 62
Byram
Cuthbert 209, 242,
270
George 187, 253,
273
Peter 5, 49, 65,
110, 147, 167, 209,
210, 242, 270
Richard 5
William 186, 267
William Jr. 253
Byrum
Cuthbert 292, 337,
355, 386, 415, 448,
477, 509
George 290, 332,
356, 391, 415, 449,
476, 507
Nimrod 356, 386,
418, 459, 478, 521
Peter 292, 337, 355,
386, 417, 459, 478,
521
Peter Sr. 548
Sarah 357, 395,
417, 459
Senate 477, 509
William 289, 325,
357, 396, 416, 452,
477, 509
William Sr. 289,
325

C

Cahal
James 434, 466
Cain
James 110, 169,
479, 511
Calamees
Marquiss 29
Calameese
Marquis 110, 145,
161
Calameez
Marquis 110, 146
Calamus
Marquiss 110, 144
Calender
Philip 245, 374,
409, 544
Callagan
John 537
Callendar
Philip 237, 266
Callender
Phillip 207, 308,
346, 494, 526
Callinghan
John 546
Calmeus
Marquis 7
Calmeze
Marquis 50
Calvert
George 6, 110, 172
John 6
Camberford
James 479, 511
Campbell
Hugh 110, 172
William 203, 227,
537, 539, 543
Cane
Daniel 292, 330
Canzy
John 38
Capon
Thomas 276
Carey
----- 50
Carl
William 418, 447

Carlile
John 62
Carnet
Benjamin 292, 332
Carney
Benjamin 358, 389
J. 281
Jessey 479, 511
John 66, 110, 153,
479, 511
Joshua 78, 92, 223,
255
Josua 292, 332, 358,
389, 418, 454
Thomas 110, 160
Carny
Joshua 180, 212
Carpenter
John 50
Richard 110, 155
Thomas 7
Carrell
Nicholas 11
Carroll
Nicholas 110, 142
Carryl
Nicholas 110, 145
Carson
Alexander 40
Carter
----- 110, 171
Ann 225
Anne 211
Benjamin 253
C. 279
Catherine 212, 226,
256
Charles 61, 211,
242, 292, 307, 336,
351, 358, 374, 391,
407, 418, 434, 456,
471, 479, 516, 542,
552
Col. 110, 148, 150,
157, 159, 160, 163,
174
Col. Charles 265
George 374, 407,
434, 463
H. 280

Harris 180, 213, 223, 255, 256, 292, 331, 358, 389, 418, 450, 479, 511
Henry 308, 339, 373, 401, 434, 462, 493, 524
J. 279, 282
James 50, 66, 110, 165, 180, 213, 226, 256, 292, 325, 418, 450, 479, 507
James Jr. 50
Jedediah 180, 255, 258, 282, 292, 329, 358, 389, 418, 450, 479, 511
Jedidiah 225
Job 61
John 66, 73, 78, 92, 180, 212, 215, 226, 256, 273, 292, 326, 329, 358, 399, 418, 450, 479, 516
John Jr. 253
John Sr. 187
Joseph 50, 66, 78, 92, 194, 246, 308, 344, 373, 403, 434, 468, 494, 526
Katherin 180
Landon 110, 165, 203, 227, 539
Luce 92
Lucey 79
Renn 479, 508
Robert 10, 110, 111, 141, 143, 148, 149, 150, 156, 157, 160, 165, 173, 308, 347, 494, 532
Robert Jr. 111, 169, 170
Robert W. 192, 246, 374, 407, 434, 471
S. W. 283
Carty
Timothy 36
Cary
----- 111, 147, 152, 153

Edward 207
Cash
John 254, 418, 456
Peter 418, 456, 480, 521
Cashal
James 494, 525
Cason
Thomas 66, 92
Casson
----- 372, 401
Thomas 78, 184, 201, 232, 250, 307, 339, 432, 462, 542
Casson's Estate 492, 523
Catlet
John 26, 111, 155
John Jr. 26
Catlett
John 7, 111, 151, 165
Cave
William 40, 50
Caves
Thomas 308, 348
Ceed
James 21
Chadburn
Amos 20
John 25
William 20
Chadwell
Brian 292, 327, 418, 452, 479, 511
Briant 358, 389
Bryan 211, 275
Bryant 237, 242
George 34
James 34
John 6, 34
John Jr. 34
Joseph 34
William 34, 293, 338, 539
Chalmers
Daniel 50
Chambers
John 184, 200, 231, 249
Joseph 36

Chamblin
Brian 50
Chamlin
Aaron 23
Brian 23
Brian Jr. 23
William 23
Champ
John 7
William 111, 159, 163, 165
Champe
John 111, 171
Chandler
Henry 212
John 37
Wilkinson 292, 335
William 111, 158, 174, 265, 358, 394
Williamson 418, 456, 479, 517
Chanuller
John 61
Chapman
Joseph 7, 31
Mrs. 73
Nathaniel 50, 51, 66, 111, 171
Philip 203, 227, 246, 373, 405, 538, 545
Phillip 191, 307, 351
Sh. 282
Taylor 50, 66, 78, 92
Thomas 6, 111, 141
William 111, 144
Chatham
William Fitzhugh 184, 232
Chelkett
William 434, 463
Chesshire
Mary 292, 336, 358, 394
Chilton
John 14, 45, 111, 154
Mark 111, 148, 154, 161, 172
Widow 45

William   41, 308,
    339, 493, 524
Chinn
    Andrew 318, 350
    Joseph   188, 259,
        277, 308, 340, 373,
        401, 493, 524
    Perry 292, 335, 358,
        389, 418, 452, 479,
        508
    Susanna 188
    Susannah 308, 340
Chinon
    Joseph 433, 462
Chissom
    Elizabeth 292, 335,
        358, 393, 418, 447,
        479, 519
Chiveral
    John 213, 234, 252,
        275, 358, 391
Chiverall
    John 185, 292, 337,
        479, 519
Chiverault
    John 418, 459
Chloe
    John Jr. 273
Church
    Robert 111, 166
Citchen
    William 494, 529
Clark
    Ann 183, 307, 339
    Anne 199
    George 39, 41
    John 39, 61
Clarke
    Anna 230
    Anne 249
    George 50
Clements
    Margaret 50
Clemings
    John 259
Clemmons
    George 19
    John 308, 340, 358,
        389, 418, 452, 493,
        524

Clerk
    Ann 278, 379, 409,
        410
    William 374, 409
Clifton
    ----- 111, 160
    Burdett 50
    Burdit 66, 78, 92,
        111, 161
    H. 279
    Henry   180, 215,
        225, 255, 292, 327,
        358, 389, 418, 450,
        479, 516
    William   50, 111,
        160
Cloe
    James   180, 255,
        359, 399
    James Jr. 292, 330,
        359, 399, 418, 460,
        479, 520
    James Sr. 292, 330,
        418, 459, 480, 521
    John 292, 328
Clors
    James Jr. 274
Clow
    J. 280
    James 215
    John 235
Clowe
    James 223
Coal
    Richard 544
Coale
    Charles 19
Coats
    George   292, 331,
        358, 396, 418, 447,
        479, 516
Cock
    Elisabeth 78
Cocke
    ----- 111
    Catesby   111, 112,
        153, 154, 158, 162,
        163, 164
Cocks
    Enough 358, 400
Coffer
    Francis 6

Widow 112, 169
Colbert
    George 112, 167
    Sarah 6
Cole
    George 200
    Richard 203, 227
    William   292, 326,
        358, 393, 479, 511
Coleclough
    Benjamin 6
    Rachael 50
Collet
    John 112, 157
Collins
    Molton   112, 145,
        155
    Thomas   207, 236,
        244, 268, 308, 349,
        374, 409, 434, 472,
        494, 529, 545
Colney
    Elijah 494, 528, 531
    Elisha   373, 403,
        434, 464
    George 494, 532
    Joseph 373, 403
Colquahoon
    Walter 374, 409
Colquhoun
    Walter   308, 349,
        494, 530
Colquhown
    Walter 266
Colquohound
    Walter 434, 469
Colson
    Charles 66, 78, 92
Colvert
    John 112, 172
Combs
    Cuthbert 185, 233,
        253, 271, 292, 328,
        358, 399, 418, 457,
        479, 509
    Fielding 358, 396
    John   66, 78, 92,
        112, 144, 145, 187,
        218, 233, 253

Vincent Jr. 232,
250, 373, 401, 403,
434, 463, 494, 525
Vincent Sr. 201,
232, 308, 346, 434,
464, 494, 525
Voncent Jr. 308,
340
Craighil
William 244
Craighill
Nathaniel 236
William 207, 236
Crap
James 78, 542
James Jr. 543
James Sr. 538
John 537
Crapp
John 543
Crass
James Jr. 203
James Sr. 203
John 203
Crawford
----- 6
Creel
John 7, 112, 148,
149
Critchett
James 434, 471
Crooper
Richard 112, 113,
162, 163, 167
Crop
J. 282
J. Jr. 282
J. Sr. 282
James 92, 308, 342
James Jr. 190, 227,
246, 374, 408, 434,
468, 494, 526
James Sr. 192, 227,
246, 308, 342, 374,
408, 434, 468, 494,
526
John 190, 227, 246,
308, 342, 374, 408,
434, 468, 494, 532,
539
Crosby
Daniel 113, 144

George 50, 113,
144, 146, 147, 155,
165
George Sr. 6, 113,
155
Uriah 66
Uriel 92
Cross
James 66
Crosy
Uriel 78
Crump
John 113, 156
William 61, 62
Cumberford
Edward 31
James 212, 418, 452
Cumings
William 274
Cummings
Alexander 7
Asa 547
John 78, 92
William 547
Cummins
Asa 185, 218, 235,
253, 274
Asey 292, 326, 358,
386
Asia 479, 509
Asie 419, 460
Moses 218
William 186, 253,
292, 325, 358, 386,
418, 454, 479, 510
Zachariah 366, 398
Curtice
Aaron 308, 339,
373, 401, 433, 462,
493, 525
Elijah 309, 348,
373, 406
George 183, 307,
339, 373, 401, 434,
463, 493, 524, 539
George Jr. 307, 339
George Sr. 307, 339
John 184, 307, 309,
349, 351, 373, 403,
434, 464, 493, 523

Richard 184, 308,
351, 373, 403, 434,
464, 493, 523
Thaddeus 494, 527
Theodocius 434,
464
Theodotia 314, 343
William 184, 250,
308, 346, 373, 402,
434, 465, 494, 527
Curtis
Aaron 199
George 542
John 113, 173, 542
Theodoshe 184
William 542
Curtiss
Aaron 230
George 200, 230,
249, 276
J. 278
John 200, 231, 249
Richard 201, 231,
250, 277
Theodore 278
Theodosia 249
William 202, 232
William Sr. 278

D

Dade
Baldwin 66, 79, 92,
537
Cadwalader 79
Cadwallader 66, 92
Cadwallader Jr. 66
Cadwaller 51
Francis 50, 66, 79,
113, 162
Henry 51
Horatio 539
Rose 66, 79, 92
Townsend 50, 77,
79, 86
Townsend Jr. 51
Townshend 66, 79,
92, 537
Daffin
Vincent 374, 406

Dick
  Moses   359, 395,
    419, 452, 480, 511
Dickenson
  Hannah   293, 331,
    359, 394, 419, 456,
    480, 507
Dickerson
  Edward   188, 219,
    260
  William   189
Dickie
  John   539
Dickinson
  Hannah   275
Diggs
  Edward   216, 234
Dilley
  John   419, 459, 480,
    522
Dillion
  John   180, 256, 359,
    398
Dillon
  John   293, 329, 419,
    450, 480, 507
Disher
  Lewis   374,   409,
    419, 454
Dishman
  Sam   45
  Samuel   45
Dishmon
  Samuel   114, 163
Dishue
  Lewis   480, 520
Dodd
  James   314, 343
Dodson
  Jervas   114, 162
Dogen
  John   37
Doggett
  George   542
Doile
  David   546
Dolehy
  William   25
Doleman
  Raleigh   210
Donaldson
  William   62

Donalson
  William   61
Donathan
  Gerard   309,   339,
    374, 401
  Gerrard   434, 463
Donavan
  James   319,   351,
    374, 409
  Joseph   434, 466
Doniphan
  Alexander   66,   79,
    92, 114, 171
  Garrard   200
  Gerrard   230, 249,
    276
  Matthew   8, 66, 79
  Mott   92, 93
Doniphon
  Matt   50
Dooling
  John   68
Doratha
  James   318, 350
Dorgan
  Timothy   114, 150
Dormant
  Michael   114, 174
Dorment
  Michael   114, 174
Dorril
  William   114, 171
Dorrill
  -----   114, 157
  William   114, 168
Dorsen
  John   217
Dorson
  Christopher   293,
    330, 359, 389, 419,
    452, 480, 520
  John   185, 251, 359,
    389, 419, 452, 480,
    507
  Spencer   359, 396
  William   293, 330,
    359, 396, 419, 452,
    480, 517
Doudle
  Brawner   309, 345
  James   309, 345

Douglass
  Archibald   259, 273
  Catherine   66
  Cathin   92
  Cathrine   79
Dougless
  Archibeld   190
Douglis
  Archabald   480, 507
  Archabeld   359, 391
  Archebald   293, 338
  Archibild   419, 447
Dowdle
  James   374,   406,
    435, 468, 494, 528
Downing
  -----   114, 171
  George   37
  William   30,   114,
    142
Downman
  B. Joseph   494, 530
  J. B.   277
  Joseph B.   231, 249,
    374, 401, 434, 463
  Joseph Ball   309,
    342
  R. W.   261, 268
  Raleigh   99, 201
  Rawleigh   184, 293,
    332
  Rawleigh W.   480,
    522
  Rawleigh   William
    359, 391, 419, 452
  Travers   45
Doyall
  Dennis   293,   333,
    334, 359, 386, 391,
    419, 447
  Dennis Jr.   419, 447,
    480, 515
  Dennis   Sr.   293,
    333, 480, 515
  Patterson   293, 334,
    359, 385, 419, 447,
    480, 517
Doyle
  Dennis   547
  John   543
  Patterson   241, 270

Moses 67, 80, 212, 243, 294, 336, 420, 452

Moses Jr. 268, 360, 386, 420, 452, 481, 511, 548

Moses Sr. 268, 294, 333, 360, 386, 481, 519, 548

William 243, 267, 291, 294, 332, 336, 358, 400, 420, 450, 481, 510, 548

William Jr. 360, 388

Frittoe
 Moses 93

Froughner
 John 309, 346

Fugate
 Benjamin 230, 276
 Daniel 230, 277
 Francis 254, 276
 Francis Jr. 199, 230
 Francis Sr. 199, 230
 G. 281
 Gerrard 180, 224, 256
 Jeremiah 181, 256, 360, 389
 Jerremiah 294, 338

Fuget
 ----- 61

Fugett
 Benjamin 309, 340, 494, 524
 Daniel 309, 340, 435, 463, 494, 524
 Frances 310, 340, 435, 463
 Frances Jr. 310, 340, 435, 469
 Francis 309, 340, 495, 533
 Francis Jr. 494, 524

Fugitt
 Benjamin 374, 404, 435, 463
 Daniel 374, 404
 Francis Jr. 374, 402
 Francis Sr. 374, 404
 Gerard 260

Fulk
 James 8

Fuller
 Stephen 7, 8

Furr
 Thomas 117, 155, 156, 174

G

Gaddes
 Alexander 94

Gaddess
 Alexander 77, 225

Gaddis
 Alexander 215, 256
 Ann 295, 329, 361, 395, 421, 456, 482, 520

Gaddiss
 W. 281

Gainer
 James 26

Gallehew
 Solomon 185

Gallowhorn
 Thomas 545

Gant
 William 295, 326, 360, 385, 421, 452, 482, 507

Gardner
 Mary 117, 171
 Phillip 295, 335, 361, 386, 421, 449, 482, 508
 Susanna 117, 171
 Thomas 117, 171, 174

Garison
 George 252
 Moses 181

Garner
 Jacob 310, 339
 John 231, 310, 340, 375, 402, 435, 462, 495, 524
 Jones 291, 336
 Jonus 357, 400
 Philip 212, 241
 Thomas 8

William 375, 407, 435, 462, 495, 524

Garrard
 D. 283
 Daniel 100, 191, 204, 227, 246
 James 99, 210, 542, 552
 Mary 295, 329, 482, 516
 W. 280
 William 181, 218, 257, 295, 329, 361, 395, 421, 444, 455, 542, 552

Garrison
 Aaron 181, 361, 397, 422, 460, 482, 517
 Aron 295, 330
 Eliza 234
 Elizabeth 217, 273, 295, 330, 361, 399, 482, 509
 George 185, 234, 269, 272, 295, 332, 361, 391, 421, 450, 482, 511
 John 185, 217, 234, 252, 272, 294, 323, 360, 386, 421, 449, 482, 507

Garryson
 George 216

Gaskin
 Isaac 256

Gaskins
 Isaac 213, 225, 295, 330, 361, 399, 421, 459, 482, 512
 J. 279

Gatewood
 Richard 317, 350

Ga[...]rd
 [see Garrard above]
 James 538

Gee
 Benjamin 361, 395
 Joseph 361, 395
 Keziah 361, 399
 William 361, 395

George
  Benjamin 23, 214
  Nicholas 67, 80
  Nick 93, 94
  William 68, 233,
    272, 295, 337, 361,
    388, 421, 460, 482,
    520
German
  John 117, 150
  Thomas 117, 151
Gerrard
  Gerrard 200
  William 67, 80, 94,
    225
Gess
  Mathew 27
  Moses 27
  William 27
Gibbons
  John 31
Gibson
  Jacob 9, 117, 172
  Jonathan 117, 156
  Joseph 117, 151,
    167
Gie
  Benjamin 421, 450,
    482, 516
  John 421, 450, 482,
    510
  Joseph 421, 457
  William 421, 456,
    482, 516
Gill
  Thomas 367, 388
Gilpin
  Israel 207, 310, 341
  Joseph 310, 341
Gimbo
  William 319, 352
Gladding
  John 117, 142
Glass
  Henry 543
Glebe for the poor
    80
Glebe land 80
Gleekis
  William 45

Godby
  Edward 210, 242,
    268
Godfrey
  William 117, 167,
    168
Goin
  William 9, 117, 143
Going
  James 117, 156
  Thomas 117, 169
  William 117, 142,
    169
Golahorn
  Solomon 186, 252
Goldsmith
  J. 282
  John 252, 295, 325,
    360, 385, 421, 449
Gollehorn
  Solomon 435, 464
  Thomas 435, 465
Gollehorne
  Soloman 495, 523
Gollerhorn
  John 188
Gollihorn
  Thomas 495, 523
Gollohan
  John 200
Gollohon
  Solomon 233, 274,
    278
  William 266
Gollohorn
  John 310, 343, 348
  John Jr. 310, 348
  Sollomon 310, 343,
    361, 395, 482, 517
  Solomon 375, 402,
    421, 459
  Thomas 310, 343,
    375, 403
  William 189, 294,
    323, 361, 388, 421,
    460, 482, 517
Golohan
  Solomon 213
Goloohorn
  John 254, 259, 375,
    409
  Solomon 253

William 260
Gorden
  Samuel 375, 409
Gordon
  Bazell 435, 469
  Samuel 310, 349,
    495, 529
Gorman
  James 19
Goslin
  John 8
Gough
  Francis 216, 235
  Hannah 217, 295,
    338, 361, 395, 421,
    452, 482, 510
  James 361, 395,
    421, 452, 482, 512
  Thomas 67, 80, 93
Gouring
  Mathew 62
Gowin
  William 117, 143,
    166
Gowring
  Mathew 61
Gradey
  William 80
Grady
  Edward 34
  Patrick 9, 52
  William 67, 93, 204
Graham
  Edward 117, 154,
    165, 167
Grant
  Andrew 80, 94
  Ann 36
  George 21
  John 51
  W. 539
  William 212
Grat
  John 548
Graves
  ----- 375, 403
  Benjaman 310, 344
  Benjamin 193, 204,
    227, 246, 375, 403,
    543
  Catharine 495, 528

Grimes
  Charles 28
  Edward 28
  John 28
Groves
  Samuel   181, 214,
    257, 269, 294, 323,
    361, 399, 421, 450,
    482, 519
  Thomas   310, 348,
    375, 403, 435, 465
  William   181, 214,
    295, 310, 329, 344,
    361, 398, 421, 450,
    482, 512
  William Sr.   310,
    344
Grubbs
  Richard 118, 150
  Thomas 19
Grubs
  William 25
Grymes
  John 118, 159
  Nicholas 61, 62
  Phillip 61, 62
Guant
  William 243, 268
Guess
  Joseph 9, 118, 168
Gui
  Benjamin 295, 328
  John 295, 328
  Joseph 295, 328
  Kissiah 295, 328
  William 295, 328
Gullery
  Thomas 495, 526
Gum
  Epram 495, 533
  John 252
Gun
  John 361, 386, 421,
    459, 482, 521
Gunn
  John 271, 295, 334
Gunnel
  William 118, 156
Gunnell
  William   118, 154,
    157

Guthrie
  Thomas 268
Guthry
  Thomas   207, 236,
    244, 375, 407
Guttery
  Thomas   310, 341,
    435, 462
Guy
  Benjamin 278
  J. 281
  John 218, 224, 256
  Mrs. 225, 256
  William 218, 278
Gwatkins
  Charles 25
Gwin
  ----- 118
  Major 8

H

Habern
  David 190, 299, 333
Hackney
  William 5, 118, 150,
    174
Hackny
  William 118, 145
Hagan
  John 547
Hagard
  James 24
  James Jr. 24
  Richard 24
  William 24
Hall
  Benjaman 311, 345,
    375, 403
  Benjamin 204, 227,
    243, 436, 470, 495,
    528
  Edward 32
  Hanah 193
  Hannah   204, 227,
    247, 311, 345, 375,
    405
  John 9, 29, 32, 118,
    151, 153, 311, 345,
    436, 467, 496, 532
  John Jr. 32

Joseph 35
  Mary 245
  Michael 61, 62
  William 118, 169
Halley
  Francis 212
Hallin
  Margaret   (widow)
    118, 154
Hallowday
  William 422, 448
Hally
  Henry 118, 149
Hamersly
  Francis 22
Hamilton
  George 550
Hammerly
  Francis 224
Hammond
  Gervis 61, 62
Hamston
  Edward 52
Hancock
  John 9
Hand
  William 19
Haner
  Harmon 545
  William   245, 246,
    269, 310, 349, 549
Hanes
  William 237
Haney
  William 204, 265
Hannan
  George 219
Hansbro
  Lydia 271
  Peter 271
Hansbrough
  James   68, 81, 94,
    217, 235
  James Jr. 547
  Ledia   296,   338,
    422, 452
  Lettice 234
  Lidia 482, 507
  Lydia 219, 362, 398
  Morias   68, 81, 83,
    94
  Morias Jr. 547

Peter 68, 81, 99, 187, 234, 252, 295, 323, 361, 386, 422, 449, 482, 507, 546, 550
Peter Jr. 94
Peter Sr. 81
Smith 546
Hansdell
Chitton 310, 351
Hany
William 436, 471, 495, 529
Hardin
Henry 29
Henry Jr. 29
John S. 181
John Scot 182
Thomas 182
Hardine
Charles 80
Harding
C. 281
Charles 67, 94, 118, 119, 143, 152, 153, 185, 211, 218, 235, 251
Cuthbert 186, 251, 271, 296, 328, 361, 386, 422, 449, 483, 515
Enough 362, 392
G. 280
George 67, 181, 211, 223, 257, 295, 323, 362, 389, 422, 450, 483, 512
Henry 45, 52, 68, 81, 94, 119, 144
J. S. 281
James 362, 386
John 251, 257, 271, 296, 328, 361, 386, 422, 449, 483, 508
John S. 223, 257, 483, 513
John Scott 295, 323, 362, 389, 422, 453
Jonathan S. 215
Mark 119, 156

Thomas 181, 215, 223, 257, 280, 296, 332, 362, 386, 422, 452, 483, 510
William 187, 216, 234, 251, 274, 296, 328, 362, 392, 422, 455, 459, 483, 508
Hardman
Thomas 34
Hardy
Henry 119, 144
John 181, 214, 224, 269, 296, 326, 362, 399, 422, 459, 483, 518, 538
Harlan
Jesse 208, 548
Harmon
Ishamel 545
Harper
John 119, 144
Harrard
W. 280
Harris
Charles 119, 172
John 62
Thomas 119, 167
Harrison
----- 119, 158
Burr 9, 32
Capt. 9
Charles 9
Col. 119, 153
Cuthbert 119, 151
John 272, 296, 327
Robert 544
Thomas 9, 10, 23, 38, 119, 153, 166, 217
Thomas (Rev.) 226
Thomas Jr. 23
William 9, 52, 119, 142, 145, 171
Harrod
William 362, 395, 422, 458, 483, 519
Harrol
Moses 213
Harrow
----- 119, 162

Hartin
B. 99, 100
Hartshorn
John 52
Harvey
----- 119, 141
James 119, 141
Harvy
James 119, 171
Harwood
Allice 376, 408, 436, 469, 496, 533
John 208, 311, 346, 544
William 181, 257
Hawkins
John 231
Hawley
Francis 257
Widow 9
William 9
Hawlin
Widow 119, 154, 173
William 45, 119, 171
Hawlins
Widow 119, 154
William 119, 154
Hay
Prisalla 94
Prisilla 67, 80
Thomas 67, 80, 94, 189, 258, 272, 296, 327, 362, 396, 422, 447, 483, 512
Hayney
William 376, 409
Haynie
Spencer 543
Hays
Thomas 218
Heabeard
Widow 9
Heckason
John 546
Hedges
John 32
Robert 9, 30, 119, 153
Hedgman
----- 119, 141

William 544
Humphry
  Daniel 376, 408
  McCausland   376,
    410
  William 375, 407
Humphrys
  Daniel   436, 470,
    495, 528
  Walter 19
  William   193, 227,
    436, 468, 495, 526
Humstead
  James 24
Hunter
  Adam   249, 269,
    310, 311, 350, 351,
    375, 376, 402, 409,
    436, 467, 469, 496,
    533, 542
  James 68, 81, 94,
    120, 173, 200, 542
Hunter's Forge 208
Hurl
  John 121, 157
Hurle
  John 121, 168
Hurst
  John 45, 52, 68
  Joseph 227
  Moses 208
  William 208
Huse
  Virgen 296, 337
Huster
  J. 245
Hyden
  Daniel 212
  Henry   210, 242,
    267
Hyser
  James 208

I

Indicott
  Joseph 537
Innes
  John 217
  William 362, 385

Innis
  John 297, 323
  William   186, 235,
    252, 297, 325, 423,
    452
Ironwork   Company
  121, 142

J

J......
  Henry 208
Jackman
  Thomas 121, 167
Jackson
  ----- 10
  Francis   121, 164,
    166
  George   312, 344,
    544
  John 28, 121, 160,
    174
  R. 283
  Robert   192, 228,
    247, 312, 344, 376,
    403, 437, 468, 496,
    526, 538, 544
  Robert Jr. 204, 544
  Robert Sr. 204
  Rosamond 192, 228
  Rosamund 247
  Rosana   376, 410,
    496, 526
  Rosanah 437, 468
  Rosanna 312, 344
  Samuel 10, 121, 172
  Thomas   10, 121,
    147
  William 53, 68, 81,
    94, 121, 144, 312,
    344, 437, 467, 496,
    526
Jacobs
  John 38
  Joseph 121, 163
  Nat 23
  Robert 496, 528
  William   202, 232,
    254, 278, 312, 350,
    376, 406, 437, 465,
    496, 528

James
  Cloe 256
  Daniel 204
  G. 283
  George 52, 68, 81,
    95, 192, 247, 312,
    339, 345, 376, 410,
    437, 470, 496, 533,
    544
  Isaac 242
  John   40, 53, 200,
    231, 250, 270, 312,
    339, 376, 410, 437,
    472, 496, 528, 542,
    552
  Jonathan 537
  Joseph 40, 546
  Richard 121, 146
  Thomas   10, 40,
    538, 544, 548
Jameson
  Alexander 187, 252,
    296, 323, 363, 392,
    423, 455
  Jameson 484, 512
  John 484, 514
Jamieson
  Alexander 81
Jamison
  Alexander 68, 95,
    218, 233, 271
Janeways
  Margery 10
Jarman
  Thomas   121, 151,
    168
Jefferys
  John 68
Jeffress
  Joseph 71, 97
Jeffreys
  Joseph 84
Jeffries
  James 210, 538, 547
Jeffriss
  James 100
Jeffry
  Thomas 52
Jeffrys
  Alexander 36
Jenkins
  Rob.t 52

Mathew 23
Samuel 53
Wilford 10, 68
William 23
Kemp
James 39
Kemper
Jacob 121, 172
John 121, 172
Peter 122, 173
Kendal
Charles 216
George 217
John 216
William 53, 188
Kendall
Aaron 363, 398, 484, 519
Ann 242
Anthony 297, 337, 363, 393, 423, 453, 484, 512
Aron 297, 327, 423, 458
Charles 186, 235, 272, 297, 335, 363, 389, 423, 453, 484, 509, 547
Daniel 212, 270, 297, 334, 363, 391, 423, 453, 484, 512
George 547
Henry 212, 243, 270, 297, 332, 363, 393, 423, 449, 484, 510, 548
James 99, 268, 297, 334, 363, 387, 391, 423, 456, 484, 519, 547
James Kee 297, 335
Jeremiah 547
Jesse 212, 241, 261, 268, 270, 537
Jessey 297, 327, 363, 388, 424, 458
Jessy 484, 515
John 81, 95, 186, 234, 252, 274, 297, 335, 363, 387, 423, 456, 484, 515, 547
Joseph Sr. 270

Joshua 68, 81, 95, 212, 242, 270
Joshua Jr. 212, 548
Joshua Sr. 548
Josua 297, 335, 337, 363, 393, 395, 423, 449, 453
Josua Jr. 484, 520
Josua Sr. 297, 337, 363, 393, 484, 510
Moses 297, 335, 363, 387
Peter 271, 297, 328, 363, 388
Samuel Sr. 539
Warden 214
William 81, 95, 122
Wordon 423, 457
Kendloe
Daniel 257
Kenney
James 66, 95
John 496, 523
Thomas 484, 520
Kenny
Andrew 496, 526
James 53, 68, 81, 122, 147
John 200, 250, 278, 312, 343, 376, 403, 437, 465
John Jr. 496, 531
Thomas 201, 233, 250, 312, 340, 376, 401
Kent
----- 10
Isaac 10
Samuel 122, 154
Kenyon
James 184, 200, 231, 249, 278, 312, 347, 376, 407, 437, 467, 542
Kerk
Jeremiah 437, 466
Jesse 437, 469
Ketchen
James 363, 390, 437, 466
Merriman 363, 390

Merryman 297, 336, 484, 512
Richard 296, 335
William 437, 465
Kincher
Mary 189
Kindall
Bartley 548
John Jr. 548
Kindle
James Sr. 548
Jesse 547
Kinean
Abraham 53
King
Elisabeth 68, 81
Elizabeth 95
Joseph 10, 53
Oliver 39
Thomas 236, 546
Weathers 215
William 122, 171, 215, 223
Withers 78, 95, 223
Kingcart
Thomas 122, 158
Kirby
James 312, 346, 376, 407
Kirk
J. 283
James 297, 332, 363, 390, 423, 453
Jeremiah 99, 312, 347, 376, 407
Jesse 193, 204, 228, 247
Sarah 297, 332, 423, 453, 484, 519
William 19, 548
Kirkbride
John 546
Kirtlin
Richard Jr. 122, 149
Kitchen
Anthony 69
Charles 254, 312, 343, 496, 525
James 250, 312, 343, 376, 403
James Jr. 254

Mc

Olliver
  J. 284
  John 228, 247
Ollover
  Hezekiah 486, 519
Olover
  Hezekiah 425, 460
Orea
  Daniel 12, 26, 126,
    151, 157, 158, 166
  John 12, 26, 126,
    151, 157, 158, 166
Osborn
  Thomas 126, 161
Overall
  ----- 126, 151
  Elizabeth 299, 327,
    365, 390, 425, 460,
    486, 521
Overhall
  ----- 57
  Elizabeth 274
  Widow 54
  William 12
Owens
  John 127, 147
Owsley
  Thomas 12, 127,
    143, 158, 165, 168

P

Packstein
  John 366, 393
Packston
  John 299, 324
Page
  Col. 127, 150
  John 12, 54, 127,
    141, 146
  Magery 12
  Man 127, 150, 174
  Mann 83, 97, 127,
    167
Pain
  Richard 127, 161
Painter
  Robert 100, 241,
    270, 300, 333, 366,
    392, 426, 455, 486,
    513

Paise
  Thomas 12
Pallmer
  R. 284
Palmer
  John 543
  Joseph 543
  Raleigh 205, 228
  Rawleigh 192, 543
  Rawleigh Jr. 543
  William 549
Palmon
  Pate 247
Pare
  John 310, 345
Parker
  Abraham 366, 390
  Alice 21
  Fielder 127, 164
  John 31, 127, 170,
    172
  Richard 31
  Samuel 366, 400,
    426, 461, 487, 518
Parmer
  James 300, 326
  Rawleigh 315, 342
  Rawley 379, 408,
    440, 466
  William 300, 328
Parmes
  Raughley 499, 533
Parrock
  Thomas 62
Parsons
  William 25
Partridge
  Richard 54
Parvitt
  William 548
Paten
  George 313, 345
Paterson
  ----- 216
  Fanny 378, 405
  John 547
  Stephen 208
Pates
  Aaron 183, 199,
    230, 249, 315, 340,
    378, 402, 439, 463,
    498, 524, 543

  Allice 499, 525
  Lewis 499, 524
Patison
  John 261
Paton
  James 191, 205,
    228, 538
Patrick
  Patrick 42
Patten
  Rachal 315, 345
  Rachel 440, 471
  Rachell 379, 408
  William 186, 252
Patterson
  George 306, 345,
    440, 468, 499, 527
  H. 271
  Henry 242
  Hesekiah 300, 331,
    365, 387
  Hezekiah 440, 469,
    499, 533
  John 236, 271, 300,
    331
  Perry 315, 345, 379,
    408, 440, 465
  Perry W. 499, 528
  Stephen 237
  Thomas 242, 315,
    345, 378, 404, 440,
    465, 499, 529
Pattin
  John 182, 366, 387,
    499, 529
  Rachell 499, 533
  William 300, 334,
    366, 394, 487, 518
Pattison
  Gilbird 127, 169
  John 41
Patton
  George 271
  J. 284
  James 247, 545
  John 274
  William 228, 426,
    449
Paxon
  John 268

Pottes
  Calvert 219
Potts
  William 218
Pow
  Elizabeth 440, 469
Powell
  Joseph 62
  Thomas 300, 335,
    366, 393, 426, 461,
    486, 507
Prat
  Leonard 61
Pratt
  Burket 54
  John 12
  Thomas 70, 83, 96
Preston
  John 128, 144
Price
  Thomas 54, 70, 72,
    83
  William 243
Prichard
  Benjamin 216
Prim
  John 216
  Kitchin 61
  Thomas 538
Primm
  James 234, 241,
    268, 300, 333, 366,
    392, 426, 453, 486,
    507
  John 187, 234, 252,
    253, 268, 300, 334,
    365, 387, 426, 449,
    486, 515
  Margaret 300, 334,
    366, 387, 426, 449,
    486, 516
Prince
  John 291, 334, 356,
    388
Pritchard
  Benjamin 187, 233,
    253
  Lewis 211
Pritchet
  Benjamin 271, 299,
    325, 366, 396, 426,
    455

  Lewis Sr. 243
Pritchett
  Benjamin 486, 515
  Lewis Jr. 537
Prockter
  George 12
Proctor
  Hezekiah 543
Pryce
  Thomas 96
Pullen
  Gedaliah 100
  Jedediah 190, 539
Pulliam
  Jeremiah 546
Pullin
  J. 284
  Jedidiah 228, 247
Purler
  John Chapman 31
  Mary 31
  William 26
Purlow
  William 12
Pusee
  James 498, 525
  Stephen 499, 525
Puzee
  Stephen 269
Puzey
  Olden 440, 471
  Stephen 201, 250,
    315, 346, 378, 404,
    440, 464
Pyland
  Robert 128, 162

Q

Quarles
  Anne (widow) 128,
    161
  John 128, 161
Quidle
  James 21
Quin
  Thomas 23

R

Radford
  John 128, 171
Raiby
  Joseph 187
Raimy
  Butler 367, 396
  Presly 301, 327
Rakestraw
  Thomas 367, 386,
    427, 458, 488, 519
Ralls
  Ascha 218
  Charles 186, 217,
    234, 251, 274, 488,
    516
  Edward 216, 234,
    251
  Hebron 271
  Henry 266
  Hepborn 427, 449
  Hepbron 488, 521
  Jesse 182, 215, 258
  John 70, 83, 97,
    128, 145, 151, 215
  John Jr. 70, 83, 97
  Kenez 427, 449,
    488, 517
  M. A. 282
  Mary Ann 182, 427,
    458, 487, 510
  Raleigh 234, 274
  Rawleigh 427, 449
  Rawling 488, 516
  William 188, 215
Ramey
  Butler 427, 453
Randall
  George 212, 241,
    270
  Richard 61
  William 259, 275
Randol
  George 301, 333,
    367, 388, 427, 454,
    487, 515
  John 301, 333, 367,
    397, 487, 513

Sims
James 97, 131, 144, 302, 333, 368, 390, 428, 453, 488, 509
Presly 302, 324, 368, 394, 428, 455, 489, 521
Rhoadnum 368, 394, 428, 450, 488, 509
Richard 71, 223, 302, 324, 368, 369, 387, 398, 428, 454, 488, 510
Richard Jr. 258, 302, 324, 488, 508
Richard Sr. 182, 258, 302, 333, 428, 457
Simson
Alexander 32, 205
Eliza 249
Elizabeth 232, 276
George 131, 145
John 37
Thomas 131, 168
William 27
William Jr. 27
Sinclair
Alexander 55
Singleton
----- 131, 163
Edward 548
Robert 13, 46, 131, 166
Sinkler
Alexander 40
John 40
Wayman 40
Sintor
John 271
Sisk
William 97
Skanes
John 21
Skidmore
Josia 276
Skinker
----- 131, 168, 205
Capt. 131, 148
J. 539
Samuel 131, 165

T. 285
Thomas 99, 191, 229, 248, 317, 347, 380, 408, 442, 470, 501, 533, 538, 542
Skinner
Elisha 368, 388
Ezekiel 489, 519
John 537
Skrin
Anna 131, 167
Elizabeth 131, 167
William 131, 167
Slaid
William 24
Slater
George 131, 154, 158
Slaughter
Joseph 368, 395, 428, 451, 489, 515
Slaven
Jesse 249, 316, 343, 380, 406, 441, 464
Sleator
George 131, 154, 173
Smallwood
----- 13
B. 52
William 71, 84, 97
Smiddy
Benjamin 182
Smith
----- 46, 224
Catherin 34
George 131, 155
Henry 55, 71, 84, 97, 131, 144, 241, 317, 348, 368, 387, 441, 466, 500, 527, 547
Henry H. 268
Henry Jr. 71, 84, 97
Henry Sr. 317, 348
J. 280, 284
Jacob 131, 148, 149
John 13, 36, 39, 132, 162, 182, 193, 206, 213, 229, 248, 301, 302, 316, 329, 331, 341, 368, 380,

[John, contd.]
392, 406, 428, 441, 442, 451, 466, 471, 488, 500, 513, 527, 532, 538, 545
John Jr. 442, 471, 500, 532
Johnston 364, 391
Joseph 71, 82, 317, 348, 350, 368, 387, 500, 530, 547
Mary 36
N. 284
Nathan 488, 513
Nathaniel 241, 302, 333, 368, 390, 428, 455
Peter 13
Ralph 545
Robert 21, 280, 302, 330, 537, 547
Robert William 549
S. 284
Samuel 191, 206, 228, 248, 316, 341, 380, 408, 441, 468, 538, 544
Stephen 544
Steven 538
Thomas 31, 55, 71, 84, 97, 539
William 12, 39, 537, 547
Smith & Young & Hyde
----- 380, 410
Snape
Robert 245
Snellens
Enoch 379, 405
William 379, 405
Snelling
Enoch 183, 254, 441, 465
John 231, 278, 317, 351, 441, 466, 545
William 278, 317, 351, 545
Snellings
Enoch 199, 230, 316, 341

Enouch 500, 523
John 184, 500, 527
William 184, 202,
232, 441, 465, 500,
524
Snipe
Nathaniel 209, 245,
268, 316, 344, 379,
404, 441, 466, 500,
531, 546
Nathaniel Jr. 546
Robert 209, 267,
546
Snow
Thomas 22
Snoxall
Ann 189, 303, 336
Edward 189, 302,
324, 369, 398, 428,
448, 489, 517
John 303, 337, 368,
388, 428, 448, 489,
514
Sarsfield 302, 337,
367, 385, 428, 448,
488, 510
Snoxfield
Edward 260
Somers
(orphans of) 55
Sooter
A. 284
Andrew 191, 206,
229, 248
John 192, 206, 229,
248
T. 284
Sorvell
Thomas 209
Souillivant
Benjamin 500, 524
Daniel 500, 524
Darby 309, 339,
500, 524
Darby Jr. 500, 524
Francis 500, 525
Lettice 500, 524
Southard
Lawrence 61
Spaldin
Francis 40
John 40

Sparrow
Mathew 62
Speckt
Andrew 442, 471
Spelman
----- 132, 160
Spence
Patrick 13, 46
William 192, 205,
229, 248, 380, 405,
441, 468, 500, 527,
537, 545
Spencer
Francis 13
Spicer
Absolum 12
Spiller
Craven 302, 326,
368, 394
John 25
Warington 25
William 7, 25, 132,
163, 164, 166
William Jr. 25
Spillman
Elizabeth 274
Spilman
Elizabeth 259, 302,
327, 368, 393
Spry
----- 132, 142
John 13, 132, 141,
146
Stafford
Thomas 132, 160
Stamps
Thomas 132, 151
Stanley
John 548
Stanton
Lenn 37
Stark
----- 132, 161
Benjamin 97
Hanah 185
Hannah 233, 303,
337, 368, 395, 429,
460, 488, 513
James 71, 216
Jeremiah 84, 97,
186, 216, 368, 394,
547

Jerremiah 301, 324,
428, 455, 488, 508
John 301, 302, 324,
367, 368, 369, 387,
393, 398, 428, 456,
488, 489, 513, 518
John Jr. 302, 324
John Sr. 428, 455,
489, 513
Mrs. 216
William 186, 301,
302, 324, 329, 368,
390, 392, 394, 428,
450, 451, 488, 489,
510, 516
Starke
Ham 271
Hanah 252
J. 279
James 21, 55, 84,
223
Jeremiah 233, 251
John 182, 225, 258,
275
W. 282
William 55, 183,
225, 233, 253, 258
Starn
Francis 547
Steen
Francis 428, 455
Stephens
Richard 380, 405,
500, 532
Richards 442, 469
Robert 132, 143
William 368, 395
Stern
Charles 302, 324,
367, 385, 427, 447,
489, 513
Francis 100, 302,
327, 367, 385, 488,
508
John 302, 327, 368,
387, 428, 455, 489,
515
Sterne
Charles 267
Feam.s 267
Francis 241

Sterns
  Francis 211
Stevens
  Robert 132, 145
  Thomas 210
Steward
  David (Rev.) 55
  James 25
  William 84, 97
Stewart
  Joseph 55, 71
Stipes
  John 442, 472
Stith
  John 71, 84, 97,
    132, 162
  Robert 537
Stone
  Barton 212, 214
  Burton 258
  Eli 61, 62
  Francis 132, 149,
    154, 163, 175
  H. 281
  Hawkin 183, 214,
    225, 253, 302, 327,
    368, 396, 428, 451,
    489, 513
  J. 284
  J. Sr. 281
  Jesse 191, 248
  Jessey 302, 334,
    369, 397, 429, 458,
    489, 522
  John 13, 46, 61, 62
  Joseph 182, 192,
    205, 229, 248, 276,
    316, 339, 379, 402,
    441, 463, 500, 525
  Josia 368, 397, 429,
    460
  Josias 71, 84, 98,
    226, 258, 489, 518
  Josias Sr. 215
  Josius 302, 330
  Richard 273, 302,
    331, 368, 395, 428,
    451, 488, 509
  Thomas 132
  Valentine 215, 223
  W. 281

William 40, 132,
    148, 184, 202, 232,
    250, 276, 302, 315,
    329, 339, 379, 402,
    441, 442, 463, 471,
    500, 525
William B. 183,
    225, 251, 368, 395,
    428, 450, 489, 511
Stork
  Jeremiah 71
  John 302, 330, 428,
    455
Striblin
  Joel 427, 447
  Samuel 369, 398,
    429, 460
  Thomas 132, 164,
    427, 447
Stribling
  Benjamin 13, 55,
    205
  Cokely 71, 84
  Elizabeth 193, 229,
    248
  Joseph 191, 248
  Thomas 132, 147
  Widow 13, 55
Stringfellow
  .....ames 205
  ----- 209
  George 236, 245,
    267, 315, 350, 380,
    410, 442, 472, 501,
    533, 544
  Henry 315, 350,
    442, 472
  J. 284
  James 192, 229,
    248, 316, 346, 380,
    405, 442, 468, 538,
    544
  Robert 84, 98
  T. 284
  Townshand 316,
    341, 500, 529
  Townshend 380,
    409
Striplin
  Elizabeth 380, 408
  Joel 379, 404
  William 380, 405

Stripling
  Elizabeth 317, 344,
    442, 472
  Joel 500, 527
  Joell 316, 345
  Samuel 317, 348
  Thomas 500, 527
  William 317, 351,
    441, 466
Strode
  John 542
Strother
  Anthony 183, 199,
    229, 249, 276, 315,
    339, 539, 543
  George 315, 339,
    379, 404, 441, 464,
    500, 527, 543
  Thomas 191, 205,
    228, 248, 538, 542
  William 46, 132,
    151
Strutfield
  William 132, 157
Struttfield
  William 13
Stuart
  C. 279
  Charles 70, 84, 97,
    182, 213, 225, 258,
    302, 326, 428, 451,
    489, 513
  David (Rev.) 132,
    148
  Elizabeth 188
  James 190, 259
  John 70, 79, 84, 97,
    132, 161
  W. Gibbons 537
  William 79, 97
  William (Rev.) 70,
    84
Sturdy
  Robert 41
  William 538
Sturman
  William 132, 147
Suddart
  Henry 55
  Robert 55
Suddarth
  Henry 42

Suddath
  William 253
Sudden
  John 380, 409, 441,
    462
  Thomas 258
Suddon
  John 236, 500, 527
  Thomas 217
Suddoth
  Benjamin 546
  Benjamin Jr. 546
  Robert 71
  Thomas 190
Sudduth
  H. 279
  Henry 271, 302,
    326, 368, 388, 428,
    448, 489, 513
  Moses 200, 428,
    448, 489, 515
  Thomas 302, 331,
    368, 395, 428, 448,
    489, 513
Sudthard
  William 500, 528,
    530
Sudtherd
  Moses 317, 351
  William 316, 346,
    380, 406, 441, 464
Sulivan
  Daniel 543
  Francis 249
  John 543
  Jonas 259
  Martin 543
  William 542, 543
Sullaven
  Gabrel 428, 456,
    488, 513
Sullivan
  Ben 199
  Benjamin 254, 277
  D. 277
  Daniel 183, 199,
    230, 277
  Darby 183, 276
  Darby Jr. 254, 276
  Darby Sr. 254
  Derby 199
  Derby Jr. 199, 230

Derby Sr. 230
  F. 278
  Francis 199, 230
  Gabriel 200, 230
  John 200, 230, 276
  Jonas 231
Sullivant
  Owen 34
Sumner
  Joseph 13, 37
Suter
  Andrew 543
Suthard
  Harry Jr. 270
  Moses 231, 545
  Thomas 260
  William 232, 269,
    545
Sutherly
  Will 310, 349
Suton
  John 380, 408, 500,
    527
Sutor
  Andrew 316, 345,
    379, 404
  Jesse 316, 341
  John 316, 341, 441,
    468
  William 316, 345,
    379, 404, 500, 532
Sutton
  John 13
Swann
  Asa 317, 347
  Phillip 317, 351
Sweeting
  Edward 35
Swillivant
  Ann 316, 343
  Benjaman 316, 341
  Benjamin 379, 405,
    441, 463
  Daniel 317, 344,
    379, 405, 441, 463
  Darby 316, 341,
    441, 464
  Darby Jr. 379, 405,
    441, 464
  Darby Sr. 316, 341,
    379, 405, 441, 463
  Frances 441, 464

Francis 317, 351,
    380, 405
  Gabriel 316, 340,
    379, 402
  Lettice 316, 340,
    379, 402
  Lettuce 441, 462
Swindley
  Thomas 132, 171
Sylva
  Jane 260
Symmonds
  William 232
Syms
  Richard 214

T

Tackett
  Lewis 132, 163
Tacquest
  Lewis 132, 164
Tacquet
  John 26
  Lewis 26
  Lewis Jr. 26
Tacquett
  Lewis 132, 149
Talbot
  William 62
Taler's
  ----- 132, 170
Taliafero
  John 539
Tarpley
  Col. 132, 150
  John 133, 165
Tarply
  Col. 133, 150
Tate
  W. 285
  William 194, 206,
    229, 248, 317, 348,
    442, 468, 501, 533
Tayler
  Richard 133, 170,
    173
  William 381, 410
Tayloe
  John 46, 133, 172

Taylor
 Alexander 303, 336, 369, 395, 429, 455, 489, 513, 546
 Col. 53, 133, 162
 Hannah 490, 522
 J. 285
 James 41
 Jesse 192, 248, 317, 347
 Jessey 490, 520
 John 41, 55, 71, 133, 158
 Richard 133, 168, 188, 190, 259, 272, 274, 275, 302, 331, 369, 390, 429, 454, 489, 507, 547
 Robert 317, 349, 442, 466, 501, 530
 Samuel 442, 470, 501, 533
 W. Sr. 281
 William 182, 209, 236, 244, 266, 303, 317, 326, 350, 369, 398, 429, 442, 455, 472, 501, 534
 William Sr. 214, 223, 258
 Zachariah 191, 248
 Zachary 229
Teal
 William 133, 146
Tebbs
 Daniel 13, 46, 133, 164
 Robert 276
Tedwell
 ----- 133, 151
 Richard 133, 150, 157, 158, 166
Temmons
 John 501, 529
Templeman
 Edward 206, 243, 268, 318, 349, 369, 387, 429, 450, 489, 519
 James 206

Jane 317, 340, 380, 401, 442, 462, 501, 525
Moses 206, 501, 524
Tennant
 Thomas 369, 398, 429, 460, 489, 515
Terrier
 John 231, 249, 380, 402, 443, 472
Terrur
 John 501, 525
Tesly
 John 501, 528
Thacker
 Samuel 133, 171
Tharp
 John 489, 515
 Thomas 369, 392, 429, 450
Thatcer
 Joshua 259
Thatcher
 Joseph 279
 Joshua 189, 271
Thomas
 Allen 490, 520
 Benjamin 71, 84, 98
 Catherine 133, 156
 Daniel 133, 156
 Evan 133, 157
 Hugh 133, 156
 James 133, 148, 159, 170, 174
 John 538
 Owen 14
 Robert 62
 Simon 55, 70, 84
Thompson
 Elijah 429, 458, 489, 520
 James 317, 346, 381, 406, 548
 John 442, 466
 Samuel 303, 333, 369, 398, 429, 458, 489, 514
 William 98
 Zacariah 190
 Zachariah 317, 347
 Zacharias 544

Thomson
 James 209
 Samuel 215, 269, 279
 Z. 285
 Zachariah 248
 Zacharias 229
 Zachary 206
Thorn
 Ephraim 133, 155
 George 133, 173, 429, 454
Thornbury
 ----- 49
 John 71, 84, 98
 Samuel 71, 84
Thorne
 William 26, 133, 166
Thornley
 John Jr. 539
Thornto
 Charles 210
Thornton
 Anthony 13, 55
 Charles 241, 270, 303, 335, 369, 387, 429, 447, 489, 515, 547
 F. 537
 Francis 71, 84, 98, 133, 162, 539
 George 200
 John 539, 542
 John (Rev.) 232
 T. 279
 T. (Rev.) 269
 Thomas 185, 201, 317, 340, 380, 401
 William 46
Thorp
 Amos 549
 John 210, 367, 387
Thorpe
 T. 210
Thraelkeld
 Elijah 369, 398
 George 369, 398
Thralekeld
 Elijah 303, 335
 George 303, 335

Absolam 192, 206, 229, 248
Absolum 317, 347, 380, 406, 442, 469, 501, 525
Benjaman 317, 342
Benjamin 381, 408, 442, 470, 501, 532
G. 285
Griffin 99, 193, 206, 248, 380, 406, 442, 470, 547
Griffith 229
James 192, 206, 229, 248, 285, 317, 343, 380, 404, 442, 469, 501, 532, 538, 545
John 546
T. 539
Thomas Jr. 543
William 317, 343, 543
William Griffin 317, 347, 501, 525, 537
Turnum
Thomas Jr. 548
Tuton
John 134, 171
Tuttle
John 369, 392, 429, 454, 489, 514
Twinham
Thomas 543
Tyler
A. 278
Alexander 217
Alice 199, 230, 249, 318, 351, 442, 472
Allice 381, 406, 501, 528
Charles 14, 134, 172
H. 134, 172
Henry 55, 71, 84, 98
John 318, 351
T. G. 278
T. S. 303, 337
Thomas 382
Thomas E. S. 179, 286, 305 552

Thomas G. 202, 261, 429, 460, 490, 520
Thomas S. 369, 400
Thomas V. 206
William 46, 545
Zachary 206

U

Underwood
Frances 490, 519
John 268, 318, 348, 546
Zachary 232

V

Vant
James 547
Vaspar
James 235, 274
Vaughan
Ann 369, 396, 490, 517
Vaun
Ann 303, 330, 429, 457
Veal
----- 134
John 46
Maurice 134, 163
Veale
John 14
Maurice 14
Vernon
Abner 209, 311, 350, 549
Vickers
Elias 14
Villars
George 538
Violet
Edward 134, 143, 146
Vivian
Thomas 134

Vivion
Thomas 56, 134, 173
Vowles
Charles 318, 350
Chaveles 381, 401
Henry 318, 350, 381, 411, 443, 472, 501, 530
Richard 381, 411
Richards 443, 472
Thomas 209, 236, 269, 318, 350, 544
Zachariah 318, 350, 501, 530

W

W....ms
George 225
Wadington
Francis 14
Wainwright
John 134, 153
Waiten
James 443, 465
Walker
George 134, 146
Henry 134, 172
James 318, 347, 369, 391, 430, 460, 491, 519, 548
Mary 188
Ralph 134, 141
Rd. 279
Richard 212, 260, 269, 303, 325, 369, 385, 429, 447, 490, 516
S. 285
Soloman 206
Solomon 192, 248, 318, 345, 381, 404, 546
Thomas 14, 134, 156, 501, 524
W. 54
William 35, 54, 57, 72, 85, 98, 202, 232, 250, 273, 277, 318,

George 304, 334
J. 273, 279, 281
James 303, 304,
  324, 334, 370, 393
John 183, 185, 217,
  251, 304, 329, 333,
  369, 385
John Jr. 235, 370,
  397
John Sr. 234, 304,
  330, 370, 392
M. 281
Mark 183, 211, 225,
  370, 397
P. 280
Peter 226, 303, 328,
  370, 396
Philemon 26, 135,
  149, 150, 172
Philemon Jr. 26
Thomas 26
William 183, 226,
  258, 304, 334, 370,
  393
Watkins
  Charles 135, 163
Watson
  Andrew 135, 172
  James 304, 337
  William 268, 304,
    337, 370, 399, 429,
    451, 491, 518
Watters
  Philemon 136, 150
Watts
  Francis 38, 56
  Joseph 40
  Richard 14
  Thomas 14
Waugh
  ----- 69, 136, 147,
    163
  Capt. 136, 169
  David 14, 36
  G. L. 278
  George 200, 381,
    401, 443, 466
  George Lee 318,
    349
  Gowrey 71, 84
  Gowry 98, 230, 552
  Hannah 218

Jacob 136
James 56, 71, 85,
  98
John 14, 37, 56, 71,
  85, 98, 136, 163,
  166, 172, 175
Joseph 11, 14, 36,
  39, 56, 71, 84, 98,
  136, 160, 169
Lee George 501,
  527
Mary 56
McCagby 318, 340,
  381, 402, 443, 462,
  501, 524
McChazy 201
Mica 250
Mrs. 136, 141
R. F. 278
Robert T. 318, 349
Tayler 71
Waugh, Gowry 136,
  170
William 56
Way
  Allan 266
  Allen 304, 335, 369,
    388, 430, 454, 490,
    509
Wayman
  Edward 40
Wayton
  James 61
Weadon
  Augustin 370, 399,
    430, 459, 491, 522
Weak
  George 381, 404
Weaks
  Benjaman 382, 410
  Benjamin 443, 471,
    502, 531
  George 443, 465,
    501, 527

  Thomas 319, 347,
    381, 406
  William 219
Weather
  James 501, 530
Weathers
  Charles 318, 348

James 318, 348,
  381, 410, 443, 471
John 258
Webb
  Aaron 194, 244,
    269, 318, 341, 381,
    404, 443, 470, 502,
    531
  M. 285
  Moses 244, 381,
    404, 443, 470, 502,
    531
Webster
  Charles 37
  Edward 37
Week
  James 229
Weeks
  G. 285
  George 193, 209,
    229, 546
  James 206, 544
  John 260
  William 189, 260,
    545
Weithers
  John 217
Welch
  Langton 502, 530
  Thomas 136, 174
Wellford
  Robert 184, 231,
    250, 277, 319, 351,
    381, 406, 443, 471,
    502, 533
Welliford
  Robert 201
Wells
  Cartey 85, 98, 136,
    143
  Carty 56, 72
  Charles 56
  E. 280
  Edward 548
  Elizabeth 183, 214,
    223, 258, 304, 335,
    370, 394
  G. 280
  George 183, 214,
    224, 258, 304, 335,
    370, 394, 430, 455,
    490, 514

Thomas 304, 335,
371, 400, 430, 460,
490, 514
Wert
George 270
West
----- 136, 146, 158
Ann 14
Charles 199, 230
E. 285
E. Jr. 285
Edward 72, 85, 86,
193, 229, 318, 342,
538, 539, 543
Edward Jr. 193,
248, 318, 342, 543
Edward Sr. 248,
318, 342, 381, 408
Francis 266
George 429, 448
Ignatius 546
J. 285
John 136, 143, 160,
192, 229, 248, 318,
342, 345, 381, 406,
443, 466, 468, 490,
502, 514, 533, 537,
544
John Jr. 501, 527,
543
John Sr. 381, 406
Joseph 537, 548
Nasey 537
Thomas 319, 349,
382, 410, 443, 468,
502, 530
W. 280
William 72, 85, 99,
183, 189, 214, 225,
258, 261, 265, 304,
330, 370, 393, 396,
429, 430, 454, 455,
490, 491, 514, 518,
546
William Jr. 265,
304, 331
William Mills 543
William Sr. 304,
331
Weston
Robert 542

Whalebone
Thomas 206, 537,
543
Whaley
James 136, 150
Wharton
Henry 216
Whealer
John 136, 173
Wheeler
----- 10
John 14, 41, 56,
136, 155, 165, 169
William 72, 85, 98
Wheeller
----- 11
Whitcomb
Richard 37
White
A. 285
Ann 206, 381, 406,
443, 468
G. 285
George 183, 193,
200, 206, 229, 248,
249, 277, 318, 319,
341, 343, 348, 381,
404, 408, 443, 462,
463, 468, 501, 527,
529, 537, 539, 543
George Jr. 319, 348
Jacob 23
John Willson 136,
166
Nancy 319, 347
Robert 538
T. 285
Thomas 194, 206,
229, 248, 318, 342,
381, 406, 543
William 20, 136,
164
Whitecotton
Husband 36
Mealy 36
Whitefoot
Cotton 72
Whiteing
John 72
Whitesides
William 25

Whitfield
John 490, 515
Whiting
John 85
Whitledge
John 23
Thomas 14, 23,
136, 150, 163
Thomas Jr. 23
William 23
Whitson
----- 136, 146
Joseph 20
Joshua 14
Richard 37
Samuel 19
William 14
Whitt
George Sr. 381, 402
Wiggenton
P. 65
Wiggington
Henry 72, 85, 98
James 72, 85, 98
Peter 72, 98, 272
S. 280
Sarah 224
William 275
Wigginton
Henry 14, 56, 136,
146
John 56
Peter 136, 147
Sarah 370, 398
William 14, 136,
147, 211
Wigington
Henry 19
John 20
Sarah 183, 258
William 19
Wiginton
Benjamin 214
Sarah 214
Wilkerson
Gerard 539
Wilkins
----- 136, 142
Wilkinson
----- 137, 169
Minor? 137, 159
William 137, 154

Woodard
  Mary 443, 470, 502, 531
Woodbridge
  William 14, 46
Wooderd
  Mary 318, 341, 381, 407
Woodgerd
  Henry 304, 337, 370, 394, 429, 451, 491, 518
  Jessey 370, 394, 430, 454, 490, 508
  Richard 304, 337, 370, 398
Woodside
  William 549
Woodsmall
  James 215, 223
Woodward
  Henry 233, 265
  Mary 209
  Mrs. 244
  Richard 267
Woodyard
  Henry 217
Wormsly
  Susanah 370, 400, 430, 458, 491, 519
Wort
  George 304, 333, 370, 393
Wren
  John 539
Wright
  Joseph 137, 151
  Robert 443, 462
  Samuel 443, 470, 501, 502, 529, 533
  T. 279
  Thomas 183, 214, 224, 258
  W. 285
Write
  Ann 502, 533

Y

Yancey
  John 86, 99

John Jr. 72
Yates
  Robert 72, 86, 99
Yeatman
  John 545
Yelton
  James 547
Young
  Bryan 15, 137, 172
  Bryant 137, 171, 173
  Frances 254
  Francis 233, 269
  Henry 18, 21, 33
  J. 278
  John 24, 137, 148, 149
  Joseph 249, 319, 352
  Leonard 319, 341
  William 15, 72, 86, 192, 229, 248, 285, 319, 341, 371, 382, 391, 410, 430, 443, 448, 467, 491, 502, 517, 527

Z

Zyley
  John 319, 349

Unidentified

[...]ron
  Daril 538
.....
  John 223
.....der
  John 208
.....ng
  Thomas 208